Understanding
READING
COMPREHENSION
Processes and Practices

Education at SAGE

SAGE is a leading international publisher of journals, books, and electronic media for academic, educational, and professional markets.

Our education publishing includes:

- accessible and comprehensive texts for aspiring education professionals and practitioners looking to further their careers through continuing professional development

- inspirational advice and guidance for the classroom

- authoritative state of the art reference from the leading authors in the field.

Find out more at: **www.sagepub.co.uk/education**

Understanding
READING
COMPREHENSION
Processes and Practices

WAYNE TENNENT

Los Angeles | London | New Delhi
Singapore | Washington DC

Los Angeles | London | New Delhi
Singapore | Washington DC

SAGE Publications Ltd
1 Oliver's Yard
55 City Road
London EC1Y 1SP

SAGE Publications Inc.
2455 Teller Road
Thousand Oaks, California 91320

SAGE Publications India Pvt Ltd
B 1/I 1 Mohan Cooperative Industrial Area
Mathura Road
New Delhi 110 044

SAGE Publications Asia-Pacific Pte Ltd
3 Church Street
#10-04 Samsung Hub
Singapore 049483

Editor: James Clark
Assistant editor: Rachael Plant
Production editor: Imogen Roome
Copyeditor: Elaine Leek
Proofreader: Leigh C. Timmins
Marketing manager: Dilhara Attygalle
Cover design: Naomi Robinson
Typeset by: C&M Digitals (P) Ltd, Chennai, India
Printed by CPI Group (UK) Ltd, Croydon, CR0 4YY

Library of Congress Control Number: 2014935448

British Library Cataloguing in Publication data

A catalogue record for this book is available from
the British Library

ISBN 978–1–4462–7317–3
ISBN 978–1–4462–7318–0 (pbk)

At SAGE we take sustainability seriously. Most of our products are printed in the UK using FSC papers and boards.
When we print overseas we ensure sustainable papers are used as measured by the Egmont grading system.
We undertake an annual audit to monitor our sustainability.

For George

CONTENTS

ABOUT THE AUTHOR

Wayne Tennent is a Senior Lecturer in Education at the University of East London. He worked for a number of years as a class teacher in London. He also spent some time working away from the UK, teaching in Greece, Brunei and New Zealand. He has completed a PhD that investigated ways to develop children's comprehension in group reading contexts.

ACKNOWLEDGEMENTS

Thanks to family and friends, particularly June, Mary, Don, Nigel, John, Jim, Jonesy, Nikki, Venessa and Brian.

Thanks to colleagues, particularly Jane Hurry, Helen Mitchell, Paula Bosanquet and David Reedy.

Thanks to friends, colleagues and children in the following organisations and schools: The United Kingdom Literacy Association; Gants Hill School Improvement Learning Community; the Rochford and Rayleigh reading project schools; the Barking & Dagenham reading project schools; Hamilton Primary School, Colchester, Essex LA; and Earlham Primary School, Newham LA.

Particular thanks to the teachers and educators whose work informs the Practices section of this book: Ian Casey, Cranbrook Primary School, Redbridge LA; James Grant, Lauriston Primary School, Hackney LA; Pippa Couch, art educator; Sophia Morley and Fran Norris, Hamilton Primary School, Colchester, Essex LA; and Ben Meyjes, Highlands Primary School, Redbridge, LA. It has been a privilege to work with you, and see the impact you have had on children's reading.

Special thanks to Gaye Byars.

SAGE would like to thank the following reviewers whose comments helped to shape this book in its early stages:

Julie Bowtell, University of Hertfordshire
Dr Cathy Burnett, Sheffield Hallam University
Howard Cotton, Plymouth University
Naomi Flynn, University of Winchester
Louise Lambert, University of Northampton
Elaine Matchett, Birmingham City University

CHAPTER 1

LOCATING READING

Chapter Overview

This chapter aims to locate reading comprehension within the wider construct of 'reading'. It argues that any conception of what comprehension is, or might be, will relate to a wider conception of reading. The simple view of reading (Gough and Tunmer, 1986) has become a prominent conceptual framework for the teaching of reading. The manner in which this view conceives reading is examined. Research findings related to the simple view that inform the teacher of reading are presented. Following this, a number of issues are raised that are perhaps not made obvious by the simple view, including how it might be interpreted and the fact that comprehension itself is comprised of component parts. It is suggested that to support children's comprehension of text, other perspectives on reading need to be considered.

CAN BABOONS READ?

To consider what is meant by 'reading comprehension' it is useful to consider what is meant by reading in the first place. An interesting article appeared in *The Independent* newspaper in 2012 under the headline:

'Literate' baboons can tell genuine words from nonsense

In the article, John Von Radowitz outlined a research study conducted by French scientists that investigated the ability of baboons to discriminate between real words and nonsense words. These baboons were presented with 'dozens' of genuine

English words and more than 7,000 nonwords. The baboons were able to recognise the real words with an accuracy rate of nearly 75% (Von Radowitz, 2012).

This study raises a number of questions. For example, why on earth would anyone fund such a study? Also, the baboons had to engage with in excess of 7,000 words: is this a good use of their time? What could they possibly have learnt from this? Actually, these are not flippant questions, though they may appear so.

Reading is not a natural act

One point to consider relates to the fact that we are not 'hard-wired' to read; and by read in this context we mean to decode and interpret *writing systems* (whether they are alphabetic and map sounds to letters, or logographic and map syllables to symbols, as in Chinese). As a species we have adapted our visual and aural perceptions which once would have kept us clear of predators and helped us track prey, to the task of developing writing systems, and then learning how to read them (Wolf, 2008). The word 'learn' is used advisedly. Our early evolutionary ancestor would have had to learn to 'read' the tracks of a possible predator to see if they were fresh, and to listen to see if the predator was still in the vicinity. They would perhaps have used some sort of language to communicate this information to nearby fellow humans. Clearly, they didn't think, 'Oh look! Those are the tracks of our most dangerous predator', and then just stand there. If they had, they might possibly have been eaten and the species would have died out. Instead, our ancestors would have had to comprehend the situation from the given 'text' (the footprints). They would have had to analyse, evaluate and respond – probably by running away. Wolf (2008) notes how through neuroscience we know that the same parts of the brain that deal with visual and aural information are centrally active when we have to decode written text, and that other parts of the brain that deal with understanding and interpreting are also activated as we try to make sense of it. Indeed, there is no part of the brain that is designed specifically to deal with written text.

What the baboon study does, and as Von Radowitz outlines in his article, is provide some evidence to suggest that the ability to adapt these skills may pre-date humankind. The study also suggests that the ability to adapt these 'hard-wired' skills to the task of recognising a writing system may not be unique to humans. Interesting perhaps, but what relevance does it have for you as a teacher of reading? The key point to note here is that this study reminds us that reading is not a 'natural' act; if it was we would all be able to do it effortlessly. It would be like breathing. But it is not. It needs to be taught.

Reading may mean different things to different people

A second point to consider relates to the description of the baboons as being 'literate'. Von Radowitz may have been using some journalistic licence, and not a little irony, to make the story appear more interesting, but it does make us examine what we consider 'literate' to mean. Barton (2007) has traced the etymology of 'literate' and cites the *Oxford English Dictionary* as noting a reference to the word from 1432. At this time it meant to be educated and in holy orders. From 1924 the term came to be more clearly defined as being able to read and write. This definition would describe literacy as a set of reading and writing skills that simply need to be learnt; being 'literate' would mean that the task of learning these skills has been achieved. This view of being literate was dominant in education until about the 1980s (Pahl and Rowsell, 2011), although Au (2004) would argue that this definition is still the one that is generally accepted.

Reflecting upon these definitions, you may wonder whether 'literate' is the correct term to use when applied to our baboons. The 1432 definition requires us to consider the term 'holy orders'; and also to consider what it means to be educated. In Western Europe at this pre-industrial time, reading would largely have taken place in monasteries and entailed the study of holy texts. This type of study would have been conducted by monks who were likely to have been born into wealthy families (Beare, 2000). Clearly this part of the definition would not apply to our baboons. But are they educated? In all likelihood the response to this would be 'no'. One rationale for this response would probably state that though they might have been able to differentiate between (some) words and nonwords, they have no *understanding* of what these words mean. Turning to the 1924 definition, a similar point might be made. We could say that they have developed some literacy skill in that they are able to recognise (some) words. However, it might be argued that because they are unable to *comprehend* the word, they cannot be described as literate. The point for you as a teacher of reading is to consider what actually constitutes reading.

Dialogue Point

Defining terms

Through dialogue with colleagues, consider the following questions:

- What does it mean to be educated?
- What does it mean to be literate?
- What is reading?

At this stage, taking a line of argument that considers the relationship between the recognition of words and the ability to understand them is a pertinent one. In the course of studying the teaching of reading it is likely that the term 'reading wars' (Stanovich and Stanovich, 1999) will be encountered. This refers to a time (apparently) when there was a polarised debate as to how reading – particularly early reading – should be taught; whether there should be an exclusive focus on developing a knowledge of letters and sounds (phonetic knowledge) before engaging with the meaning of texts, or whether children should be immersed in the meaning of texts at all times without necessarily focusing on phonetic knowledge. As Levy (2011) points out, very few educators assumed these polarised positions; and indeed there is general agreement that for children to become skilled readers they need to develop a phonetic knowledge of written texts as well as the ability to make meaning of (or comprehend) them (Snow et al., 1998).

It is perhaps not surprising then that the conceptual framework for reading described as the 'The simple view of reading' (Gough and Tunmer, 1986) has come to prominence, as it defines reading in relation to these two components specifically.

THE SIMPLE VIEW OF READING

The simple view of reading is a psychologically-based framework which suggests that, in its simplest form, reading is composed of two key over-arching components: word recognition and linguistic comprehension.

Gough et al. (1996) capture this in the following hypothetical 'formula':

Reading = decoding x comprehension

By decoding, Gough and colleagues mean context-free word recognition; the ability to recognise written text effortlessly. It does not relate to any kind of understanding of what that written text might mean. This relates to the spoken language comprehension part of the equation, by which the authors mean the interpretation of words, sentences and discourse.

The description of this as a *hypothetical* 'formula' is apt. A formula of this nature suggests numbers can be used to represent decoding and spoken language comprehension, which in turn will provide an overall score for reading. This is not the case here. This is emphasised by the use of the multiplication symbol to describe the relationship between decoding and comprehension. A reader may be unable to decode a text, but may have some level of language comprehension. They would score a *hypothetical* 'zero' for decoding and score positively for comprehension:

Reading = decoding x comprehension

0 x 1

If these two scores were added together, the reader would achieve a positive score for reading, when clearly they have read nothing. A multiplicative relationship means a zero score for decoding would mean a zero score for reading overall.

The same is true if the situation is reversed. It may be possible to decode the text, but if the reader has no comprehension of the language then the score for reading would also be zero.

Reading = decoding x comprehension

$$1 \times 0$$

The rationale for presenting this as a formula is to show that if we want to say someone is reading, they need to be able to demonstrate *both* decoding ability and a comprehension of the text.

📁 ## The simple view of reading: both decoding ability and comprehension are required

A worked example

1. I don't know the code but I can use my spoken language comprehension

The following text is an actual English sentence; it uses the exact spellings of English words but it uses the font Wingdings 3.

See if you can work out what the sentence says. (To begin with, can you work out what the first word says?):

∧↑⇨ →⇩⇦↙↗⇨⇨▲⇨△ ▲▶↔⇨↑⇨⇦ ◀↑⇨ ⇦⇨↙↙.

In trying to make sense of this you probably used a number of strategies. You applied your knowledge of English sentence structure and probably decided that the first word is 'The'. Without probably even thinking about it, you decided that the second word is a noun and that the third word is a verb. You were probably hoping that the fourth word is also 'the', but it appears to have different orthography (or letter pattern) from the first word in the sentence (but remember, capital letters have a different shape to lower case letters). You might have also noted the spelling pattern in the last word, which ends in a double letter.

Throughout this activity you are certainly trying to discern some sort of alphabetic principle. However, because you do not recognise the orthography of the letters it is very difficult to make sense of it. It is also very time-consuming.

A visual image might help, however. State in one sentence what is happening here, in the picture on the right:

© isitsharp/istockphoto

Providing a visual image means that the need to decode the written text has been removed. Wyse et al. (2013: 135) would describe this as using 'visual image interpretation', and you can probably make a statement that shows your comprehension of the picture.

And indeed,

∧↑⇨ →✦⇨↙↗⇨⇨▲⇨△ ▲▶⟷⇨↑⇨⇨ ◀↑⇨ ⇨⇨↙↙

does translate into

The   goalkeeper   punched   the   ball.

You comprehended the visual image by applying what you know about football. The player allowed to use their hands (or fists) is called a goalkeeper and sometimes they might punch the ball rather than catch it. So you were probably able to state something that approximates in meaning to the 'Wingdings 3' sentence. Of course, approximating is not actually good enough because while the reader may get the gist of the text this may not reflect the exact wording. This still leaves room for a misconception.

The key point here is that you were able to apply your spoken language comprehension in relation to the visual image and make sense of what was happening. It is highly unlikely that you were able to access the written text. As such, according to the simple view, you were not reading.

The simple view of reading notes that readers need to know 'the code' of the language to be able to read written text.

2. I know the code but I can't apply my spoken language comprehension

But what if you do know 'the code'? Does this mean reading has taken place? See if you can decode the following text and work out its meaning:

Ron im illy bashtruf. Ini vasby ti desh pinskehmough.

Ini vasby ti poosh football.

In common with our friends the baboons (perhaps), you probably recognised two of the words in these sentences: Ron (probably someone's name) and football. You were probably able to decode every word (although you may have been uncertain as to the pronunciation of 'pinskehmough': 'ow' as in 'plough'; 'o' as in 'though'; 'uff' as in 'tough'; 'ock' as in 'lough', 'off' as in 'cough' ...?), but your reading rate probably slowed down to ensure the accurate decoding of unknown spelling patterns. Again you probably attempted to apply your knowledge of grammar to mark such things as nouns and verbs. In this situation you were applying your knowledge of the alphabetic principle, but because you did not recognise the words you could not assign meaning to the text (and perhaps you did not even try). In effect you were 'barking' at the text. By this we mean being able to decode written text with ease and fluency while making no attempt to understand it.

Again, this is not reading, and decoding without comprehension is not enough.

RESEARCH BASED ON THE SIMPLE VIEW OF READING: SOME FINDINGS

A number of research studies have investigated the relationship between decoding and spoken language comprehension and these have uncovered findings that have relevance to you as a teacher of reading.

Decoding text is more difficult for younger children

Gough et al. (1996) investigated the relationship between word recognition, reading comprehension and listening comprehension. They did this by way of a meta-analysis. A meta-analysis involves sifting through completed studies that fit the criteria being investigated (in this case, studies that have focused on the relationship between word recognition, reading comprehension and listening comprehension), noting the findings in the data and then reanalysing them to find common trends. In all, they looked at seventeen studies that focused on monolingual speakers and separated their analysis into four age-related groups: Grades 1/2 (6–8-year-olds), Grades 3/4 (8–10-year-olds), Grades 5/6 (10–12-year-olds), and college age. They found a strong correlation existed between word recognition and reading comprehension in younger children. This correlation became less strong the older the children were. This means that for younger children the ability to comprehend written text is more dependent on word recognition ability than for older children.

Catts et al. (2005) had similar findings. In a longitudinal study they tracked 604 children in their second (7–8-year-olds), fourth (9–10-year-olds) and eighth (13–14-year-olds) grades of schooling to test their language reading and cognitive abilities. Using a number of tests (which again included word recognition, listening comprehension and reading comprehension), they found that difficulties with reading comprehension could be explained by word recognition difficulties for a number of the younger children. Word recognition issues were less likely to explain comprehension difficulties for older children.

This probably comes as no surprise. For younger readers, particularly beginning readers, decoding is a more effortful task because they are still learning that each letter (or cluster of letters) relates to a particular sound (grapheme–phoneme correspondence). Perfetti et al. (1996) describe this as a 'decoding bottleneck' (see Box below) because the task of attending to the words in text consumes the majority of the child's processing capacity. As they encounter the words more regularly in text this skill becomes more automatic and takes less effort. Frith (1985) describes this as moving from the alphabetic stage, where children develop an awareness of letter/sound relationships and begin to segment words into syllables and sounds, as with *c – at* or *c – a – t*, to the orthographic stage, where they no longer need to sound out words on a regular basis, and are able to recognise a large number of words instantly and automatically. The majority of children get better and quicker at decoding text as they get older and therefore have more cognitive resources to spend on making sense of it. So teachers should be aware of the importance of getting the words off the page.

📂 **Perfetti et al.'s (1996) 'decoding bottleneck'**

When children (and adults as well) attempt to read written text they do so with limited processing capacity. This means that we all have limited cognitive resources we can apply to the task.

This can be demonstrated by looking at the bottles in shown below. Imagine these bottles show all the space two people have in their head when they are reading a written text, and that the water in the bottle shows how much of their limited processing capacity they have to spend on *decoding* the text.

For the first person it takes a lot of effort to decode the text and as a result they have less 'space' (or processing capacity) to spend on trying to make sense of it. This is what Perfetti et al. mean by a 'decoding bottleneck'. For the second person, decoding the text has been a relatively easy task and they have more available resources to comprehend it.

There are specific processes required to comprehend written text, which are different from those required for decoding

An inter-dependent relationship clearly exists between the two processes of decoding and comprehension because they are both necessary for reading. The simple view provides an understanding that both these linguistic processes need to be applied fluently and efficiently (Snowling and Hume, 2005) for written text to be understood. The worked examples above highlight the fact that the complete absence of either one of these two components means that reading cannot take place.

Gough et al. (1996), however, suggest these components can be also disassociated. This probably comes as no surprise. The worked example above showed that both decoding and comprehension were needed to read and are thus inter-dependent; but it also showed that the two can be separated. You comprehended the picture that supported the undecodable text and you decoded the nonsense text without making any sense of it.

Indeed, studies have actively attempted to separate the components of word recognition and comprehension. The Catts et al. (2005) study is one. Another is the Aaron et al. (1999) study that analysed the performance of 139 children in Grades 3 (8–9-year-olds), 4 (9–10-year-olds) and 6 (11–12-year-olds) on a range of tests including reading comprehension, listening comprehension, nonword and irregular word reading, vocabulary and tests of word reading speed. Sixteen children were noted to have some kind of reading difficulty. For most of these children the source of the difficulty tended to be specific to *either* word recognition ability or comprehension, not both.

This finding suggests that for effective reading to occur there must be processes taking place that are specific to either word recognition or comprehension. Comprehension is different from word recognition and will therefore require different teaching approaches.

Specific reading difficulties can be located

Disassociating the two components also provides the opportunity to locate where children might be having specific difficulties with reading. Again, in the Aaron et al. (1999) study the authors investigated whether there were identifiable subgroups of poor readers within the group of 16 children they had identified. They described this subgroup of children as having some kind of reading disability. They found that two of these children had reading profiles that showed a deficiency in decoding skill alone, and a further two were deficient in listening comprehension alone. Three children showed weaknesses in all areas, suggesting a third subgroup with a mixed reading disorder. Thus, they were also able to identify specific areas of reading deficit.

In this way, the simple view may help to provide a clearer outline of children's reading profiles. For example, a child with good spoken language comprehension but poor word recognition might be considered dyslexic. Proponents of the simple view would suggest this informs the teacher as to types of teaching strategies they might use.

There is a link between reading comprehension and listening comprehension

One further finding of interest suggests there is a link between reading comprehension and listening comprehension. In the same meta-analysis, Gough et al. (1996) found a general trend in their data which suggested that the older the subjects, the stronger the relationship between reading comprehension and listening comprehension. Once again, this is supported by Catts et al. (2005), who found that older children who were having reading comprehension difficulties were likely to have listening comprehension difficulties too, rather than any associated difficulty with word recognition.

Gough et al. explain this link by noting that reading and listening comprehension require access to similar linguistic processes; the only difference is the point of access. Written text is accessed via the eye; listening requires access via the ear. As Cain (2010) notes, listening comprehension and reading comprehension are not exactly the same thing. Nonetheless, the link between the two has implications for us as teachers; if we want to support children's reading comprehension then there might be a call also to support their listening skills.

INTERPRETING THE SIMPLE VIEW – READING AS A LINEAR PROGRESSION

The simple view of reading has had a significant impact – whether implicitly or explicitly – on how reading is taught in many parts of the world, including the United States (Davis, 2006), Australia and New Zealand (Wilkinson et al., 2000) and Ireland (Concannon-Gibney and Murphy, 2010). In England, the *Independent Review of the Teaching of Early Reading: Final Report* (Rose, 2006) recommended that the simple view of reading should be adopted as the conceptual framework for the teaching of reading in all state primary schools in England (pupils aged 4–11 years).

Yet what is interesting here is the manner in which this simple view has been interpreted. We have already noted by analysing the 'formula' that for reading to take place both decoding and comprehension are required. Alongside this, it was also noted that various studies have disassociated the components of word recognition and comprehension and treated them as separate entities. While this has clarified the fact that these components make different, discrete demands upon readers, it might be argued that this separation has led to the simple view being interpreted (explicitly in some contexts, less so in others) in a linear manner; that the decoding aspects of reading need to be addressed first before comprehension can be looked at.

Indeed, advocates of the simple view do seem to support this. Gough et al. (1996) state that for beginning readers the texts they read by themselves in these earliest stages will for the most part not be particularly challenging to their language comprehension system: the problem that early readers have is to gain access to this system from the print. They argue that for 'reading' to take place in these early years the emphasis will have to be on developing decoding skills – children need most at this point to develop visual word recognition processes. As children get older they will develop a mastery of decoding skills. The emphasis will then begin to switch away from decoding and the focus of reading will turn towards comprehension. This suggests that as reading skill develops, the associated language processes become more important than the ability to decode.

Perfetti et al. (2005) also argue that the need to establish appropriate word recognition skills should take priority over the development of metacognitive skills. Indeed, they suggest that attempting to develop metacognitive skills alongside word recognition skills is detrimental to the latter. Presumably they are referring to the 'decoding bottleneck' outlined earlier in this chapter, where limited processing capacity means that the greater amount of cognitive resources spent on decoding text leaves less cognitive resources available to spend on comprehending the text.

The linear view manifested in classroom practice: addressing the decoding component

How this has become manifested in classrooms is perhaps best captured in the phrase 'learning to read, reading to learn'. This phrase (which has become a mantra in some circles) surfaced in an article by Chall et al. (1990) which proposed that from Kindergarten to Grade 3 (4–8-year-olds) the focus of reading should be on 'learning to read', by which they mean decoding – getting the words off the page. Following this, from Grade 4 onwards the focus should then shift to 'reading to learn', by which they mean comprehension broadly. This equates to what van den Broek et al. (2005) describe as the 'the commonly-held view' of teaching reading, and is based on the premise that once decoding ability is in place, comprehension should more easily follow.

A consequence of this is that there has been a foregrounding on the word recognition component, most clearly evidenced by the movement towards the implementation of phonics instruction across the English-speaking world. Strauss and Altwerger (2007) note that The Elementary and Secondary Education Act (2001) – otherwise known as 'No Child Left Behind' – has made phonics the only legal approach to the teaching of early reading in the United States. In Australia, the *National Inquiry into the Teaching of Literacy: Teaching Reading* (Department of Education, Science and Training, 2005) stated that 'an early and systematic emphasis on the explicit teaching of phonics' (p. 9) was a feature of successful reading instruction, and this is now embedded in the Australian Curriculum (2011). In New Zealand, phonics has not been incorporated into policy – possibly because of a strong historical link to the whole language approach (Soler and Openshaw, 2007). However, Blaiklock and Haddow (2007) outline a study where a systematic phonics programme was implemented successfully alongside the whole language approach, leading the authors to call for its wider adoption – something Patel (2010) also calls for. In England the *Independent Review of the Teaching of Early Reading: Final Report* (Rose, 2006) stated that reading accuracy is most effectively supported through the systematic (planned and regular) teaching of phonics and cites the meta-analyses completed by Torgerson et al. (2006) in support of this. Rose advocated the exclusive use of synthetic phonics, which emphasises relating phonemes to graphemes and blending them together to make words, rather than analytic phonics where children are taught to recognise phonemes in whole words and segment them. Wyse and Styles (2007) note that Torgerson et al. (2006) did not comment on the specific type of phonics instruction; they only stated that the instruction should be systematic. Regardless, as a result of this review, synthetic phonics programmes have become an everyday feature in English primary classrooms and the pre-eminence of synthetic phonics is enshrined in the new curriculum (Department for Education (DfE), 2014).

So the impact of the simple view on the word-recognition aspect of reading has been substantial in terms of *what* should be taught, and in some instances also *how* it should be taught.

TURNING TOWARDS COMPREHENSION

The ability of children to comprehend text is proving to be an issue internationally. Here are some examples to show this:

- In England, it is estimated that one in every ten children is likely to have a specific reading comprehension difficulty that will cause them to perform below expected levels (Nation and Snowling, 1997).

- In the United States, Kamil et al. (2008) analysed the results of the National Assessment of Educational Progress (NAEP) in Reading (2007) report, and found that 69% of Eighth Graders (13–14-year-olds) were unable to comprehend text to a level appropriate to their grade.

- In Australia, Woolley (2007) states that Year 3 (8–9-year-olds) is a recognised point at which comprehension difficulties are likely to surface for a significant number of Australian children, which leads to a stagnation in reading development.

In the previous section we saw how attempts to address the decoding component described in the simple view of reading led to a focus on phonics. Given these three scenarios it would make sense to look to the research relating to the comprehension component. And at this point things start to become more complex.

It was noted earlier that one of the findings from research suggested that the process of comprehension was different from that of decoding. Evidence from the Aaron et al. (1999) study was cited to support this. However, what is not made clear in the Aaron et al. study is what exactly the process of comprehension involves. Once we start to investigate this, we may come to the conclusion that we need to widen our perspective on reading beyond the simple view. I'm going to suggest three reasons why this might be the case. Each of these reasons is up for discussion.

Comprehension is not a 'unitary construct' – it has component parts

In the description of poor performance on comprehension in different countries, you may have noted the following phrases:

- perform(ing) below expected levels
- unable to comprehend text to a level appropriate to their grade

What is interesting to note here is that reading comprehension ability is being related to some concept of age-appropriate norms. This suggests a tacit acknowledgement that reading comprehension skill is an acquisitive process. Now, this can be substantiated in relation to the development of word recognition skill. For example, Frith's (1985) staged model of word reading acquisition was briefly mentioned earlier, noting how children move from the alphabetic stage (where children develop letter/sound awareness) to the orthographic stage (where word recognition becomes automatic). Frith notes a stage prior to this, known as the logographic stage, where children are not aware that individual letters and letter combinations represent specific sounds; rather, they recognise familiar words and letters through visual features such as shape or size. For example, they might recognise the 'M' for a McDonald's restaurant. Alongside this model of word reading acquisition, a sequential model of phonological awareness – the awareness of the sound structure of spoken words without recourse to print (Stahl and Murray, 1994) – has been proposed by Torgesen (1999). This describes a process whereby children initially become aware of, and manipulate, rhyme and alliteration through to being able to manipulate individual sounds in words by way of blending and segmentation.

There is, however, a problem with applying a concept of development and age-appropriate norms to the comprehension process. This is because the nature of this acquisition has not been mapped in any sequential manner as it has for the word recognition processes. We have no definitive description of an 8-year-old comprehender. The reason for this is that comprehension is not a 'unitary construct' (Duke, 2005: 93), but is rather comprised of discrete components.

An analysis of the statement below can show this:

Professional thieves operate at this station

This was a public notice I once saw in London. Sharing this statement with teachers over the last few years has raised a number of interesting responses (and the list following does not capture them all):

- Some of the children in my class would think 'operate' had something to do with hospitals and doctors.

- It's a statement of fact but it must be meant as a warning

- It means that you have to keep your bag close to you.

- Does 'professional' mean they are qualified? Surely that can't be right! It must just mean they are good at their job.

- Wouldn't it be funny if 'station' meant a police station!

- You'd have to know what a thief is.

- Why don't they stop them then?

- I bet it means that if you get robbed, it's your own fault. The station authorities won't take responsibility.

- I got a picture in my head of Liverpool Street rail station [in London]. It's really busy. I can't be sure it's there though. It depends on where the sign was.

- It doesn't say that what the thieves are doing is wrong.

An analysis of these responses shows that the act of comprehending requires the activation of a number of processes. Decisions have to be made about word meanings; pronouns have to resolved; appropriate background knowledge has to be retrieved from memory and applied; cultural understandings (in this case about what behaviours are acceptable or not) are accessed; some overall 'picture' of the scene is developed; checks are made for sense; meanings might not be stated explicitly and gaps in understanding have to be resolved; possible interpretations are expressed; oh, and words have to decoded. In essence, linguistic, cognitive and knowledge factors are being applied simultaneously, alongside a range of other factors, such as decoding ability. Indeed, it might be argued that a person's entire reading experience is being accessed – in this instance, all just to make sense of six words strung together.

The point to consider here is that though the simple view of reading takes note of the importance of language comprehension, language comprehension itself is highly complex. There is a wealth of research in each of these component areas (which we will begin to investigate in the Processes section of this book), but it is very difficult to pull all of them together into one workable construct of comprehension. This explains Kintsch and Rawson's (2005) point that when we provide a child with an overall score for comprehension, it does not actually mean a lot. This creates a difficulty for the teacher of reading: when you are teaching comprehension, what are you actually teaching?

The linear view of reading relegates comprehension to a secondary component

It was noted earlier that the simple view has been interpreted in a linear manner: decoding first, comprehension second. In taking a linear view of the teaching of reading there is a danger that the comprehension component will be treated as being of secondary importance. Wyse and his colleagues have been particularly vociferous on the dangers of taking a linear approach to the teaching of reading, and they warn against presenting the decoding and comprehension components in a decontextualised manner (Wyse et al., 2013). They argue that failing to address children's comprehension abilities at any stage is dangerous because of the link made by Cain and Oakhill (2006) between poor comprehension and poor educational attainment generally.

Interestingly, the argument against a 'decoding first, comprehension second' approach to the teaching of reading is given some credence by Gough et al. (1996) themselves. They note that a typically developing child at the age of 5 will have mastered many aspects of spoken language. They will have a vocabulary of several thousand words and they will be aware of the phonology and syntax of the language. Basically, children arrive in schools with a spoken language comprehension in advance of their ability to decode. From the perspective of teaching, it might seem odd to avoid supporting this development until the decoding component has been mastered. Moreover, this raises the issue of when this shift in priority from decoding to comprehension should take place. Only when fluent decoding is in place? Taking the linear (or 'commonly held') view in its strictest sense this would suggest there would be very little attempt to address reading comprehension *per se*, prior to entry to secondary education with some children.

Investigating comprehension requires a wider conception of reading

The simple view of reading captures the two key components raised in our initial discussion on the literacy (or not) of baboons. These were the need to apply phonetic knowledge to written text and to make sense of it. It might be argued, however, that this is an over-simplification of what reading is perceived to be. Hall (2003) notes four different perspectives that might be taken to the act of reading. Two of these have been referred to earlier in the context of the 'reading wars'.

The cognitive-psychological perspective describes the view that the simple view of reading is most closely associated with. It is assumed that children learn to read in stages and the emphasis should initially be focused on developing phonetic knowledge. As noted above, this is most obviously associated with a focus on the systematic teaching of phonics.

The psycholinguistic perspective describes the polar opposite view as described in the 'reading wars'. Hall notes that proponents of this approach consider the authenticity of the reading task to be of paramount importance. It is the engagement with the language and its meanings which is central. It is characterised by encouraging children to use syntactic and semantic clues to get to the meaning of unknown words. So the reader is encouraged to use contextual clues and there is likely to be less emphasis on phonetic knowledge.

Moving on from these two accounts, the sociopolitical perspective begins to view literacy, and therefore the act of reading, in relation to the issue of empowerment. An earlier task in this chapter involved considering what it meant to be a reader. In one sense the question could be reversed. Consider those children and adults who cannot 'read'. How are they positioned in society? The answer to this question is likely to support Hall's view that reading is not a neutral act. It is 'bound up with ethnicity, gender, social class, disability and so on' (Hall, 2003: 189). Certainly, numerous studies have shown the link between attainment in school and social class. Indeed, consider the initial discussion on literacy and how in 1432 being literate involved being in 'holy orders'; and how the opportunity to achieve this was largely based around wealth. Also consider the power of the church at this time, and how this might have been related to the ability to read. This perspective assumes a more critical approach (Hall, 2003), which will involve making the reader aware of Hall's 'bound up' aspects noted above when they engage with text.

Another perspective that encompasses elements from beyond the classroom is the sociocultural perspective. This perspective reminds us that reading takes place in a social and cultural context. The earlier discussion about what it means to be literate got as far as the 1924 definition. Though it was argued that the view of reading as a set of skills to be learnt might still be prevalent in some quarters, more recent perspectives are of relevance to the teacher of reading. For example, one view sees literacy as a social practice (Gee, 1999) relating to our everyday lives. Indeed, reading takes place not just in the school domain, but also in churches, mosques and the home (Pahl and Rowsell, 2011). Also the nature of reading is changing because of engagement with new technologies. For example, children might be using social media such as Facebook, which is likely to provide a very different literacy practice from typical school-based literacy practices. This use of technology may also mean that children are engaging with text in different ways. Rather than simply reading books one at a time from page one onwards, they are dealing with multiple texts online bringing together information from different sources (Goldman et al., 2013). These newer perspectives remind us that all reading takes place within a context – it has a purpose, and this purpose may not relate to the context of school alone. They also highlight the fact each domain might operate from a different idea of what comprehension actually means.

Do we know what reading practices children are engaged with outside the classroom? In this context one might argue that being able to read (or being literate) is not simply about being able to decode a writing system; it is about myriad types of understandings in which that writing system exists. For you, as a teacher of reading, the issue is about knowing the types of texts that children engage with on a daily basis and the manner in which they are used.

Dialogue Point

Perspectives on reading and comprehension

Four perspectives on reading were presented above:

- Which perspective (or perspectives – none of this is 'hard and fast') most closely supports your view of what reading is?
- Consider how comprehension might be perceived differently from each of these perspectives.

CONCLUSION

Wyse et al. (2013) describe reading comprehension as 'the essence of reading because it entails readers understanding the written word expressed in texts' (p. 155). Accepting the role ascribed to reading comprehension in this statement would mean that the baboons in the study outlined at the beginning of this chapter cannot be described as literate. And there is probably general agreement on this.

This description of reading comprehension, however, also brings us back to the key point of this chapter, which is what do we consider reading to be in the first place? This is a critical question because to some extent this will determine what we consider the comprehension of written text to entail. At this point you will have noticed that no attempt has been made to define comprehension as yet, precisely because any definition must account for what reading is perceived to be.

Currently, prominence is given to the simple view of reading (Gough and Tunmer, 1986), which perceives reading as being composed of two key components: word recognition and language comprehension. It can be argued that the simple view of reading does two things that are important for the teacher of reading to note in relation to comprehension. The first is that it foregrounds comprehension in the reading process. We are forced to engage with the term and what it might mean. Second, it states that without comprehension we cannot say that reading has taken place (much as Wyse et al.'s description does). Decoding alone is not enough.

Issues that you as a teacher of reading need to consider are whether a linear approach should be taken to reading (decoding first, comprehension second), and how we negotiate the fact that comprehension is not one thing but a number of component parts. Also, hopefully, you will have considered your own perception of what reading is, and should be. This perception may chime very closely to the construct of reading outlined by the simple view; it may accept the simple view as a base starting point and seek to incorporate other perspectives into it; or alternative perspectives may be adopted more fully.

The next chapter will consider how reading comprehension might be defined, taking account of how this might vary depending on how the construct of reading is perceived. But it is worth considering one further point before moving on, one that relates to the simple view of reading. As noted above, Gough et al. (1996) state that children entering formal education are likely to have little or no decoding ability. In one sense then, formal 'instruction' in decoding can put an understanding of letter-sound correspondence into the heads of children. Children can be taught *what* sounds letters make and *how* they can be sounded out. The teacher of reading can even tick a box to say which ones each child knows.

Gough et al., however, also note that children entering school will have a spoken language comprehension in advance of decoding ability. This means that they can already comprehend; they already have something in their heads. They are developing their own understanding of the world, which takes place in a unique social, cultural and familial context. And it is this that is applied to the written texts they engage with. So the teacher of reading can show children *how* to comprehend text (as the second part of this book will demonstrate); *what* each child makes of the text they read will be dependent on their experience of the world. And this is what makes investigating children's reading comprehension so fascinating.

School-based activity

Engage a group of children in dialogue and find out the following:

- What do they think 'reading' is?
- What kinds of reading activities do they engage in?
- How similar are their perceptions of reading to yours?

CHAPTER 2

LOCATING COMPREHENSION

Chapter Overview

This chapter aims to locate what we mean by comprehension specifically. It makes clear that reading comprehension is different from spoken language comprehension. A number of definitions of reading comprehension are presented; however, it is argued that coming to a conclusive definition is problematic. The reasons for this are twofold. First, readers make sense of texts in unique ways depending on their knowledge and experiences; and second, comprehension is a componential construct, and not everyone will agree on these constituent process components. Possible components are analysed by investigating how reading comprehension has been conceptualised by various theorists.

A NON-COMPREHENDING 'READER'?

Applegate et al. (2009) relate the tale of a frustrated graduate student who had completed a school-based reading assessment with a 'strong' reader. The student was concerned that although the child in question was able to decode a presented text fluently, she appeared to have difficulty in understanding it. The student was encouraged to discuss this with the child's teacher, and apparently the teacher stated the following: 'Oh, she's my best reader, for sure. She's just not a good comprehender' (Applegate et al., 2009: 512).

Chapter 1 explored a study that investigated the ability of baboons to discriminate between words and nonwords. This raised a number of questions. We could ask very much the same questions in this scenario of the non-comprehending reader; we just need to change who was involved (teachers and children instead of scientists and baboons) and what was investigated (reading fluency and comprehension instead of the recognition of words and nonwords). So in this case we might ask, why on earth would this graduate student undertake such a test of a child's reading fluency and reading comprehension? What can this information possibly tell them? What's in it for the child? Is this a waste of their time?

Whereas this line of questioning may have appeared flippant (at least initially) in relation to the ability of baboons to recognise words, in this situation relating to a child's apparent inability to comprehend text this is clearly not the case. So what's different? Well, one might argue that the difference is obvious; and it is a difference of perspective – teacher or scientist? Taking a teacher's perspective, the uncomprehending child scenario goes to the heart of teaching and learning. If teachers do not have this information on a child's reading ability they will not know what to teach next; and if this happens the child will indeed find their time in class wasted. In the long term this is likely to impact upon their academic achievement. As Cain and Oakhill (2006) have noted, children experiencing reading comprehension difficulties are likely to attain less well in education generally.

Key questions arising

There are a number of equally pressing questions that need to be considered in relation to the teacher's statement above, however. These are as follows:

- What is the teacher's conception of reading generally?

- What is the teacher's conception of the role of comprehension specifically?

- Is this anything more than an anecdote, or is it common to find children in classrooms who can decode and read fluently but who cannot comprehend?

Unpacking these questions serves three purposes. The first question provides a link to the previous chapter and reminds us that we must consider comprehension within wider conceptions of reading. The second question allows us to consider what we might mean by comprehension and what it might entail. The third question begins to link our conception (or possible conceptions, as we shall see) of comprehension to the classroom.

CONCEPTIONS OF READING

The first question requires us to consider the teacher's conception of reading. In one sense, this points us back to the first chapter as we are forced to ask again, 'What is reading?'. The child, we are told, in this anecdote could *read* fluently but not *comprehend*. Given this, can she be described as 'reading'? The simple view of reading would suggest not, because it states that *both* word recognition and comprehension are required. However, we do not know the age of the child. Perhaps the child is a young reader and more of her capacity is used on decoding even though she appears to be fluent. In Chapter 1 we investigated Perfetti et al.'s (1996) description of the 'decoding bottleneck' and this has relevance for younger readers particularly. Neuroscience tells us that when novice readers are learning how to decode text, it is written large on the brain; this is literally the case. A large portion of the brain responsible for visual and auditory perception is 'lit up' when we learn to decode. As we become proficient decoders, less of this brain space is required (Wolf, 2008). So the child's age might provide one explanation for the lack of comprehension. Another explanation related to this might be that the teacher has a linear view of reading and believes that decoding must precede comprehension. Alternatively, this may not be the teacher's view but may be symptomatic of a wider belief that reading should be taught in this linear fashion, dictated by the curriculum over which the teacher has no control. Again, whether you think this is the correct approach is something you will have to decide, and this will relate to what you perceive reading to be. Without wanting to labour the point, it is important to take a position on this. Considering reading in the context of baboons is surreal; in the context of a child's education – and indeed their future life chances – it is not.

CONCEPTIONS OF COMPREHENSION

This leads us on to the second question; and this one relates to the term 'comprehension' itself. For the teacher in our scenario to suggest that the child is not a good comprehender, she must have some conception of what comprehension entails. This must also be the case for the graduate student who has come to the same conclusion that the child is not a good comprehender. However, although they have come to the same conclusion, we cannot be sure that they conceive of comprehension in the same way. So our next question to consider is, 'What do we mean by *comprehension*?'. Finding an answer to this question may seem straightforward; intuitively terms such as 'making meaning' or 'making sense' might spring to mind. However, as we shall see, these are not the same thing.

To begin unpacking this it is worth considering how we define the term 'comprehension'.

Reading comprehension is not the same as spoken language comprehension

The first point to consider is largely unproblematic. When we attempt to define the term we need to make clear that, in this instance, we are referring to *reading* comprehension: the comprehension of written text – not spoken language. Clearly, spoken language comprehension is important to reading, as acknowledged by the simple view of reading. When we talk to someone and when we read, we use many similar processes, but as Cain (2010) notes, they are not exactly the same. When we read we access information via the eye, when we listen we access information via the ear; writing is permanent, speech is transient;

when we read we cannot seek clarification, when we talk we can; when we read each individual word is spaced separately, when we listen the words tend to run into each other with no breaks. For these reasons our comprehension of oral and written texts may not be the same, even if the content is. So reading comprehension requires reference to written texts.

DEFINING READING COMPREHENSION

Having established that reading comprehension is different from listening comprehension, our question becomes more specific: 'What is *reading* comprehension?'

Dialogue Point

Exploring definitions of reading comprehension

Below are a number of definitions of reading comprehension.
   Before reading the definitions consider how you would define reading comprehension. Share your thoughts with colleagues and note similarities and differences
   After reading the definitions consider the following with colleagues:

- Which words/terms seem to be repeating?
- Which definitions appear limited and why?
- Which one (or ones) do you tend to favour?
- How close were any of these to your own definition of comprehension?
- To what extent do these help to refine your own definition?

   You will notice that they span a wide period of time. Just because something is old, doesn't mean it is irrelevant, so don't let this cloud your thinking.

A search through the literature reveals the following definitions of reading comprehension:

- 'Retrieving the sense of individual words, combining clauses to make sentences, and make meaning from successive sentences and paragraphs.' (Cain, 2010)

- 'The skill of reading to extract knowledge or reading with understanding.' (Moyle, 1972)

- 'A process in which readers construct meaning by interacting with text through the combination of prior knowledge and previous experience, information in the text, and the stance the reader takes in relationship to the text.' (Pardo, 2004)

- 'When a reader attempts to comprehend text a mental representation of the content as a whole is constructed, whether this is a sequence of events or a place.' (Johnson-Laird, 1983)

- 'The process of simultaneously extracting and constructing meaning through interaction and involvement with written language.' (RAND Reading Study Group, 2002)

- 'Comprehension is getting questions answered. As we read … we are constantly asking questions, and as long as these questions are answered, as long as we have no residual uncertainty, we comprehend.' (Smith, 1985)

- 'Intentional thinking during which meaning is constructed through interactions between text and reader.' (Durkin, 1993)

- 'Reading comprehension is the construction of the meaning of a written text through a reciprocal interchange of ideas between the reader and the message in a particular text.' (Harris and Hodges, 1995)

- 'The process undertaken by the reader as they attempt to establish meaning from written text.' (National Reading Panel, 2000)

Emerging key strands

Some important key strands emerge from these definitions. We note the use of such words as 'interaction' and 'construction', which tells us that comprehension is an active process. This is important because reading can be considered to be a 'receptive' activity (we 'receive' the words on the page; in contrast writing is a 'productive' activity), but we do not engage with text passively. We 'build' understanding as we read successive statements in a text. We note from these definitions, largely through implication, that comprehension is a process, something that is developed. The manner in which we interact with text is likely to change with age and experience. The importance of words and sentences in the construction of meaning is also implied in this interaction, though Cain states this explicitly. Johnson-Laird highlights the fact that we turn these words and sentences into a mental representation, which to simplify and put crudely means we create some sort of 'picture'. The word 'meaning' appears in most of these definitions, which supports our intuitive response of 'making meaning'. Most definitions make reference to 'text' and relate this specifically to the written words on a page. This would support the point made above that reading comprehension is different, from spoken language comprehension. So while these definitions are phrased differently, it would appear that there are some key strands that are shared.

Problems of defining reading comprehension

There is no conclusive definition of reading comprehension, however. To prove the point, some texts with a central focus on reading comprehension spend more time grappling with its complexities than in trying to define it explicitly, for example Cairney (1990) and Pearson and Johnson (1978) (both excellent books that share the same title, interestingly – 'Teaching reading comprehension'). This is because defining reading comprehension is no easy task; rather, it is problematic for two reasons.

1. Readers 'make sense' of text in unique ways

The first reason relates to the fact that readers 'make sense' of text in unique ways. The term 'make sense' is used advisedly, and to show this we need to look more closely at the terminology used in the definitions. It was noted that as the shared key strands emerged some terms were repeated across the definitions; but these terms actually bear further scrutiny. For example, we have to be clear about what we mean by 'text' and what we mean by 'meaning'. Some would suggest that a text can be written, but it can also be visual, for example. This would include images seen as pictures or films. This is explored in greater depth later in the Practices section.

For now, we will focus on 'meaning' as there are inherent problems with defining this term. Winograd and Johnston (1987) make a distinction between 'meaning' and 'sense'. Referring to the work of the influential Russian educator Lev Vygotsky (1978), they describe 'meaning' as relating to 'socially shared knowledge' and 'sense' to the 'individual's experience'. Now clearly, if reading comprehension is related specifically to getting 'meaning' from text, the implication for the teacher of reading (comprehension) is that the individual's experience is not going to be as important as ensuring that this shared knowledge is 'transmitted' to the child. It would be up to the teacher to interpret the text for the child. This in turn raises the question of whose knowledge is being shared and whether this is likely to lead to the marginalisation of groups who do not share this knowledge. This would be a particular issue in socially and culturally diverse classroom contexts.

Indeed, it might be argued that no young reader is likely to have a fully formed understanding of this 'socially shared knowledge', and that they *have* to bring their personal experiences to the texts they read to make it coherent. Therefore it is no easy task to say whether a text has been comprehended because readers are capable of establishing different 'shades' of meaning; and texts are likely to be understood in different ways. So whilst we can agree with Johnson-Laird that as we read we develop a mental representation (or picture), it is unlikely that two individuals will build exactly the same picture from the same text. This is implied in the Smith (1985) definition which describes comprehension as 'getting questions answered'. While this standpoint can be justified, it does in turn raise another question in itself: Can we be sure that we will all ask the same questions? And for the teacher of reading (comprehension), which questions do we want children to ask of texts? Pardo perhaps states this most explicitly when she notes the importance of the knowledge the reader brings to the text and the reader's stance to the text. And this is because as readers we bring unique experiences to the texts we engage with, and inevitably we will make 'sense' of it in different ways. Thus, to define reading comprehension as the search for, or the establishment of, meaning from printed text is inadequate.

2. Where does comprehension start and finish?

The second reason relates to the decisions we make as to where comprehension starts and ends. To give an example, Rasinski and Padak (2008) suggest that text comprehension could refer to simply retelling information, to providing information not explicitly stated in the text, to applying the information that has been read to the completion of another task, or to the ability to make judgements about the quality of a text. These are four different ways in which the reader might interact with text and it is important to consider whether we think each of them is *necessary* for comprehension. For example, does text comprehension *have* to involve the application of information to another task? Or does comprehension *have* to include the ability to make a judgement about the quality of a text? Is this the same thing as 'making meaning' or 'making sense'?

This leads us once again to Smith's (1985) idea that comprehension relates to the questions we ask about the text. We can take this idea further. To do this we can go back to our scenario of the uncomprehending child reader and consider what we are *not* told about this anecdote. There are three important pieces of missing information. First, we do not know the age of the child. We have established and discussed this earlier in the chapter. Second, we are not told which text the child was asked to read. We can presume that the text was within the child's decoding ability – she decoded it fluently. As the decoding burden was minimal, in theory the child could concentrate solely on comprehension. Finally, we do not know what questions the child was asked about the text. Presumably this was how the graduate student made the judgement that the child was unable to comprehend the text, but obviously different questions require the responder to display different kinds of thinking. For example, taking the story of Jack and the Beanstalk, asking the question 'Who did Jack meet on the way to the market?' is a very different question from 'Was Jack's mother right to send him to bed without any supper?'.

The questions the child was asked in our scenario remains a missing piece of information that would be worth exploring. So let's create a similar scenario which might help to address this. Imagine you presented an average 10-year-old child reader with the following text (which would be well within their decoding ability at this age):

> The iron gates of the school swung open and the stern teacher rang the shiny, loud bell. He shouted at the children telling them to line up quickly. The gaunt, hungry children lined up in the yard in front of the imposing, red-brick building.

and then imagine you asked this 10-year-old the following questions orally:

1. Where did the children line up?

2. What's a school?

3. Do you think the children liked going to school?

4. When do you think the story took place?

5. Do you think it's a good thing for children to go to school?

6. The author uses the term 'gaunt'. Do you think this is an appropriate expression?

7. Why might the development of the schooling system have been important in relation to the needs of capitalist factory owners during nineteenth-century industrialisation in Britain?

Q
8 8

Dialogue Point

Unpacking reading comprehension by questioning

Consider the text above and the related questions. Consult with colleagues and answer the following questions:

- How are the questions different?
- Do we need to answer them all to understand the text?
- If not, where does comprehension begin and end?

Clearly, these questions are very different and require the reader to formulate very different responses. The first question requires the reader to show a literal comprehension – the answer is explicitly stated in the text. Question 2 requires the reader to show their knowledge of a specific word. In this instance, the word is 'school'. Schooling is an experience that is shared by people in cultures across the globe, but can we assume it means the same thing to everyone? Indeed, can we assume our understanding of 'school' will remain the same as we grow older? Question 3 requires the reader to make a type of inference based on available evidence. The reader will need to have made sense of the text as a whole and then look to find some clue from within the text itself to answer it. Question 4 requires the reader to apply background knowledge which they retain in long-term memory. This is a story about Victorian schoolchildren in England; if the reader does not have this knowledge – or if they have this knowledge but cannot retrieve it from long-term memory – it will be more difficult to make sense of it. Question 5 requires the reader to provide an opinion. For example, we may think that it is a good thing for children to go to school because education is important. It might have given them greater opportunities in life. Question 6 requires the reader to consider the author's use of language critically; and Question 7 attempts to engage the reader in the broader social and cultural contexts of the time. You would be correct in assuming the final question has been phrased in such a way that we would not expect a child of 10 years of age to be able to answer it, but it does have a purpose; it is also designed to raise the question of how we locate the limits of reading comprehension. At what point does comprehension stop? Gathering responses to Questions 5, 6 and 7 and stating that these reflect the readers' comprehension might be considered contentious. It might be argued that they are irrelevant to comprehension as they stem *from* the text but are not *about* the text, *per se*. Or should comprehension require the reader to address aspects that appear 'beyond' the text, and if so, then how far beyond? So there is a need to consider where the boundaries are set for comprehension. And this is particularly important for the teacher of reading (comprehension) as this helps us to decide what we need to teach.

One way to support us in this relates to the previous chapter where we began to develop a concept of comprehension as being composed of component parts.

Earlier, we looked at the phrase 'Professional thieves operate at this station'. We noted the variety of responses that this simple phrase might require the reader to make. It was stated that this was because comprehension is difficult to describe as one thing – it is componential. So another reason why it is not straightforward to define reading comprehension is because what one person might consider to be a component of comprehension, another person might not. Certainly, all the definitions stated above take this into account to some extent; where they differ is in what they consider these components to be. So in the same way as we have questioned what it means to 'read' in Chapter 1, we can also question what it means to comprehend; and as with reading, not everyone will define comprehension in the same way. Indeed, it can be argued that any definition of comprehension will be linked to what we are willing to accept as being its component parts. So for this reason it is worth beginning to unpack some of these components of comprehension.

Unpacking the components of comprehension

Perhaps the easiest way to unpack the components of comprehension is to consider how various theorists have conceptualised it. By this, we mean the kind of theoretical framework that has been developed through which the construct of comprehension can be analysed. A common way of conceptualising comprehension is to think of it in terms of levels. A simple example of this is noted by Wyse et al. (2013), who describe comprehension on two levels: literal, where an understanding of the text is gained 'at a surface level' (p. 156), and inferential, which requires the reader to engage with text at a deeper level and 'pick up the nuances implied' (p. 156). By analysing the composition of these levels the key components of comprehension can emerge. In this example, to gain a literal comprehension of a text the reader will need to engage with the 'surface' features that will involve accessing their knowledge of vocabulary and sentence structure. So, vocabulary and sentence structure are likely to be two key components of comprehension.

Wyse et al. outline the literal and inferential comprehension levels without any great detail, but they do not appear to conceptualise these levels hierarchically – that one level needs to be attained before progressing to the next more difficult level. Wyse et al. appear to conceive of literal and inferential comprehension levels as simply being different. However, a number of levelled conceptualisations do suggest the components of comprehension are developed in a hierarchical manner – which in turn would mean that the components of comprehension are developed by readers separately and over time. In contrast, some levelled conceptualisations view them as working in a more interactive manner, which would suggest a more simultaneous acquisition of component skills. Both hierarchical and interactive conceptualisations are investigated below. If you notice the references, many of them are not very recent. Don't let this distract you – they may be old but they are not necessarily dated. The task here is to note the component processes that are prevalent within each level and see whether they reappear across the different theories.

Conceptualising the components of comprehension through hierarchical levels

The first example can be seen in the National Literacy Strategy (NLS) (1998) in England (although this has since been superseded). In the Glossary of Terms that accompanied the NLS Framework for Teaching, three levels of comprehension are described: literal, inferential and evaluative.

> Literal: the reader has access to the surface details of the text, and can recall details which have been directly related.
>
> Inferential: the reader can read meanings which are not directly examined. For example, the reader would be able to make inferences about the time of year from information given about the temperature, weather etc., and from the characters' behaviour and dialogue.
>
> Evaluative: the reader can offer an opinion on the effectiveness of the text for its purpose.
>
> (The National Literacy Strategy; Department for Education and Employment (DfEE), 1998)

Interestingly this three-level description appeared to double as a definition for comprehension itself.

A second example can be noted in Barrett's Taxonomy of Cognitive and Affective Dimensions of Reading Comprehension (Clymer, 1968). This taxonomy suggests that there are five component dimensions to comprehension, which are as follows:

> Literal Comprehension, which includes both the recognition of ideas and details when encountered and the ability to recall them later.
>
> Reorganisation, which includes skills such as classifying and summarising.
>
> Inferential Comprehension, which involves making conjectures and hypotheses about the text when information is not explicitly stated.
>
> Evaluation, which requires the making of judgements about the text.
>
> Appreciation, which involves engaging with the more literary elements such as imagery and the author's choice of words.

A third example is Moyle's (1972) five-stage model, which is as follows:

> Literal stage – reporting what the author says in the sequence he [sic] presents it. Acting upon simple instructions.
>
> Interpretive stage – re-expressing the author's meaning in one's own words, isolating main ideas, and supporting ideas, outlining the information or argumentation involved.
>
> Evaluative stage – assessing the quality, accuracy and truthfulness of what is said by reading between the lines as well as within them and comparing

new material with knowledge accumulated from past experience. This can be undertaken at two levels – the intellectual and the emotional.

Memorisation of those parts thought to add to past reading and experience.

Action – using the knowledge gained to answer the questions which provoked the reading in the first place; directing thinking into new areas or new activities; seeking further knowledge or understanding in related areas.

A number of features appear in each of these levelled conceptualisations from which we might draw some key components of comprehension. For example, they all seem to start with words and sentences as a precursor to the making of inferences, before moving on to the evaluation and appreciation of the text. There is a sense that prior knowledge is important as well as memory. This is particularly so of long-term memory, which holds the store of our prior knowledge.

There is much to consider with these, however, both in terms of their hierarchical nature and the components they suggest are important. The NLS three-level construct of comprehension provides a starting point. There appears to be an assumption that literal comprehension will be attained before an inferential comprehension; and that an evaluative comprehension is the one that children should aim to achieve. There is no evidence to support this. Indeed, Kintsch and Kintsch (2005) point to the fact that these levels are also used in the United States, although they do not appear to have been based on any research findings.

On a more important note, we have to question whether evaluation is a component of comprehension at all. Is it necessary for the reader always to have an opinion on something they have read? If I read an instructional text that comes with self-assembly flat-pack furniture I am unlikely to make a comment on the effectiveness of the instructions, unless of course the finished product bears no resemblance to the picture on the side of the box. The point to consider is whether evaluation should be considered to be part of comprehension, *per se*.

Evaluative comprehension also appears in Barrett's taxonomy. This taxonomy was developed to support teachers' questioning of children's reading and to assist in designing test questions. It might be argued that this is not strictly a levelled model of comprehension; indeed, it describes the five elements as dimensions. However, there is a sense of hierarchy once again here in that the final dimension, appreciation, requires the reader to access all the other dimensions before it can be addressed. And once again, a similar issue arises in considering whether it is necessary to 'appreciate' a piece of text in order to comprehend it.

Should 'appreciation' and the ability to recognise imagery be components of comprehension? It is possible to argue that the ability to engage with imagery could be considered within a hierarchical context because it involves an in-depth engagement with language. Alternatively one might argue that the ability to engage with imagery is underpinned by the ability to make inferences.

Where Barrett's taxonomy is interesting is that it does engage with the 'making meaning' and 'making sense' argument by suggesting that the final three levels – inferential comprehension, evaluation and appreciation – all require the reader to access personal experience.

Moyle's five-stage model is similar in some ways to the other two models presented, in terms of how the stages are named. What is interesting is that Moyle describes these named levels differently. For example, in his evaluative stage he talks of the need to 'read between the lines'; a term more commonly associated with inference making. As such, inference making appears to be placed within the evaluation stage, as does Barrett's 'appreciation' dimension. Moyle's final stage, action, is also interesting as it suggests that we cannot say something has been comprehended unless it has been applied in some way.

And finally we must consider the distinction between literal and inferential comprehension. Describing literal comprehension as being about the surface features or details, which involves recall of details, assumes that no inference making has taken place. In actual fact, to achieve a literal understanding of text we often have to make inferences, most clearly seen through how we make sense of pronouns. Take the following sentence:

'The girl closed the door and walked along the path to the front gate. It was cold.'

If we do not think too much about this piece of written text the conclusion might be drawn that the weather was in some way poor. But why? There is no mention of the weather. All we have to go on is the pronoun 'it'. But 'it' could refer to the door, or the path or the front gate. The text does not really give us a clue. So we have to make an inference that it is about the weather. We have to make an inference to get a literal understanding. This is a particular type of inference called an anaphor, which relates to pronouns. We will explore these in more detail in Chapter 6. For now, what this shows us is that there is more than one type of inference and that inferences have different purposes in reading.

These three hierarchically-levelled conceptualisations of comprehension describe various components of comprehension at specific levels of development. It might be argued that they actually confuse these components with the development of comprehension ability. As noted above, we need to make inferences of a specific type to gain a literal comprehension of text. Alongside this, when we ask children to comment on a character's actions they are required to make the same type of inference as when considering an author's actions. Again, we will explore inference making more fully in later chapters. The central point to be made here is that the key components of comprehension work simultaneously and in an interactive manner.

Conceptualising the components of comprehension through interactive levels

Some theorists have conceptualised the components of comprehension as *levels*, but rather than viewing these levels as being in a hierarchical relationship, they view them as working interactively. For example, Graesser et al. (1996) differentiate between two explicit types of comprehension:

Shallow levels of comprehension refer to an understanding of the surface features presented in texts. This includes lexical processes, syntactic parsing and how the explicit text is interpreted. The reader has to recognise the words printed on a page. For this to occur, the reader must have developed an ability to decode the words on the page, and they must also have an understanding of word meanings.

Deep levels of comprehension refer to implicit interpretations of text involving the use of inter-related components. These include the use of retained knowledge stored in memory, and the use of pragmatics, which involves the appropriate application of this background knowledge (Seifert, 1990) and an awareness of the social context of the text (McTear and Conti-Ramsden, 1992).

In contrast, Irwin's (1991) framework has five levels:

The microprocesses level: the reader comprehends individual words and phrases.

The integrative processes level: the reader connects words and sentences and makes 'slot-filling' inferences to fill any gaps.

The macroprocesses level: the reader understands and organises all the elements of a story or the components of a factual statement and consolidates them to form a mental model.

The elaborative processes level: the reader embellishes on the content of the printed text and enriches the mental model by connecting prior knowledge, making predictions, visualising, analysing, synthesising and evaluating.

The metacognitive processes level: the reader monitors their comprehension and addresses any problems.

Differences can be noted between the interactive frameworks noted here and the hierarchical frameworks noted above; and these tend to refer to the description of the levels themselves. Irwin, for example, places evaluating within the elaborative processes level, rather than conceiving it to be a level in itself. It is also worth noting that neither of these two models makes explicit mention of the need to make inferences.

On the whole, however, these two examples support the components outlined in the hierarchical frameworks. It might be argued that they actually extend the number of components. For example, Graesser et al. (1996) note how we bring our social and cultural knowledge to bear when we engage with texts. This is an important point because it acknowledges once again the fact that we bring our previous experiences to texts we read. It is not simply about 'making meaning' but also about 'making sense'. Also, Irwin (1991) notes the metacognitive process of comprehension monitoring. This is the act of consciously checking that what is being read makes sense, the opposite of 'barking' at text – something we described in the previous chapter as fluent decoding without any attempt to understand.

Placing the components of comprehension into a conceptual framework

Taken together, these conceptualisations of comprehension highlight a number of key components that can inform the teacher of reading. They tell us what is going on in a child's head when they read. We can locate the processes that readers undertake in the pursuit of understanding text. Figure 2.1 demonstrates the range of processes and factors that are likely to be of relevance to the teacher of reading. At the centre of the figure is the product of comprehension, which we might term the understanding of text. For text to be understood, the reader has to access a number of components in three broad domain areas: linguistic processes, knowledge factors and (meta-)cognitive processes. Specific components can be located within each of these broad domain areas. For example, vocabulary and syntax are components related to linguistic processing; domain knowledge and general knowledge are components related to knowledge factors; and memory, comprehension monitoring and inference making are components related to (meta-) cognitive processes. We shall investigate each of these components separately in the Processes section that follows. Separating the components allows us to see their unique contribution to the comprehension process, however it is important to remember that these processes work interactively. It is because these components work interactively that no links have been made between them in Figure 2.1.

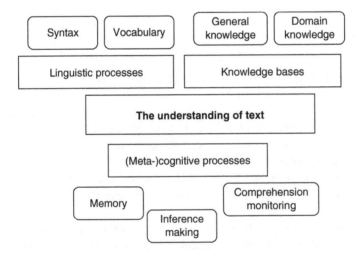

Figure 2.1 The components of comprehension in three broad domain areas

Beginning to relate the components of comprehension to the classroom

Having established that there are some key process components and some further important factors that support reading comprehension, we can now reconsider our uncomprehending child reader at the beginning of this chapter. The third question we might have asked about this scenario was whether this phenomenon of good, fluent decoding and poor comprehension was anything more than an anecdote, or whether this is a more common occurrence. As teachers of reading we need to know whether this is an isolated incident or whether there is any evidence to say that this issue is more widespread.

In fact, there is evidence to suggest that this is a common scenario. For example, Applegate et al. (2009), in response to anecdotal evidence of this nature, completed a study that investigated the relationship between reading fluency and reading comprehension. In their study they found that of the 171 children in their sample of fluent readers (which they define as those readers considered to read quickly, accurately and with expression), 57 (33%) struggled with text comprehension, and a further 62 (36%) were proficient generally but needed further support. Added to this, and as noted in Chapter 1, it is claimed by numerous researchers that up to one in every ten children in an English classroom is likely to have a specific reading comprehension difficulty (Cain, 2010; Nation and Snowling, 1997; Yuill and Oakhill, 1991). Clearly there is a discrepancy between these estimates and this is likely to have been caused by the nature of the measurements used. The Applegate et al. study findings were based on tests the researchers had developed themselves, whereas the 'one-in-ten' poor comprehension estimation is extrapolated from scores on standardised tests from numerous studies. Standardised tests give an individual score that is compared to scores achieved by a very large sample on the *same* test. Broadly speaking, researcher-designed reading tests tend to focus on the specific area being investigated. They tend to give a sensitive measure of this focus area, but can be less sensitive in regard to other related areas. In contrast, standardised tests give a general score, but may not tell us much about specific areas of interest. Neither approach is perfect, but neither should either be dismissed. The point to consider here is that there is evidence to suggest that children with poor comprehension are likely to be encountered in classrooms; and the implication of this for the teacher of reading is that these children need to be taught how to comprehend text. What is perhaps less clear is where the source of difficulty lies. Looking at the components of comprehension outlined above, and presented in Figure 2.1, there are many possible reasons as to why the child wasn't able to comprehend the text. The failure may have been due to other factors; for example, the child may consider the goal of reading to simply be about good fluent decoding. Alternatively, it may have been caused by difficulties in inference making. A further alternative is that there might be a number of processes and factors working together to have a negative impact.

CONCLUSION

Comprehension has been described as the goal of reading (Nation, 2005; Rasinski and Padak, 2008), and by Durkin (1993) as 'the essence of reading'. These two statements are interesting because they are not the same. One suggests comprehension is an end in itself; the other suggests something located 'within' (presumably within the interaction between the text and the reader). These two descriptions capture the 'making meaning' and 'making sense' distinction outlined earlier in the chapter. This is an important distinction because there are implications for how reading comprehension is taught. Many of the definitions given earlier focus on 'making meaning' rather than 'making sense'. This would suggest that comprehension is simply knowledge to be 'transmitted'. Yet we know that the understanding of any text will be unique precisely because each reader brings their own life and reading experience to it.

Comprehension is also difficult to define because of its componential nature. What we choose to include in these component processes will depend upon where we think comprehension begins and ends. By this point you should have an opinion on this already. For example, you may choose not to include Barrett's appreciation dimension. Whether this opinion relates to current curriculum and assessment procedures in your teaching context is a separate issue that will need to be explored.

It was also noted that viewing the components as hierarchical levels may not be productive. Hierarchical levels are suggestive of a developmental path. Now although we assume comprehension to develop with age, and there is plenty of evidence to support this, we do not know what this development looks like. If we did, we would be able to address the comprehension needs of every child (and there would be no need for this book). No doubt you can see why. The reading comprehension process is exceedingly complex. It involves a number of discrete components that work in an interactive manner. Research has taken us a long way in our understanding of this, however; and by understanding the component processes in greater detail it would certainly help us understand the comprehension needs of the children we teach. As such, the next few chapters will focus closely on these component processes in some depth.

 Dialogue Point

Comprehension, the curriculum and assessment

By this time you should have taken a position as to which components you think are necessary for comprehension.

Share this position with colleagues.

Gather together curriculum documents and assessment tools that are used in your teaching context. Choose two separate key stages and consider the following with colleagues:

- Which components of comprehension are we encouraged to teach?
- Is there a sense that some components are more important than others?

SECTION 1

PROCESSES

Vygotsky (1978) described the acquisition of knowledge as involving the 'intramental' and the 'intermental': the psychological and the social. 'Intramental' relates to psychological processes involved with learning, and the 'intermental' reminds us that this learning takes place in a social context.

In this section on 'Processes', the focus is on the 'intramental'. To understand reading comprehension, it is important to remember that it is not a 'unitary construct' (Duke, 2005: 93): it is not one thing. Rather, it is a mesh of inter-related component parts. In this section we will unpack these component parts to see how they contribute to comprehension. The components will be considered in relation to the three broad domain areas outlined in Chapter 2.

Chapter 3 is called 'Knowledge: of life and language'. It focuses on two components of comprehension: the prior knowledge we bring to the act of reading any text, and the knowledge of language which is applied to it. This covers the two domain areas of linguistic processes and knowledge factors. Chapter 4 introduces the domain area of (meta-)cognitive processes by investigating the role of memory in comprehension and the metacognitive ability to monitor comprehension as we read to ensure that it makes sense. Chapters 5–7 extend this focus on the (meta-)cognitive processes domain by taking a detailed look at the role of inference making. These chapters aim to offer teachers an in-depth outline of an area that is considered to be centrally important to the comprehension of text. Chapter 8 investigates some key findings from various models of text comprehension. The aim here is to reassert the point that these components work interactively.

CHAPTER 3

KNOWLEDGE: OF LIFE AND LANGUAGE

Chapter Overview

This chapter investigates comprehension from the perspective of two knowledge components. The first perspective considers the importance of life experience and how knowledge gained from this supports the reader in text comprehension. This prior knowledge is considered in relation to generic knowledge, which relates to knowledge the reader has gained of the world in general; and domain knowledge, which relates to the knowledge they may have in a specific area, knowledge which not everyone will have. The second perspective considers the knowledge of language. It focuses on the linguistic processes involved in text comprehension in relation to our knowledge of words (vocabulary) and our knowledge of grammar structures (syntax). Two major implications are raised through the analysis of these two components of comprehension: children attempting to comprehend text will bring different prior knowledge to it, and will display different levels of linguistic proficiency.

'Twas brillig, and the slithy toves
Did gyre and gimble in the wabe:
All mimsy were the borogoves,
And the mome raths outgrabe.

'Beware the Jabberwock, my son!
The jaws that bite, the claws that catch!
Beware the Jubjub bird, and shun
The frumious Bandersnatch!'

And so begins 'Jabberwocky' by Lewis Carroll ([1871] 2003). Working with a group of trainee teachers on this text, it was interesting to see how they dealt with it. Some of them were very confident. It transpired that these trainees were English Literature graduates who had either encountered the work of Lewis Carroll before, or were at least aware of how poetry works and noted such things as the rhyme scheme very quickly. Others were less confident: they couldn't understand all the words and found it difficult to assign meaning to some parts of it. (They found the second verse easier than the first though.)

So how would children make sense of it?

Well, very much in the same way as adults actually. Children bring knowledge to each text they read. In this chapter we will look at this knowledge from two perspectives: knowledge we have gained through life and the knowledge we have of language.

KNOWLEDGE OF LIFE

Life knowledge refers to knowledge we have gained through prior experience. The importance of this prior knowledge to the comprehension of text has long been accepted by researchers and theorists in this area. Indeed, many years ago Bartlett (1932) suggested that information from text is not simply stored in our heads, but interpreted in relation to what we already know. It is through the application of this prior knowledge that we notice relationships between different parts of texts and thus achieve a coherent understanding of it (van den Broek, 1994). Bartlett raised another very interesting point by suggesting that this process of applying prior knowledge to comprehend text is potentially a two-way interaction: our prior knowledge allows us to interpret new information, but this new information can also allow us to interpret our existing knowledge differently. This is an interesting point for the teacher of reading to consider because it reminds us that the comprehension of text – and thus the act of reading – supports the learning of new knowledge.

We can learn by reading books. This seems blindingly obvious, doesn't it? But let's unpack it a little further because there are couple of points that need to be made explicit when considering the role of knowledge in text comprehension.

Comprehension takes places in the context of socially and culturally constructed knowledge

First, we must remember that, as Mercer (1995) reminds us, all knowledge is constructed, and it is constructed in a social and cultural context. This context provides a reference point that helps us to describe how the world works. Those who share this context also share the knowledge associated with it and this will help to inform their interpretation of it. Text comprehension takes place within this context. The meanings that we as readers assign to any text are framed by the social and cultural context we are familiar with. So the interaction is not simply a two-way interaction between the reader and the text; it involves the context too.

Comprehension takes place in the light of what we already know

As Bartlett (1932) noted, encountering new information can make us view our existing knowledge differently. Thus, 'new' knowledge builds on established knowledge. Even when really clever people (the Einsteins of this world) come up with a new idea or theory, it is still developed in the context of pre-existing (socially and culturally located) knowledge. Thus, when readers seek to attain meaning from text they do so in relation to the knowledge they already have. The implication of this is that readers – of any age – are not blank canvasses. They bring something to each reading episode.

So when we consider the role of knowledge we must consider the knowledge the reader brings to the text and the context in which this knowledge was created.

Dialogue Point

Exploring the knowledge we bring to text

You are currently engaging with a book about comprehension. It contains domain-specific knowledge. Later in this chapter, we will look at the role of vocabulary, morphology and syntax in comprehension.

Make a mind map to show words or ideas that you have about these. Share your mind map with colleagues and consider two points:

- What do you know of these things?
- Where did you gather this pre-existing knowledge from?

Now, read these sections of the chapter and add to your mind map. Share findings with colleagues. Can you add more by sharing from their mind maps?

Types of knowledge

Research into reading comprehension has generally split knowledge gained through life experience into two specific types: generic knowledge and domain knowledge. Both types reflect the fact that the knowledge we have is shared to a greater or lesser extent.

Generic knowledge

Generic knowledge is knowledge that can be widely shared. It is accessed, or has the potential to be accessed, by anyone in relation to their everyday experience. You might see generic knowledge labelled sometimes as world knowledge. This is fine if we consider it as an individual's knowledge *of* the world. It is not knowledge shared *by* the world as a whole because, as we have already noted, knowledge is culturally located; what constitutes generic knowledge will differ between societies.

According to Graesser et al. (1994), generic knowledge includes knowledge of scripts, stereotypes and schemata. Knowledge of *scripts* can be related to genre theory (Kress and Knapp, 1992), which suggests that in all social situations certain scripts are adhered to. So, for example, even when we go to the post office to buy a stamp, there is a general script which is followed. It might include a formal salutation, particular requests around postage (class of stamp, for example), expressions of gratitude and farewells. Knowing this script provides social access; in contrast, not knowing the script leads to exclusion. This becomes more obvious with such things as the language associated with the law. *Stereotypes* refer to how particular groups or phenomena might be expected to think and behave. We note the behaviour and attitudes of some members of the group and assume that all members of the group share these attributes. *Schemata* relate to how we organise our thoughts about different aspects of the world, and the links we can make to this when engaging with new information.

When we apply generic knowledge to text, we are most likely to apply it in relation to narratives. As Bruner (1986) notes, stories tend to be reflective of everyday life and experience. Bruner (2002) also stated that 'Stories are a culture's coin and currency' (p. 15), and thus they play an important part in the sharing of knowledge within and between generations.

> 📁 **Generic knowledge applied to a story: an example**
>
> If we read a story with a fox as a character we might expect that character to behave in a certain a way and that certain things will happen. Why? Well it is historical. When (Western) society was more agriculturally-based, foxes were (and still are) considered a threat to farmyard animals. They are clever at gaining access and they kill randomly. We have built a schema based on (historical) life experience about foxes. The stereotype is that all foxes are cunning and untrustworthy. And so we bring this knowledge to stories that feature foxes, or even a character whose name is 'Fox'. Originally these would have been oral stories but these have been transferred into written texts. An example would be Robert Nye's wonderful story entitled 'Lord Fox' (1997). This story is set in the border country between England and Scotland several hundred years ago. It features a mysterious central character called Lord Fox, who is indeed cunning and untrustworthy. So we can begin to see how (a culturally located) generic knowledge is applied to written text in the context of a story.

Domain knowledge

Domain knowledge involves the use of knowledge *specific* to a prior experience, theme or subject. So, for example, if someone has a passion for a particular sporting team, hobby or pop group, the knowledge related to these is unlikely to be universal. Domain knowledge is often associated with an expertise. An expert may be considered to be someone who has an extensive knowledge in a particular domain. This could indeed include such things as knowledge of a particular sporting team, but can also apply to such things as car mechanics or neurolinguistic processing. Expertise in areas such as these may or may not involve some course of study.

The fact that it can be applied to study brings us to how domain knowledge relates to text comprehension. In contrast to generic knowledge, which is more commonly associated with narrative texts, domain knowledge is more usually applied to non-fiction, or expository, texts. Domain knowledge can be applied to narrative texts of course – a knowledge of horse racing will probably support the reading of a Dick Francis novel (actually, Moravcsik and Kintsch (1993) suggest that story knowledge is itself a type of domain knowledge). Also, with the postgraduate trainees reading 'Jabberwocky' it was noted that some of them were more able to engage with the text because they had knowledge of how poems can be structured, and this is also a type of domain knowledge.

Research in this field has yielded some perhaps unsurprising but certainly important results. For example, Moravcsik and Kintsch (1993) found that participants with a high knowledge domain were able to attain a deeper understanding. In another interesting study Yekovich et al. (1990) found that inferences about a text could be made by apparently 'low-aptitude' individuals, if they were familiar with the domain. As they point out, what may be termed as 'aptitude' is dependent not just on how well the reader is able to process text – but also upon the knowledge the reader brings to it.

🗁 Domain knowledge applied to a non-fiction text: an example

A colleague was leading a Year 5 (9–10 year olds) guided reading session looking at the language of newspapers. It featured an article from a local newspaper about a girl of 11 who was playing rugby for a local team. The article was full of the usual clichés about her being a tomboy (reinforcing a stereotype in our generic knowledge about girls who play rugby, perhaps?).

Richard (pseudonym) was one of the group members. He wasn't an avid reader and it often took him a little longer than others in the group to achieve a general understanding; but his general reading skills were developing. What was interesting with this text was that Richard had been playing rugby for several years. As a result he had knowledge of relevant domain-specific words such as 'scrum', and he was the most adept in the group at making sense of the figurative and idiomatic language being used. He led the discussion in comprehending statements such 'waiting in the wings' (wing is a position in rugby), and 'she converted the rest of the team' (a conversion is a kicked score).

Here we can see how the comprehension of text can be supported if the reader has domain-specific knowledge to apply to it.

Knowledge of life: implications for the teacher of reading

The application of prior knowledge is essential for text comprehension regardless of whether the text is a narrative or a piece of non-fiction. However, the amount of prior knowledge readers are able to apply is likely to vary from topic to topic, and from individual to individual. This is particularly so for children. We can presume that their knowledge bases are likely to develop with age; they will have greater experience of the world and are likely to develop specific interests. For the teacher of reading, two questions become important.

1. Make explicit to children that prior knowledge should be accessed wherever possible

First we might ask, 'Do the children actually know that they need to apply their prior knowledge to text?'. Less skilled readers may believe that reading is about decoding words rather than seeking meaning (Myers and Paris, 1978). Cain and Oakhill (1999) go on to suggest that those struggling with comprehension need to be shown 'the aims and purposes of reading'. I would argue that even apparently skilled readers need to be made clear about this. Reading ability is often equated with the ability to decode text; indeed it is often the case in my experience that children in the (so-called) 'more able' guided reading groups are ones who can decode more efficiently. They have not necessarily been placed in these groups because of their comprehension ability. So even so-called 'skilled' readers in the classroom context, some of whom might more accurately be described as skilled decoders, may also need clarification as to the aims and purposes of reading.

2. Find out what knowledge children have

The second question we must then consider is, 'What knowledge are the young readers bringing to the text I've chosen?'. As we have noted, readers engage with text in the light of what they already know, they are not blank canvasses. This applies to children too. The meaning they extract from text will be formed in the light of their prior knowledge, both generic and domain-specific, and this will be different for each child.

School-based activity

Investigating the impact of prior knowledge on children's comprehension

Working with individuals or a small group of children, choose a text that you think they may have little prior knowledge about.

Choose a second text, which you think some or all might have a more detailed knowledge about.

Engage the children in a brief dialogue about each text.

Record both sessions.

Analyse the recordings and notice how they have engaged with each text. What were the similarities and differences?

Share your findings with colleagues.

KNOWLEDGE OF LANGUAGE

Knowledge of language underpins our knowledge of the world. This is because our knowledge of the world is framed by language. We learn to assign labels, or words, to objects, ideas and feelings. So it is fair to say that our knowledge of the world will include our semantic knowledge, which we can call our knowledge of word meanings or vocabulary. These words do not exist in isolation of course, and we learn to place these words in the context of other words to form sentences. Our syntactic knowledge is the ability to understand the grammatical structures used in sentences we form to attain meaning (Cain and Oakhill, 2007). Initially as very young children, we acquire our knowledge of words and grammar through listening. This is a receptive skill; it is something that comes into our heads. We begin to show our understanding of them through speech, which is an expressive skill (it is something we do). At some point we begin to engage with written text and apply our knowledge of words and grammar to reading, which is also a receptive skill. However, the manner in which we develop understanding through the receptive skill of reading is not exactly the same as how we develop understanding through the receptive skill of listening.

In this section we will look at how words and sentences, broadly speaking the linguistic processes, support the comprehension of text.

VOCABULARY

It is important to distinguish between two contexts in which the term 'vocabulary' is used. It can refer to *oral vocabulary*, which is the knowledge of word meanings, and it can also refer to *sight vocabulary*, which is the ability to recognise the visual form of a written word. Simply recognising a written word does not mean that its meaning has been understood. We can see this in 'Jabberwocky'. What does 'brillig' mean? We can recognise 'brillig' as a word while also having no idea what it means, which is why a number of the trainee students found it annoying to work with. And thus we arrive at a point worth reiterating: Decoding without comprehension is not reading. So what does it mean to say that a word is known?

What does it mean to know a word?

To say that anyone knows the meaning of a word is difficult because the nature of word knowledge acquisition is itself complex. For example, Aitchison (2003) notes that though a child can 'label' things and objects, they will have a restricted understanding of the word's meaning. Experiencing the word in a wider variety of contexts allows them to refine this understanding. Aitchison provides the example of the word *penguin*. The word may initially be a label for a toy, but as the child experiences wider contexts of the word, their understanding of what a penguin actually is, is refined. They will know its features, for example, and what differentiates it from other flightless birds.

So the meaning of a word in children's oral vocabulary may be different from individual to individual because of the context in which it was acquired, and the experience they have of this word. Thus some children are likely to have a deeper understanding of a word. This relates to what has been termed *vocabulary depth*, and studies have investigated this. Oullette (2006), for example, investigated the role of vocabulary for Grade 4 children (9-year-olds) in relation to the specific reading skills of decoding, visual word recognition and reading comprehension. She found that the depth of expressive vocabulary knowledge was closely associated with reading comprehension ability. So if we have a more detailed knowledge of a word, it helps us to comprehend the text.

The idea that children's understanding of words changes with time probably should not come as a surprise; it is likely to be something we experience as adults. I suspect (though I don't know) that some readers of this section may not, for example, have considered dividing vocabulary into two types, oral and sight, or considered the relationship between the two. This is interesting because it shows that our knowledge of words is not necessarily static, and is likely to alter with our experience of them. The knowledge we bring to a word, whether it be generic or domain-specific, is likely to change, and with it, what we believe the word to mean.

So how does this help teachers? Well on one level it doesn't; in fact it rather complicates matters. Perhaps the important point for teachers is that we know what particular words mean to a child in the context of the learning taking place. If we really need to find this out, the approach taken by Paribakht and Wesche (1997) might provide a starting point. They investigated vocabulary in relation to second language acquisition and suggested we should consider describing children's word knowledge using the following scale:

1. Never saw (the word) before

2. Heard it but does not know what it means

3. Recognises it in context

4. Knows it well

5. Can use the word in a sentence

This last point sees the word ceasing to be simply part of the child's receptive vocabulary (to do with reading and listening) and becoming part of the child's expressive vocabulary (to do with writing and speaking) (Baumann et al., 2003). So to go back to the start of this section, sight vocabulary isn't enough. We can say a word is understood only when it becomes part of oral vocabulary (whilst accepting that the meaning given to the word may be refined over time). To complicate matters further, Bromley (2007) raises two issues you might find interesting. First, there are a vast number of words in the English language (English has three times as many words as German, and six times as many as French); and second, it has been suggested that around 70% of the words we use most frequently have more than one meaning.

How reading supports vocabulary

Both oral and sight vocabulary are important to reading development. Oral vocabulary carries the knowledge of word meanings; and sight vocabulary is important because if we cannot get the word off the page we will not be able to know if we understand what it means. But actually we know that it is a recipro-cal relationship: reading is important for vocabulary acquisition.

As already noted earlier, for very young children vocabulary acquisition takes place largely through the oral mode. A child's oral vocabulary increases with age. As a child gets older, oral vocabulary knowledge is extended through the child's reading experiences. Thus, as children's reading becomes more proficient, reading itself becomes an important influence on the acquisition of new word meanings (Perfetti et al., 2005).

Cunningham (2005) explains this by noting the differences in oral and written languages as methods of communication. Speech requires the use of more com-mon words for dialogue to be maintained given the constraint of time, which means spoken language tends to be used in a less complex manner. The writer, on the other hand, has the time to access a wider lexicon. Thus, a child reader is likely to encounter a wider variety of vocabulary in written texts than through speech. This does not necessarily guarantee that oral vocabulary will be aug-mented, as these encounters with new vocabulary are often infrequent. Anderson and Nagy (1992) conclude from their various studies that children incorporate into their oral vocabulary about one of every twenty new words during reading when it is encountered only once. Children may incorporate these infrequent and unfamiliar words into their sight vocabulary and may be able to assign some sort of meaning to them, but unless the word is encountered again they may not be able to refine their understanding of the word. As Aitchison's account of children's vocabulary knowledge shows, word learning is incremental: an understanding of a word's meaning is arrived at after a number of exposures (Cain et al., 2003).

The point important to note here is that reading has the potential to augment our oral vocabulary. If we did not read, our oral vocabulary would be smaller. The implications for children (and adults) who do not read very much are obvious, and this matters for comprehension.

Vocabulary and comprehension

It matters for two reasons. First, it matters because we know that vocabulary has a pivotal role in the comprehension of text. Indeed, Kamil and Hiebert (2005) have described vocabulary as providing a bridge between the processes involved with the decoding of text, such as putting together sounds to make recognisable sight words, and the cognitive processes involved in comprehension, such as the application of memory bases, monitoring comprehension as we read to ensure that it makes sense, and the making of inferences. These processes are explored in the following chapters. The description of vocabulary as providing a bridge is appropriate, because a bridge can be crossed in two directions. As Baumann et al. (2003) note, comprehension can be supported by vocabulary, but it may also be the case that being able to comprehend allows vocabulary knowledge to be extended. Intuitively, we might indeed see the relationship between vocabulary and comprehensions as reciprocal. The point to make here is that vocabulary is in a mediating position between any written text we read and the comprehension of that specific text.

But we know that the role of vocabulary is important even before the stage of engaging with written text. And this is the second reason why vocabulary matters to comprehension. Scarborough (2001), for example, has shown that the vocabulary size a child develops by the time they are in Kindergarten (3–4-year-olds), where they will not be decoding written text, can be directly related to the reading comprehension scores they attain as 10-year-olds. Similarly, Cunningham and Stanovich (1997) found that vocabulary size at the end of Grade 1 (6-year-olds), when decoding skills are in the early stages of development, predicted achievement in reading comprehension at the age of 16. So these studies suggest that the vocabulary that children have acquired from non-school contexts has an impact on reading comprehension later in schooling.

This is important because we cannot assume that children will begin formal schooling having acquired the same amount of oral vocabulary. Indeed, Biemiller (2005) found the following pattern by the end of Grade 2 (7-year-olds):

Above-average 7-year-olds – acquired knowledge of up to around 8,000 root words

Average 7-year-olds – acquired knowledge of around 6,000 root words

Below-average 7-year-olds – acquired knowledge of around 4,000 root words

This shows that children acquire vocabulary at different rates: those who have acquired a greater number of words will have a broader vocabulary at their disposal (though not necessarily deeper). The range of vocabulary someone has is described as *vocabulary breadth*. Again, there is evidence to suggest that vocabulary breadth is important for comprehension (Tannenbaum et al., 2006). As Biemiller and Boote (2006) point out, these differences cannot be explained by schooling because vocabulary instruction does not feature on the curriculum to this extent (if it features at all).

Morphology

At this point it is worth mentioning morphology, as it is closely allied to vocabulary acquisition; and it also has a singular role in supporting reading comprehension. Morphology examines 'how meaningful word parts, *morphemes*, are arranged to create words' (Templeton, 2012: 101). Stahl (1999) suggested that it is not enough to know a word's definition, but that we also need to consider how it relates to other words, how it is used in different contexts and how other words can be derived from, or related to, it. This is where morphology becomes important. Templeton (2012) notes that linguists have separated morphology into three components, shown in Table 3.1.

Table 3.1 Three components of morphology

Compounding	Compound words formed by combining separate words	sea + side = seaside bed + room = bedroom
Inflectional morphology	Verb tense changes Number	washes – washed dog, dogs witch, witches
	Possession Comparatives and superlatives	boy's boys' great, greater, greatest grander, grandest
Derivational morphology	Adding affixes (prefixes and suffixes) to root words	condition recondition conditional unconditional unconditionally

Anglin (1993) estimated that between the ages of 6 and 11 a child's knowledge of root words doubles. However, he also estimated that there is a ten-fold increase in the number of morphologically-related words they are likely to encounter. It would seem obvious then that making children aware of the morphological links between words is likely to support vocabulary development. This is not difficult to show, even with the words in 'Jabberwocky'. Imagine we have assigned meaning to 'slithy' and 'mimsy'. Perhaps then we could develop the word 'slithily' from 'slithy'; or 'mimsily' from 'mimsy'. And we could then ask, 'Who is 'the "slithiest" tove?'. Or can one 'borogrove' be 'mimsier' than another? The point here is that being morphologically aware can help to both broaden and deepen our knowledge of words (Kieffer and Lesaux, 2007).

Morphology and comprehension

Cain (2010) describes morphological awareness as a metalinguistic skill because it involves actively reflecting on language. The benefits of being able to do this have been shown in studies. Carlisle and Fleming (2003) showed that morphological awareness predicted vocabulary scores two years later for the 7-year-olds in their study. However, morphological awareness has also been shown to have a direct link to comprehension. Deacon and Kirby (2004) found that comprehension differences with 7-year-olds in their study were explained by differences in morphological awareness: better comprehenders were more morphologically aware. Added to this, McCutchen and Logan (2011) point to a number of studies which suggest that for older children comprehension is more strongly related to morphological awareness than it is to phonological awareness (the knowledge of sounds in words).

Dialogue Point

Investigating morphology

Templeton (2012) refers to one teacher who takes a strong focus on teaching morphology and shares the mantra 'You learn one word, you learn ten!' with her class. How true is this?

Working with colleagues, see if you can generate ten words from these root words:

  hand   play   verse

And these words with Latin roots, which we don't use any more but which help us to form words:

  dict   rupt

Discuss:

- How the prefixes and suffixes change the meanings of these words
- How the grammatical function of the word changes

School-based activity

Investigating children's morphological awareness

Collect together a small number of root words.
  Working with different groups of children, see how many words they can generate from the root words.
  Consider whether:

- They were able to give meaning to the words they generate
- They created and rejected 'meaningless' words (What were these words? And why were they rejected?)
- There were any between-group differences

  Share findings with colleagues.

SYNTAX

As well as working out the meaning of individual words, readers have to work out the meaning of the sentences in which they are contained (Cain, 2010). To do this readers have to engage with syntax. Syntax relates to the grammatical arrangement of words within and across sentences. We can see this once again referring to the 'Jabberwocky' text at the start of the chapter. We may have had difficulty assigning meaning to some of the words, but the grammatical arrangement of the piece is not wholly unfamiliar. We can notice adjectives, which come before nouns ('slithy toves' and 'frumious Bandersnatch'), verbs ('gyre' and 'gimble'), and prepositions that signify place ('*in* the wabe'). In texts where the words are known we are likely to pay less obvious attention to the grammatical arrangement, but the 'Jabberwocky' text forces us to look at this more closely in order to make sense of it, or at least try to. It shows that syntactic awareness is important in supporting comprehension. Syntactic awareness relates to the ability to reflect upon (Cain and Oakhill, 2007) and manipulate (Nation and Snowling, 2000) the grammatical structures in sentences.

The oral/aural development of syntactic knowledge

As with vocabulary, children's knowledge and awareness of syntax develops with age. Garton and Pratt (1989) note that by the age of 2–3 years most children will have acquired enough syntactic knowledge to be able to combine words to make statements that follow grammatical rules. Cain (2010) suggests that children have acquired a basic understanding of grammar and syntax by the age of 5. However, this syntactic knowledge continues to be developed orally through childhood. This growth in syntactic knowledge facilitates the ability to use longer sentences. Nippold (1998) points to the work of Leadholm and Miller (1992), who collected spontaneous language samples (including complete and incomplete sentences) from children aged 3–13. This suggested that the length of sentences used by children in their everyday conversational speech continues to increase into adolescence.

Syntax and comprehension

As with vocabulary, the syntax that readers engage with in written text is not always going to be the same as the syntax used in speech. It is important then for readers to be aware of the word order in sentences as this can have an effect on how the text is comprehended. In the 'Jabberwocky' extract, for example, we might expect 'All mimsy were the borogoves' to be written as 'The borogoves were all mimsy'; 'the borogoves' are the subject of the sentence and we usually expect this to come first. Another example is with the use of active and passive sentences, where sentences that appear similar can actually have different meanings (Cain, 2010). Look at the difference in meaning between the first sentence, which is active, and the second sentence, which is passive, although the sentences are very similar:

The mother fed the children.

The mother was fed by the children.

We can see then how the grammatical structure of a sentence can impact upon comprehension. However, the relationship between syntax and comprehension is not a straightforward one. Studies have found a link between the two. Nation and Snowling (2000), for example, found that poor comprehenders had significantly more difficulty dealing with passive sentences than good comprehenders, which suggests poor comprehenders are likely to be less syntactically aware. Cain (2010) notes studies which have found that, as with vocabulary, syntactic awareness impacts upon later comprehension (Demont and Gombert, 1996; Muter et al., 2004), but Cain (2007) also suggests that this is likely to be mediated by such things as word knowledge. This makes sense; if you do not know the words in the sentence in first place, it is difficult to make sense of the sentence anyway ('All mimsy were the borogoves'?). The point to note is that syntactic awareness is required for comprehension, even if it does work in the context of such things as vocabulary.

Knowledge of language: implications for teaching reading comprehension

The teacher of reading comprehension is left with much to consider here. To begin with, we know that vocabulary is important for comprehension but that children are likely to display wide differences in vocabulary knowledge. This is likely to stem from factors outside the classroom over which the teacher has no control.

We may need to teach vocabulary, but this is not as easy as it sounds

To compensate for this, one approach might be to develop vocabulary acquisition in the classroom context with the aim of supporting comprehension. We know that vocabulary is acquired in one of two ways: through direct instruction or through incidental learning (Nippold, 1998). Incidental learning describes a situation where vocabulary is acquired without any explicit teaching and it has been suggested that this is how most vocabulary is acquired (Cunnigham, 2005; Kamil and Hiebert, 2005). Of course, in this situation it is difficult to know whether words have been learnt. Direct instruction requires a 'knowledgeable' (Nippold, 1998) person to instruct the child about the meaning of a word, and is likely to take the form of some kind of oral explanation. The problem for the teacher is to decide which words to teach and how many should be taught. Also, given the potential variation in vocabulary knowledge, a very large number of words might need to be taught. Authors such as Biemiller and Boote (2006) suggest that this can be done, but it does appear to require a radical reorganisation of how class time is used.

Help children to use contextual clues

One strategy that has been shown to be useful in helping children find the meaning of new words is by making them aware of contextual clues. Nagy et al. (1987) found that all ages in their study (8–18 years of age) could use contextual clues to discover the meaning of new words as long as they were able to decode the text. In fact, by using contextual clues we were probably able to make some sense of the second verse of 'Jabberwocky'. Using our knowledge of words such as 'beware', 'shun', 'jaws' and 'claws', we could assign meaning to 'Jabberwock', 'Jubjub' and 'Bandersnatch' (possibly types of dangerous animals or monsters). In so doing we can make some sense at least of the verse as a whole. Of course, the use of contextual clues requires inferences to be made – we infer what a 'Jabberwock' is, or might be. We also bring our prior knowledge to bear. In this case the knowledge of words such as 'jaws' and 'claws' help us to assign meaning; it also reminds us that new words are best learnt in the context of known ones (Bromley, 2007). And of course we need to know how words like 'Jabberwock' work in the context of other words, so we also apply our syntactic awareness. This emphasises the point that although we are looking at the component processes of comprehension separately, they do in fact work interactively. Another approach would be to make the children aware of such things as similes, metaphors and illustrative examples of the new word (Sinatra and Dowd, 1991).

CONCLUSION

In this chapter we have taken the theme of knowledge and used it to consider the importance of two components that contribute to reading comprehension. The first was the prior knowledge that readers bring to any reading episode (developed through life experience); and the second was the knowledge of language (or the linguistic knowledge) which the reader brings, and which helps them to give meaning to the words they read, in the context of the text they are reading. We noted how these contributed uniquely to overall comprehension, but also saw a few hints as to how these components work interactively. One point does come across strongly when these two components are considered, and it is one worth repeating. When children come to the reading of written text they are not blank canvasses. They bring both life and linguistic knowledge to each reading experience, in the same way as the trainee teachers engaged with 'Jabberwocky' (and in the same way as you are engaging with this text too). Their life knowledge is socially and culturally constructed. There is no such thing as a cultural knowledge, much in the same way that there is no such thing as an acultural text. Moreover, they are likely to bring with them varying degrees of linguistic knowledge. The trick for the teaching of reading comprehension is to find out what prior knowledge they are bringing to a chosen text, and to have some understanding of their general language proficiency.

CHAPTER 4

MEMORY AND MONITORING

Chapter Overview

This chapter investigates two further components of comprehension. The first of these is memory. Memory is presented as a cognitive component that consists of two separate systems: long-term memory and short-term memory. The role of each of these systems in the comprehension process is considered. Special attention is given to the role of working memory. The second component investigated in this chapter is that of comprehension monitoring. Comprehension monitoring is a metacognitive component and involves readers actively ensuring that they are comprehending the text as they read it. A number of implications for teachers are raised in relation to these components. These include such things as being aware of the load on working memory that texts may present; and the fact that the monitoring of text is not a skill that children are likely to have, but it is rather a strategy that needs to be taught.

Philip Pullman, author of the *His Dark Materials* trilogy, once took part in an online discussion about his work (*The Guardian*, 2011). His young readers were invited to ask him questions. One young reader, Francesca (aged 9), asked him whether he was inspired to write by J.R.R. Tolkien, the author of *The Lord of the Rings*. Putting aside the fact that we might be taken aback slightly by a 9-year-old asking such a question, Philip Pullman's response was an interesting one. Whilst acknowledging that he enjoyed reading Tolkien, he is critical of him for two reasons, stating 'He [Tolkien] always seems to be looking backwards, to a greater and more golden past; and what's more he doesn't allow girls or women any part in the story at all'.

These are criticisms that most certainly cannot be levelled at Philip Pullman, particularly when you consider his Sally Lockhart quartet of stories. In the first of these, *The Ruby in the Smoke* (1985), we get a particularly grimy vision of London in 1872 and we are presented with the liberated character of Sally. Towards the beginning of the story, Sally finds out that her father has been lost in the South China Sea while on a business trip. She goes to the offices of Shelby and Lockhart, where her father worked with his business partner, after receiving a mysterious note. As she talks to the company secretary, Mr Higgs, about the note he suddenly keels over and dies at her feet. At this moment she hears a voice in the corridor followed, by another one:

'Samuel Shelby, Shipping Agent. Got that?'

'No Mr Lockhart?' said another voice, more timidly.

'There ain't no Mr Lockhart. Mr Lockhart's lying in a hundred fathoms of water in the South China Sea, blast him. I mean, rest his soul. Paint him out, d'ye hear me? Paint him out! And I don't like green. A nice cheerful yeller for me, with them curly lines all round. Stylish. Got that?

'Yes, Mr Selby,' was the reply.

The door opened and the owner of the first voice came in.

This is potentially a disorientating scene, particularly as it follows the gruesome death of Mr Higgs and because it is so brief. Following this, Sally and Mr Shelby engage in conversation with no reference made to what just happened (and bearing in mind there is a dead man lying at Sally's feet, that's probably understandable).

So how would children make sense of it?

Well, as we discussed in the previous chapter, we would expect them to apply their knowledge of language; of the words they know and how they work grammatically in sentences. We would also expect them to apply their general world knowledge and any domain-specific knowledge that might be relevant. However, none of this would be possible without being able to recall this knowledge in the first place; and they certainly wouldn't be able to comprehend this particular event if they were unable to keep track of the action as it happens. So to comprehend text they have to refer to memory and learn to monitor what they read as they go along; and these are two more important components of comprehension.

MEMORY

Memory is a cognitive process; it is to do with thinking. However, memory is not a unitary system (Gathercole, 1998), much in the same way that comprehension is not a unitary construct, as we have already noted. Two separable, but linked, memory systems, from which information is stored and recalled, have been most notably investigated: long-term memory and short-term memory. However, as the descriptions of these next will show, separate other systems can be found within each.

Long-term memory

Long-term memory relates to the ability to remember information from the past covering a timespan of hours to years. Information stored in long-term memory can be described as 'relatively permanent' (Cain, 2010: 65). Tulving (1983) identified two distinguishable systems within long-tem memory: semantic memory and episodic memory.

Semantic memory refers to a general knowledge of the world that the remember shares with other people. Information is likely to be organised conceptually in semantic memory and will encompass views beyond the individual and be based around facts or ideas. Being able to recall and name the capital city of France is an example of semantic memory (Baddeley, 2004). In this instance it assumes an understanding of what is meant by the concept of a capital city, and a concept that we might have of a country called France.

Episodic memory, in contrast, refers to specific episodes and experiences that are personal and unique to the person who recalls them. Information is likely to be organised temporally in episodic memory. Being able to recall a visit to the dentist from the previous week is an example of episodic memory (Baddeley, 2004). In this instance we are conscious of the timing of the dental visit and can place it in relation to other events that day or week; for example, following the dental visit we might have remembered our inability to speak coherently to a local shopkeeper because of the anaesthetic. Gathercole (1998) notes the definition of episodic memory as referring to remembrances on a narrower timescale of about a week at most. Thus, episodic memory relates to highly specific remembrances that might encompass the mundane, such as remembering what food was eaten at a particular meal.

As we know, however, events are remembered on a much greater timescale than a week. These remembrances will be incomplete, with only some incidents remembered. For example, it is possible to recall attending a music concert without remembering everything that occurred (even which songs were performed). This type of remembrance is known as autobiographical memory (Conway, 1990).

Tulving (1983) suggests that there are nonetheless some similarities between episodic and semantic memory. These include the passive and automatic retention of information, and that retaining these memories is not effortful. Tulving also suggests that retrieving this information in both the semantic and episodic systems is instigated by stimuli, questions and cues. This retrieval of information is highly selective and only a small amount of the stored information will be activated.

At this point it is important to make a link between this description of long-term memory and our discussion of the prior knowledge a reader brings to the text in the previous chapter. It was noted that this prior knowledge could be a generic world knowledge or domain knowledge specific to a particular theme or subject. All this prior knowledge is held in long-tem memory.

Short-term memory

In contrast to long-term memory, short-term memory refers to the storage of information over very brief periods of time (Baddeley, 2004) and which can be recalled for only 'a limited time' (Cain, 2010: 146). The timespan for this is seconds or possibly minutes (Gathercole, 1998). The event, word or idea has to be recalled very soon after it has been encountered. This creates a potential difficulty because we have only a limited capacity for storing, retaining and retrieving information in short-term memory. How do we know this? Well, evidence for this came initially from investigations on the ability to recall sequences of numbers (digit span tasks), which showed that most people are likely to be able to recall six or seven digits at most (Baddeley, 2004). Therefore, any information held in short-term memory has to be processed quickly because it will be retained for only a short period of time before it is gone.

So now we notice a difference between how long-term memory and short-term memory function. In the long-term memory system, information is passively and automatically retained; in contrast, the short-tem memory system is active and working.

The fact that information has to be stored, retained and retrieved within a framework of limited capacity led researchers to investigate how this actually takes place. As a result, Baddeley and Hitch (1974) developed a model of working memory which recognised three separate systems: the central executive, where information is processed; the phonological loop, which deals with phonological information (the sounds that form the words); and the visuo-spatial sketch pad, which deals with such things as shape, space, colour and movement. The authors describe the latter two as 'slave systems' to the central executive system. Baddeley (2000) later proposed a fourth component of the working memory model known as the 'episodic buffer', which is a temporary storage system also controlled by the central executive (on the assumption that the central executive itself is not capable of storage and we do appear to store some information however briefly and temporarily).

At this particular point we do not need to know how each of the systems functions in detail. We do need to know about working memory though, and we need to know that working memory is activated when information in short-term memory is simultaneously stored and processed (Pickering, 2006). We need to know this because working memory has an important role in the comprehension of text.

MEMORY AND READING COMPREHENSION

The contribution of memory to reading comprehension needs to be considered in relation to the different memory systems outlined above. Reading comprehension requires the reader to create a mental representation or situation model (Johnson-Laird, 1983; Kintsch, 1998). This is considered in greater depth in Chapter 8, but basically what this means is that we relate our knowledge of vocabulary and grammar (our semantic and syntactic knowledge, which we looked at in the previous chapter) to prior knowledge held in long-term memory (whether it be semantic memory, which is conceptual, or episodic memory, which is based on personal experience). Working memory has a critical role to play in supporting the creation of these links.

Here's why. Imagine we have read a sentence in a piece of text. We then read one more. As we finish reading this second sentence, we make sense of it by relating it to the sentence, or sentences, we have read previously. This may seem obvious, but it is actually very complex because we are having to hold information in our heads while more information is coming in. This new information, composed of possibly different vocabulary and different grammar features, has to be related to the information that is already in our heads as we read. Simultaneously it also has to be related to our prior knowledge held in long-term memory. As a result we view the information we were already holding in our heads differently, to the extent that we modify what we had previously thought.

Let's take a look at the text presented at the beginning of this chapter from *The Ruby in the Smoke*, specifically where Mr Selby is talking to the man in the corridor. We will focus on the first two sentences, as this should be enough to give us some idea as to how working memory might work to support text comprehension. The first thing to bear in mind with this snippet of Philip Pullman's story is that we are looking at speech in text, so there would be especially good reason for reading this with some sort of expression, even in our heads. This relates to something known as prosody and there is some evidence to suggest reading with expression can support comprehension (Miller and Schwanenflugel, 2008).

So with this in mind, the first sentence we read is,

'There ain't no Mr Lockhart.'

As we read this, we resolve the grammatical issue presented by 'ain't no', provided we remember that the story is set in London and we have the knowledge (held in our long-term memory) that 'ain't no' is a common grammatical structure used by Londoners in speech. It is our active working memory that is already helping us to make these links and we can now hold in our head the fact there is no Mr Lockhart – whatever that may mean.

We then read the second sentence:

'Mr Lockhart's lying in a hundred fathoms of water in the South China Sea, blast him.'

As we read this second sentence we may remember that a hundred is a fairly large number (so we make reference to our concept of number, held in semantic long-term knowledge). We may remember what the word 'fathoms' means. We may know that it is a unit of measurement related to sea depth, and we retrieve this from long-term memory (and as a fathom is a concept, we have this stored in our semantic knowledge as well). We might also recall knowledge about China being a place far away and the sea being a large body of water (again, all conceptual knowledge stored in our semantic memory). We've also probably by this point resolved the meaning of the word 'lying'. Mr Lockhart is not likely to be in the South China Sea telling lies. So in our working memory then we have already processed and held four pieces of information:

No Mr Lockhart – lying (down) – hundred fathoms of water – South China Sea

We read this text in a matter of seconds (and we haven't even finished the second sentence yet) so you can see that we have the potential to encounter substantial amounts of information during the course of reading. But we know that working memory is limited and we cannot keep adding more, particularly as the new information may force us to think about the text differently. In this example, the last thing Mr Selby says is,

'… Blast him.'

Now this isn't to do with Mr Lockhart being at the bottom of the South China Sea, as much as it is to do with Mr Selby's feeling. We have moved on in the narrative and by the end of the second sentence it is starting to get more complicated. So what we do now is to integrate the information we have in our working memory already:

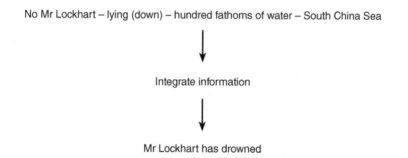

We can probably come to the conclusion that Mr Lockhart has drowned. We can now go on and engage with new pieces of information held in following sentences.

Of course, some people (including children learning to read) may not be able to hold so many chunks of information in their working memory so this example is not exact; but it does gives us some idea of how working memory works and explains why it is critical for the effective comprehension of text. It is the point at which information is held and integrated (Just and Carpenter, 1980). This process is happening in seconds and works on the assumption that we know the words conveyed in the new sentence and that we know the grammatical structure of the sentence that conveys them. We cannot assume that children will have this knowledge, however, or indeed that they have the ability to access working memory efficiently.

Indeed, studies have shown that differences in memory capacity do have an effect on comprehension. Yuill et al. (1989), for example, presented a series of six-line stories to nine skilled and nine less skilled comprehenders (7–8-year-olds). Each story featured an anomaly that was resolved within the text. The information required to resolve the anomaly was positioned in two ways: it occurred either in the sentence adjacent to the anomaly or two sentences later. Both groups performed in a similar manner when the anomaly was adjacent, but the less skilled comprehenders were significantly worse when the anomaly was at a distance. The authors concluded that the less skilled comprehenders were not able to resolve the anomalies when they were at a distance because of the increased load on memory caused by the intervening sentences.

In another study Cain et al. (2004) also found a specific relationship between working memory and comprehension in a longitudinal study that measured the performance on a range of comprehension-related tasks that included general reading ability (in terms of accuracy, rate and comprehension), vocabulary and verbal skills. They also found that performance on reading accuracy, verbal ability and vocabulary were dependent upon working memory. This means that if you have a poor working memory you are less likely to access your vocabulary knowledge, for example, when you are reading. Nation et al. (1999) noted a link between poor comprehension and poor working memory and argue that this might be mediated by semantic weaknesses, so this link between vocabulary and working memory may also work the other way around – if you have limited vocabulary it is likely to impact upon working memory.

So working memory has an important role to play in supporting the comprehension of text; both in itself and in relation to the other components of comprehension. This inter-relatedness extends to long-term memory. As stated towards the beginning of this chapter, the memory systems are linked. This was noticeable in the example above: when words and sentences are read they have to be related to long-term memory, and working memory has a role in linking this process together. A study by Goff et al. (2005), for example, investigated how word reading, language skills and memory related to overall comprehension. One implication of their study was that working memory supported the retrieval of information from longer-term memory.

Long-term memory in itself, however, is also important for comprehension, and the reason for this is obvious: if the information required to understand a piece of text is not held in long-term memory then the reader is going to have difficulty comprehending it in any case. This relates to the previous chapter, where we discussed the role of prior knowledge in text comprehension. And we saw earlier in this chapter that in just two sentences of text spoken by Mr Selby we needed to access a variety of background knowledge to ensure comprehension, including a knowledge of number (hundred), measurement (fathoms) and geography (South China Sea).

Dialogue Point

Analysing texts to see the load they place on working memory

Working with colleagues, choose two or three texts.

As with the example above from *The Ruby in the Smoke*, map the 'chunks' of information held in one of your chosen texts and note the points at which information might need to be integrated. (Remember, we cannot hold many 'chunks' in our heads at any one time.)

Continue reading the text and note the next two to three cycles of information and when they might be integrated.

Repeat this process for the other chosen texts.

Now think of some focus children you are working with (three at most). How would they cope with even these short snippets of text? Consider

- The vocabulary in the text
- The amount of information in each text
- The prior knowledge that would need to accessed from long-term memory

School-based activity

Using 'think-alouds' to investigate how children integrate 'chunks' of information

A 'think-aloud' is a useful counterpoint to a 'read-aloud'. A 'read-aloud' will tell you what a child is able to decode. A 'think-aloud' can tell you what they have understood.

Working with individual children, ask them to read some text that is relatively easy to decode, silently to themselves. Ask them to stop at specific points in the text, say after every two or three sentences (you can mark these in the text). Ask them to relate what has happened in the text they have just read.

Record their responses.

Later, working with colleagues, note the 'chunks' of information held in each section of text.

Analyse:

- How they integrated the 'chunks' of information in each section
- Whether all children integrated the information in the same way

IMPLICATIONS FOR THE TEACHER OF READING

Some specific vocabulary may need to be explained before reading

We cannot assume that children will have the necessary vocabulary and sentence structure knowledge. If they do not have these in place it will slow down the process of making sense of the word. There are implications for comprehension here because these words do not remain in working memory for very long. Explaining (or getting children to find out about) some key vocabulary before reading may support working memory.

Assess the extent to which a text links to children's background knowledge before using it

As teachers we need to consider the extent to which children are able to apply prior knowledge by accessing long-term memory. This is important with all types of text. A text on the life of an astronaut, for example, is still bound within broader concepts of space and space travel. Do they actually have the prior knowledge to apply to the text, which can be accessed from long-tem memory? More specifically, what knowledge do they hold in long-term memory? You can't find this out unless you ask them.

Think about the type of responses you would like to elicit from the children

We also need to consider what type of knowledge we are trying to access. Is it autobiographical or episodic memory? Or are we looking for something more conceptual from semantic memory? Children might access their understanding through autobiographical experience because it relates to concrete, first-hand experience. You may be looking for something more conceptual. Consider how you might structure dialogue to use autobiographical memory as a way into semantic memory.

Notice children's reading behaviours

Some children might still be having difficulty accessing a text even though you had thought carefully about the vocabulary in the text, the general difficulty of the text and ensured it links to some prior knowledge to be accessed from long-term memory. We cannot assume that children will have a well-functioning working memory. As studies have shown, this can be source of comprehension difficulty.

COMPREHENSION MONITORING

When spoken or written discourse is encountered it has to be understood. Yet as Cain and Oakhill (2007) note, with spoken discourse there is generally an opportunity to clarify any misunderstanding by referring to the speaker. So, if we imagined that Mr Selby's dialogue with the other man in the *The Ruby in the Smoke* happened in real life, and we were there with Sally, we would have the opportunity to ask, 'Who was that man and what were you talking about?'.

With written discourse it is different because it is unlikely that the reader will have this opportunity to address the writer as the text is being read (if at all). As a result, if a reader does not understand something their options are limited to re-reading the text and making inferences.

Now, it will come as no surprise to know that these two options can be linked; we may make an inference as a consequence of re-reading the text. Inference making has an important role in text comprehension and is covered in depth in the chapters that follow. At this point though, it is important to focus on issues relating to the re-reading of text. However, we are going to look at this from a slightly different perspective. Re-reading a text assumes that the text has been read, but how do we know that the text needs to be re-read? Possibly because something was not totally clear during the act of reading it. This brings us to the process of comprehension monitoring.

By comprehension monitoring we mean 'the processes by which readers evaluate their understanding of a text and regulate their reading' (van der Schoot et al., 2009: 22). This definition maps on to Baker's (1984) earlier description of comprehension monitoring as being composed of the two specific areas: evaluation and regulation. Evaluation requires the reader to decide whether there is an inconsistency in their understanding of the text; regulation is the act of solving this inconsistency. Baker states that evaluation must precede regulation. This makes sense when you think about it; you cannot solve an inconsistency unless you have spotted it in the first place.

Baker and Brown (1984) describe this practice of monitoring text as it is read to ensure that it makes sense as an example of metacognition. By this we mean that the reader is thinking about their thinking. As they read, the reader may make the evaluation that they have understood the text and can continue. Alternatively, the reader may make the evaluation that they have not understood the text, and that they may have to do something (regulation) in order for it to be understood.

Of course, this makes the process of comprehension monitoring seem straightforward: it is not. To begin with, as Baker (1984) notes, the evaluation process itself is complex: the reader has to evaluate the consistency of the text in terms of its grammar, vocabulary and how it relates to their own background knowledge. Effectively any of these (either separately or in combination) could be the reason why the text has been partially understood or misunderstood. The evaluation process requires the reader to locate the source of the difficulty. As Ruffman (1996) notes, even if the reader is aware that they lack understanding it does not necessarily mean that they will know the source of it. To further complicate the evaluation process it is also important to consider the reading goals associated with the reading task because this will dictate the approach taken to reading (van der Schoot, 2009). All reading takes place with a purpose in mind (or at least it should do) and this purpose will dictate how the reader approaches the text. For example, asking a reader to find three adjectives in a text is very different from asking them to explain whether a character in a story is likeable.

Following this, even if we assume the source of the difficulty has been discovered, the regulation process, whereby the difficulty is resolved, is not a simple one to undertake. As van der Schoot et al. (2009) note, once the cause of the misunderstanding has been discovered the reader has to undertake 'repair strategies' (p. 22) to fix it. This raises the further questions of what these repair strategies actually are, and whether the reader knows about them. Baker and Brown (1984) note a second specific area of metacognition that the reader needs to develop, which is having a knowledge about reading. This includes such things as the types of tasks they might be asked to complete, having a perception about their own reading, and having some knowledge of relevant reading strategies. Knowing these reading strategies might be important in supporting the process of repair. For example, in the previous chapter we briefly considered how it was possible to work out the meaning of a word by looking at the context in which it is used and making an inference. It is the use of this type of strategy that helps in the regulation process. To reiterate though, readers may not necessarily know about these strategies.

To comprehend the scene from *The Ruby in the Smoke* outlined at the beginning of the chapter, some readers may well have to monitor their comprehension by going through the steps of evaluation and regulation. We hear Mr Selby talking to another man in the corridor, but we don't 'see' Mr Selby until after the conversation has finished. Added to this we don't 'see' the other man at all; he doesn't have a name and we don't know anything about him (except that he converses with Mr Selby in a timid manner). And what could Mr Selby possibly mean by 'Paint him out!'? How do you paint someone out? And why would Mr Selby tell the man that he likes the colour 'yeller' (yellow) in stylish curly lines? Here, the reader might evaluate their understanding of this and decide that they cannot make sense of this; so they will move on to the next step of regulation. This may or may not involve re-reading the text, but it would certainly involve some sort of pause before proceeding onto the next paragraph. At this point, the reader might use the regulation strategy of inference making to fill this gap in understanding. We know that Mr Lockhart has died and that presumably Mr Selby will be running the company on his own. We might make the inference from this evidence that the other man is a sign-writer, who Mr Selby is employing to amend the business signage. In this way the reader has monitored their understanding and can move on.

Of course, this assumes that the reader has evaluated their understanding correctly. The cost of making an incorrect evaluation can be costly. Garrod and Sanford (1994), for example, presented some college-age students with the following scenario:

> There was a tourist flight from Vienna to Barcelona. On the last leg of the journey, it developed engine trouble. Over the Pyrenees, the pilot started to lose control. The plane eventually crashed right on the border. Wreckage was equally strewn in France and Spain. The authorities were trying to decide where to bury the survivors.

When asked to decide whether the burials should take place in France, Spain or Austria, 25% of participants in this study did not notice the anomaly of burying survivors. The reason for this, one can assume, is because of the expectation that the passengers would all have died. Clearly, these students did not read this scenario carefully enough and probably made some sort of prediction about what happened before they got to the end. How often do people survive plane crashes? Either way, the readers did not monitor their comprehension effectively.

COMPREHENSION MONITORING AND COMPREHENSION

When we looked at such things as vocabulary, syntax and memory we noted that these were all phenomena that exist separately from the reading comprehension process. Indeed, they are all components that are applied to the unique process of acquiring meaning from a formalised written system. In contrast, the comprehension monitoring process exists wholly in relation to the understanding of text. Nevertheless, studies have been completed investigating the role of comprehension monitoring in comprehension generally. These studies use tasks that require the detection of inconsistencies in texts. These include contradictory sentences, sentences that need to be unscrambled, or statements that are likely to conflict with the reader's background knowledge (Kolić-Vehovec and Bajšanski, 2007). Of course, there is a problem with this type of study because just by asking readers to note and address inconsistencies in text in the context of a study does not mean they would do this in the course of their ordinary reading (Vorstius et al., 2013). Once again this brings us back to the point of reading goals: if you are told to focus on the inconsistencies in a text then that is what you are going to do. However, findings from these studies suggest that comprehension monitoring is similar to the other components mentioned here, in two ways.

First, there is evidence to support the notion that comprehension monitoring improves with age. For example, Baker (1984) selected a cohort of good and poor readers from both Grades 4 (9–10-year-olds) and 6 (11–12-year-olds) and found that the older better readers were significantly better than the younger better readers at locating inconsistencies, and the older poorer readers were better than the younger poorer readers, though not significantly. Similarly, Hacker (1997) conducted a study that examined the ability of children in the Seventh (12–13-year-olds), Ninth (14–15-year-olds) and Eleventh (16–17-year-olds) Grades of schooling to detect specific types of errors in texts. Results showed a consistent developmental pattern whereby errors were detected more successfully by age.

Second, there is evidence to suggest that proficient readers are better at monitoring comprehension. In the same study as mentioned above, Hacker also noted that errors were detected within age by reading ability; good readers were better at detecting errors than poor readers. Also, Ehrlich et al. (1999) discovered that skilled comprehenders were better at monitoring and resolving inconsistencies with anaphors (the ability to resolve pronouns) than less skilled comprehenders. The less skilled readers also reported that they understood the texts less well. Another interesting finding was that the skilled readers spent more time re-reading texts when they noticed inconsistencies.

There is evidence here to suggest that the ability to monitor comprehension is closely related to reading comprehension ability. Once again, it is likely that this relationship is mediated by other factors. For example, in the last example the skilled comprehenders were noted re-reading the text and will have had to draw inferences to solve the inconsistencies. As such, Oakhill et al. (2005) describe comprehension monitoring to be a predictor of reading comprehension; if you can monitor a text as you read it, you are likely to comprehend it better.

Dialogue Point

Analysing texts to see the difficulties they present for monitoring comprehension

Good writers write for effect, and this means that monitoring comprehension as we read is not always a simple task, even for skilled adult readers. Children learning to comprehend from text are in the same position.

Working with colleagues, select a range of children's books, both fiction and non-fiction.

Keeping some focus on children you are working with in mind (three at most), consider the difficulties they might have in monitoring their comprehension of these selected texts as they read them.

Consider:

- The vocabulary in the text
- Grammatical structures
- The prior knowledge they will need
- Figurative language
- Idiomatic language

Now consider actions that you as a teacher can take to help them monitor the text effectively.

School-based activity

Investigating if and how children monitor their comprehension

Working with individual children (two to three), ask them to read some text that they might find difficult in terms of understanding or decoding it (or both), silently to themselves. It doesn't have to be long, but allow them to read it until the end.

Engage them in dialogue about the reading episode. Try to find out:

- How well they have understood the text
- Which parts of the text they found difficult
- How they tried to make sense of it (strategies they used)

Record their responses.

Share findings with colleagues at a later point and note similarities and differences.

IMPLICATIONS FOR THE TEACHER OF READING

The ability to monitor text as it is being read is important then for comprehension. This is because children are unlikely to understand every word in every text they are presented with. Oakhill and Cain (2007) question whether pre-reading children possess the skills required to monitor comprehension, and suggest that these are likely to develop, in tandem with other skills, with age. What this does not make clear, though, is how this develops. We cannot assume that the children are going to monitor their comprehension as if it were some naturally occurring act associated with reading. Indeed Oakhill and Cain (2007) have suggested that comprehension monitoring may be a by-product of reading.

Given this, it is likely that comprehension monitoring will need to be taught. And if this is the case, it raises the issue of whether we should consider comprehension monitoring as a skill at all when working with developing readers. In a very interesting article, Afflerbach et al. (2008) note how the terms 'reading skill' and 'reading strategy' are used inconsistently. On first appearance this may seem to be a minor argument over semantics, but actually it is very important. These authors suggest that the term 'skill' suggests something we can do automatically, whereas the term 'strategy' relates to some sort of action that is controlled and deliberate. We have to consciously apply a strategy. When readers become more automatic in their use of a strategy, then it becomes a skill.

Vorstius et al. (2013) explicitly relate this distinction between a reading 'skill' and a reading 'strategy' to the process of comprehension monitoring and suggest that it is only when children are monitoring their comprehension in an automatic manner that we can consider them to be skilled at it.

Given the fact that there are a number of components involved in the comprehension of text, we need to view comprehension monitoring as a strategy that needs to be taught rather than a skill that the children are likely to have embedded, particularly in the primary years. It is important because they are likely to be engaging with text of increasing difficulty so the strategies we might associate with comprehension monitoring are likely to have to be revisited.

Ensure that children are aware that they need to monitor comprehension

For the teacher of reading the first question that needs to be asked is whether the children they teach are actually monitoring their comprehension. This can be made explicit through how we model our own reading of text. Reading stories aloud can support this process.

Teach strategies to support comprehension monitoring

Even if children are attempting to monitor their comprehension we need to consider how effectively they are doing it. The likelihood is that they will need strategic support. Strategies to support children in this process include the explicit teaching of inference making. We noted one approach to this in the previous chapter where we thought about how we could infer meaning from context. Other strategies might include those noted in the Reciprocal Teaching approach: prediction, clarification, questioning and summarisation. We will look more closely at Reciprocal Teaching in the Practices section.

Have clear reading goals

When you ask children to read a piece of text you do so for a reason. All reading is undertaken with a purpose in mind. However, how clearly aware are the children about this purpose? What is the goal of reading? We might describe this as the learning objective or intention, but how clearly framed is this in language that children can understand?

The reading goal you set will impact upon their reading behaviour. Asking children to find adjectives will require them to scan the text. In contrast, asking them to explain a character's motivation is likely to involve inference making related to evidence available in the text. Thus the reading goal dictates how they read a text, how they monitor their comprehension and the strategies they might use.

Reading a text deeply for meaning may mean reading pace slows

Although we are not looking at it in any depth in this book, we know that fluency is important for reading comprehension (Kim et al., 2010). By fluency we mean that the text can be decoded automatically and with ease. In standardised tests of reading, which test reading rate, you get a higher reading score for reading the text rapidly. However, Vorstius et al. (2013) noted in a study they undertook that readers slowed down to read parts of text that were critical for understanding (which intuitively makes sense). The implication here is that if a child slows down in their reading it may not necessarily be because they are having difficulty with decoding; it may be because they are trying to make sense of it by monitoring their comprehension.

So while fluent decoding is important, we must be careful not to send out the message that reading is a race to the end of the text. If we teach children how to monitor their comprehension, it is likely that we will encourage them to comprehend text more deeply.

CONCLUSION

In this chapter we have considered two more components of the comprehension process: memory and monitoring. As with the knowledge components investigated in the last chapter, both memory and monitoring make a unique contribution to the comprehension of text. We noted the pivotal role played by working memory in linking the words and sentences being read with information held in long-term memory. We also noted the importance of being able to monitor our comprehension of text as we read it, and of the fact that children will need to be taught strategies to be able to do this.

The processes involved in memory and monitoring are different, but we can find two ways in which they are linked. First, they show that text comprehension is something that involves active engagement on the part of the reader. This is an important thing to remember because reading is often considered to be a receptive process (we 'receive' the words from the page; they are given to us); but receptive is not the same as passive. The processes involved with memory and monitoring allow young readers to engage with the work of authors such as Philip Pullman who have the skill of setting stories in unusual contexts and still making them relevant and accessible.

Second, while noting the unique contribution of each to comprehension, we can also see, as with our investigation in the previous chapter into the role of words and sentences, how these processes are linked to other components. One of these components has been mentioned in both chapters: inference making. This is a centrally important component of comprehension but there is some confusion as to its role. It is useful to examine this in some detail because it has huge implications for teaching. Inference making will thus form the theme for the next few chapters.

CHAPTER 5

INFERENCE MAKING: DEFINITION AND DIFFICULTIES

Chapter Overview

This chapter introduces an analysis of the role of the inference making process in reading comprehension. Inference making is a centrally important component of comprehension: written text cannot be comprehended unless inferences are made. Inference is defined and, by briefly investigating different types of text, we learn that there are many different types of inference a reader can make. We learn that for teachers to know which inferences to teach and when to teach them is problematic, not least because the conception of inference making in the field of research is different from the one that teachers are required to address in the curriculum. To negotiate this, a bi-modal categorisation of inference making is introduced, which is developed further in the following two chapters.

Legend has it that Ernest Hemingway, the twentieth-century American novelist, while having a meal with some fellow writers was challenged to write a story that was only six words long. With money at stake, Hemingway accepted this challenge and scrawled the following on a convenient napkin:

For sale: Baby's shoes, never used.

As with all legends, there are variants to the background of this story. Some have suggested that this meeting took place in a bar, although the story was still written as a result of a bet. For those who enjoy a good conspiracy theory, others have questioned whether Hemingway even wrote it at all. The Snopes.com website presents some (rather interesting) evidence that suggests these exact same words were used in an advertisement in the small ad column of a Kansas City newspaper. According to Snopes.com, someone really was trying to sell some unused baby shoes. This would call into question the idea that Hemingway considered this story to be his best work, not least because we do not know who he apparently said this to. Either way, the concept of the six-word story has become popularised enough for organisations such as FirstStory, a charity that uses professional authors to promote writing in schools across England, to use it as a basis for story-writing competitions. Also, newspapers such as *The Guardian* (2007) in the United Kingdom have asked notable authors to write their own versions.

John Lanchester came up with the following:

'It was a dark, stormy … aaaaargggh!'

And for those of you familiar with the London underground transportation network, Hilary Mantel's contribution of

'Mind what gap?' … … …,

which refines the six-word story into something far more compact, may well resonate. However, it will not resonate in the same way as the story attributed to Hemingway, as the writers are aiming for quite different reactions from the reader. Mantel's contribution is humorous, whereas the Hemingway story is noted for its pathos.

In Chapter 2, Barrett's taxonomy (Clymer, 1968) of reading comprehension was introduced which suggested that there are both cognitive and affective dimensions to the process of understanding text. Here, there was some discussion as to whether the more obviously affective dimensions of evaluation and appreciation were necessary aspects of comprehension. Do we have to form opinions about the text to understand what it is about? Do we need to engage with the more literary elements of the text? The six-word story examples presented above appear to relate more closely to Barrett's appreciation dimension, and it might be argued that we do actually need to consider the imagery and the author's choice of words if we are to engage with the text in the ways the authors would like us to – although this engagement is not necessarily about comprehension, but rather occurs as a *consequence* of how we have comprehended the text. Again, we must consider whether the comprehension of text requires an affective dimension, and if so, whether this is required all the time – or, indeed, whether the affective dimension is not required for comprehension but is actually a desirable, or even perhaps a necessary, response when we have comprehended some types of texts. This is something for you to consider.

At this point though, it is useful to consider how these six-word stories provide a context for an issue that is centrally important to the teacher of reading; and it requires us to put to one side what is *actually* stated, and consider carefully what is *not* said. In the Hemingway example we are not told who is selling the baby's shoes, or indeed why. In the effort to make sense of this, we can choose to fill in this gap with the image of grieving parents. In the Lanchester example, we can fill in the gap by creating an image of a monster (or a vampire, or Frankenstein) making an entrance within the first moments of the story. In the Mantel example, we can make sense of the story by imagining the comedy (?) of someone missing their step and falling between the train and the platform. Certainly, none of these scenarios is stated here; there are gaps in understanding that as readers we actively aim to fill. These gaps exist for a very obvious reason: no written text is completely explicit. No written text can *ever* be completely explicit.

To demonstrate the point, let's look at an example of another six-word story:

House built. Then children destroyed it.

This one is unlikely to win any prizes or to appear in a newspaper article about clever six-word stories. One reason for this is that it is not claiming to engage with Barrett's affective comprehension dimension – you do not have to understand it and then try to appreciate its literary merits (which is a good thing because I don't think there are any). Rather it is a simple narrative; or to be more precise, it is a simple narrative which, when analysed more closely, has information left unstated and which requires the reader to fill in a number of gaps. For example, the size of the house is not stated, and neither is what it looks like (Did the 'picture' of the house you created change as the story progressed?). Also we know nothing about the children (Boys? Girls? Both? Old? Young?). And there is the word 'it'. What is 'it'? There is no explicit statement as to what the children destroyed. The reader has to make the link between the word 'it' and the noun 'house'.

Of course, there are times when a writer will aim to keep the gaps in the text to a minimum. Take for example the following six word *non*-story:

Fry the onion and the garlic.

Text of this nature is likely to be seen in non-fiction; perhaps as an instruction for a specific recipe in a cookery book. It is still not entirely explicit. We do not know how big the onion should be or how much garlic needs to be fried; neither do we know why we are frying it. Realistically all this should become apparent when the recipe and instructions are taken as whole. What is interesting to note here is the apparent lack of gaps. (Although, is this really the case? Do you fry the onion and garlic separately or together? And do you need to put one in the pan before the other?)

So to reiterate, there are a number of gaps in the 'house' six-word story which the reader has to resolve in some way. To comprehend this story the reader has to fill gaps that include making links in a very obvious manner within the text. The gaps need to be filled just to achieve a literal comprehension of the text. Some of the gaps are similar to those evident in the six-word stories created by the famous authors – but not all. The writers here seem to be creating gaps for a different, more affective purpose. In contrast, the instructional writing from the recipe aims to close these gaps entirely.

So texts work for different purposes and they may feature more, or less, gaps in understanding, which the reader has to fill. These gaps are not all the same in nature; however, the reader attempts to fill them in the same way: by making inferences.

Dialogue Point

Investigating the gaps in text

We have looked at three kinds of six-word texts:

- Six-word stories that have a literary effect
- One six-word story that provides some simple action in a narrative
- A six-word non-story that presents an instruction to the reader

Tasks:

1 Write your own version of each one of these kinds of six-word texts.
2 Share these with colleagues and note where the gaps appear in the texts. Try to categorise or name the gaps.
3 With colleagues, think about the implication these might gaps might have for teaching reading comprehension.

THE IMPORTANCE OF INFERENCE MAKING TO READING COMPREHENSION

For decades various theorists have acknowledged the important role that inference making plays in the reading comprehension process. Inference making ability was described by Schank in 1976 as 'the core of the understanding process'. More recently, van den Broek (1994) stated that the successful comprehension of text is dependent upon the ability to relate different parts of text to each other. It is the process of relating these different parts of text which ensures that a coherent understanding of the text as a whole can be achieved. As van den Broek asserts, this is achieved by making inferences. More recently still, Schmalhofer et al. (2002) have stated that inference making is crucial to understanding the comprehension process as a whole. Taken together, the implication of these statements is that if inferences are not drawn then understanding cannot take place. This assertion is given further credence by Perfetti et al. (1996), who state categorically that an inability to make inferences leads to comprehension failure.

There is much research evidence to support these statements, and from the field of psychology the work of Jane Oakhill and Kate Cain has been particularly important; so it is worth considering some of their findings briefly. It was Oakhill (1982, 1984) who, in two seminal studies that compared skilled and less skilled comprehenders, initially located the inability to make inferences as a separate and specific cause of reading comprehension difficulty. In both studies, Oakhill demonstrated that less skilled comprehenders had greater difficulty in applying inferential processes than skilled comprehenders.

Cain and Oakhill (1999) took these studies a stage further. They designed a study where a poor comprehenders group who were decoding at an expected level for their age was matched with two other groups: a skilled comprehenders group of the same age who were also decoding to expected levels, and a group of *younger* children. These younger children were decoding to expected levels for their age, but had comprehension ages that were similar to the poor comprehenders group. Two types of inference were investigated, which the authors termed as 'gap-filling' – where the reader brings information from outside the text to make sense of it – and 'text-connecting' – where the reader makes connections between different statements within the text (if you reflect on these two inference types, they do actually relate closely to our analysis of the six-word stories). As one would expect, the skilled comprehenders group were more able to make inferences of either type than the other two groups. However, the younger comprehension age-matched children were able to make more 'text-connecting' inferences than the older poor comprehenders group, despite their word reading ability being less developed than these older poor comprehenders. This showed that the ability to make inferences is not solely dependent upon word reading ability. Conversely, for the older poor comprehenders group, having an expected word reading ability for their chronological age did not assist their ability to make inferences. Thus, this study provides evidence that word reading ability and inference making are functionally separate processes.

In a further longitudinal study, Oakhill et al. (2003) found that the ability to make inferences at the age of 8–9 years old related strongly to reading comprehension ability two years later. This would suggest that the ability to make inferences may well be a cause of good comprehension.

These studies (alongside a vast amount of literature that makes a similar point, but which has not been referenced here) show that although there are a number of components involved in the reading comprehension process, the ability to make inferences is centrally important. Inference making is a functionally separate component and the implication of this echoes the statement made by Perfetti et al. above; if children cannot make inferences they will not comprehend written text. The importance of inference making to the reading comprehension process therefore cannot be understated, and for this reason is something that the teacher of reading must be aware of.

WHAT IS AN INFERENCE?

In both the Cain and Oakhill (1999) study and our own analysis of the six-word stories we noted that inferences appear to take more than one form, and they are made for different purposes. At this point then it is worth clarifying exactly what is meant by an inference. Inference making has been defined by Bruner (1974) as the process of going 'beyond the information given'. A more wordy – but in many ways more precise – definition is provided by Wagener-Wender and Wender (1990), who describe an inference as 'any assertion relating to the text that is directly connected to the representation of the text and that was not given in the text itself' (p. 138). We can unpack this definition by relating it to

Hemingway's six-word story earlier. We have developed some sort of picture – or text representation – whereby someone is trying to sell some baby shoes. Given the statement that the shoes have not been worn, we might make the assertion that the people selling the shoes have recently been bereaved of a child. The assertion is the inference. There does appear to be general agreement that inference involves gaining further meaning of a text by relating it to information not explicitly given (McTear and Conti-Ramsden, 1992; Singer and Ferreira, 1983; van den Broek, 1994).

A DEFINITION OF INFERENCE TIED TO A CONCEPTUALISATION

These definitions may explain broadly what an inference actually is, but they do not acknowledge the complexity involved in inferential processing. Kintsch and Rawson (2005) go some way towards capturing this complexity. They actually describe the role of inferences as filling gaps in texts, much in the same way as we described the six-word stories earlier as having gaps that needed to be filled, and in a similar manner to Cain and Oakhill (1999) (although Kintsch and Rawson present gap filling more as a definition for inference making rather than a type of inference). What emerged from our analysis of these stories was that these gaps are not necessarily the same by nature. The implication established by our analysis was that there are likely to be different types of inference that the reader is required to make. This then raises two questions: Which inferences are we talking about, and how many are there?

The work of Kintsch and Rawson (2005) provides a useful starting point here as they place their definition of inference making within a broad conceptualisation. This conceptualisation accounts for two factors: the inference type and *when* the inference is actually made (during the act of reading or afterwards). They describe inferences as working along a continuum from automatic to controlled. This is shown in Figure 5.1.

Automatic inferences are made as the text is read (or 'on-line', as it is described in the literature) and require very little processing on the part of the reader, if they are made with greater automaticity. We make these inferences without apparently any conscious thought. As a skilled reader you probably did not even think

Automatic   Controlled

Made by the reader 'on-line' during the course of reading. They are made very quickly and make little demand on processing capacity	Made by the reader off-line after the text has been read

Figure 5.1 Adapted from Kintsch and Rawson's continuum of inference making

about the meaning of the word 'mind' in the Mantel six- (three- ?) word story. You recognised it as a verb meaning to pay attention, rather than a noun related to something that might be going on in your head. It was obvious. Mantel's story is a very short one, but if the word occurred in a longer sentence, such as 'Mind your head when you get on the boat', you would still probably arrive at this definition without any obvious conscious thought. You made this link automatically and at speed. At the other end of the continuum, controlled inferences are made after the text is read (or 'off-line'). Taking the Hemingway six-word story example, you will have read the text and understood that a pair of baby's shoes were for sale. It is only after having finished reading that you would have arrived at the possibility that the sellers of the shoes might be bereaved parents. You still probably made this inference fairly quickly; the background introduction given to how the story came into existence, and the fact that it was Hemingway, may have built you up to this. However, it still was not completed in an automatic manner. To give an idea of the timescales involved you probably inferred the correct use of the word 'mind' in milliseconds, whereas it might have taken a few seconds to suggest who was selling the baby's shoes. To emphasise the point, some people may not have made the inference about the baby's shoes at all. Kintsch and Rawson (2005) note that test questions provide another example of when controlled inferences are required.

Kintsch and Rawson's conceptualisation of inference making as a gap-filling process on a continuum from automatic to controlled is a useful one because it makes explicit a number of implications for the teacher of reading. It acknowledges:

1. the fact that the reader is required to make different types of inferences;

2. that the type of inference made will depend upon the level of text (word, sentence and text levels);

3. that the type of text is likely to be important (the inferences we make with more literary texts are different from those we might need to make when reading a science experiment, for example);

4. that inferences can be made 'on-line' (as the text is read) or 'off-line' (at some later point when reading has been completed);

5. whether the inference relates to what have been termed as 'bottom–up' skills (for example, language processing skills relating to the knowledge of words and sentences) or 'top–down' skills (for example, making predictions).

In the light of this definition and the implications raised by the automatic–controlled inference continuum, two important questions are raised for the teacher of reading, and these echo the two raised earlier in the chapter:

- Which inferences do I teach?
- When do I teach these inferences?

As we have seen, and as we shall see over the next few chapters, we have learnt much about the role of inference making in reading comprehension, through the work of such people as Kintsch, Cain and Oakhill. So providing answers to these questions would appear to be a straightforward task. However, it is not straightforward; in fact linking the research on inference making to classroom practice is problematic for three reasons. We will consider each of these reasons in turn. In the process, I am going to argue that we need to navigate our way through these problems if we want to have an understanding of inference making that has relevance to the context of classroom practice.

INFERENCE MAKING IN THEORY AND PRACTICE: PROBLEMS TO CONSIDER

Problem 1: There are many types of inference highlighted in the literature

The first problem relates to the first question posed by the teacher: 'Which inferences do I teach?' To answer this, the most obvious starting point is to look to the research on inference making in reading comprehension. Developed largely from the field of psychology, this is an extensive area of study. Various theorists have highlighted and given labels to numerous types of inferences that are made for different purposes. We have already noted two in the work of Oakhill and Cain (text-connecting and gap-filling inferences). There are many more. To begin with, and in no particular order, Table 5.1 offers thirty-one others.

Table 5.1 Inference making related to reading comprehension

Connective inferences	Logical inferences	State inferences
Reinstatement inferences	Information inferences	Implied instrument inferences
Elaborative inferences	Evaluative inferences	Inferences related to word
Predictive inferences	Past concurrent event inferences	meanings
Bridging inferences	Future event inferences	Superordinate goal inferences
Anaphoric reference	Perceptual inferences	Subordinate goal inferences
Deductive inferences	Narrative inferences	Causal antecedent inferences
Inductive inferences	Expository inferences	Causal consequence inferences
Explicit inferences	Pragmatic inferences	Character emotion inferences
Implicit inferences		Maintenance inferences
Backward inferences		Presupposition inferences
Forward inferences		

Sources: Black, 1985; Braine, 1990; Cain, 2010; Fincher-Kiefer and D'Agostino, 2004; Garrod and Sanford, 1990; Graesser et al., 1996; Johnson-Laird, 1983; Levinson, 1983; Long et al., 1990; Millis et al., 1990; Nicholas and Trabasso, 1983; Oakhill, 1984; Paris and Upton, 1976; Schmalhofer et al., 2002; Seifert, 1990; Shears and Chiarello, 2004; Singer, 1994; Swinney and Osterhout, 1990; van den Broek, 1994; Yekovich et al., 1993

Having read through the list of inference types in Table 5.1 you may be feeling somewhat disorientated because it has been presented without any definitions and without any context; and if any feeling of disorientation has been experienced, this is entirely intentional. When we (or indeed when we ask children to) infer from written text we must understand that we are undertaking a cognitively complex task. During the act of reading we will need to make some or most of these inferences depending upon such things as the type and length of text being read. The teacher of reading should bear in mind that teaching and assessing children's inference making ability is not a tick-box exercise.

Any sense of disorientation, however, can be negated by some careful analysis of the labels given to these inference types. The likelihood is that some of them will feel familiar or obvious; for example, you may feel comfortable with what is meant by inferences related to word meanings (we have just looked at one in the Mantel story), character emotion inferences, predictive inferences and deductive inferences. Other inference types can probably be worked out intuitively; for example, a causal consequence inference suggests some sort of link to cause and effect (something happening as a consequence of something else), and a connective inference suggests the relating of ideas between different parts of the text. Others may take a little research, although even then their meaning is held in the label given to it. For example, the words 'pedalling furiously' (Oakhill, 1982) may conjure up an image of someone on a bicycle. It is the bicycle that is being pedalled, although this is not explicitly stated. The bicycle is the instrument through which the action takes place. The bicycle is the implied instrument; and thus by conjuring up the image of the bicycle you have filled in a gap and made an 'implied instrument inference'.

Now, it would be possible in this chapter to give a descriptive account of all thirty-one inference types complete with definitions and examples. However, this would be inappropriate, not least because it would make for extremely boring reading. The main reasons, however, why this is inappropriate are theoretical and pedagogical. From a theoretical perspective I can think of four reasons. First, it would suggest that this list is in some way definitive. This cannot be stated with certainty. Second, it would also suggest that this list cannot be contested. Again, this is not the case. It might be argued, for example, that evaluative inferences do not exist at all. In Chapter 2 and earlier in this chapter, we noted that making an evaluation relates to the stating of an opinion. Taking the definition of inference making as filling in gaps in the text to gain an understanding, it is difficult to see how stating an opinion can be described in this way. We may be able to express an opinion *based* upon our understanding, but it does not contribute to the understanding *per se*, rather our opinion stems from our understanding. Third, we must also acknowledge that there is some overlap between these inferences; for example, there is no obvious distinction between a predictive inference and a future event inference. A final theoretical consideration for not listing, defining and exemplifying all of these inference types in their entirety here is that some of these labels feel more like categorisations. For example, narrative inferences might encompass other inferences such as 'character emotion inferences'.

From a pedagogical perspective, it is important for teachers to know the variety of inference types that a reader needs to make. However, I have avoided making a long list of defined inference types within this chapter for two reasons. First, I do not want to give the message that these can be turned into a long series of lesson objectives that can be worked through. These inferences are made continuously as the reader attempts to make sense of the text they are engaged with, and taking such a narrow focus means that much of the reading process will be missed. Using the example outlined earlier, if your objective is to teach implied instrument inferences, the danger is that you will be waiting for the word 'bicycle' and missing a whole raft of valuable insights into how the child is making sense of the text. This will be discussed in more detail in the 'Practices' section of the book. A second reason is that it is doubtful whether a long, descriptive list of inference types would necessarily support the teacher of reading. Certainly, it would acknowledge the variety of inferences that teachers need to be aware of, but there is little opportunity to explore these, and there is little value in considering and then teaching something in a superficial manner. Moreover, it does not acknowledge the relative importance that some might have.

So to answer the question 'Which inferences do I teach?' is problematic because there are so many different types. It raises another question: Do we need to know about them all? Well, if we can already see some overlap between some of them, and if we can imagine some as being relatively more important, then possibly not. Therefore we need to know which ones would have the most obvious relevance to inform our teaching of reading. So we need to be selective. This leads us onto the second problem.

Problem 2: How inference making skill develops over time is unknown

Our second problem relates to our second question: 'When do I teach these inferences?' Even if we are able to locate some types or categorisations of inference making which would support the teacher of reading, we are presented with another dilemma. What would support the teacher of reading is to know *when* these inferences should be taught and how inference making ability is likely to change over time. However, this is not something that research as yet has been able to resolve. Indeed, as Cain and Oakhill (2004) state, no model of inference making acquisition has as yet been developed.

Studies that have attempted to compare inference making ability between different groups of children have been of two kinds: those that make comparisons by age and those that make comparisons by skill. Neither of these approaches is wholly satisfactory. Studies that have compared children by age have made the claim that inference making improves with age. For example, Casteel and Simpson (1991) tested four age groups (8-year-olds, 11-year-olds, 13-year-olds and college undergraduates); and Barnes et al. (1996) tested a large number of children aged between 6 and 15 years. Combined findings from these studies include: that inference making becomes more accurate with age; that inferences are made more regularly; and that they are made more quickly. Intuitively this seems reasonable, but the major issue with these studies is that in both, the participants, regardless of age, were presented with the same text. In the Casteel and Simpson (1991) study, they suggest that the stories would be at least commensurate with the decoding abilities of their youngest readers. In the Barnes et al. (1996) study the authors state that the story they used would be suitable for an average 6-year-old reader. It is likely therefore that these texts would have been more difficult for the younger readers in each of these studies to decode, and accepting that processing capacity is limited, they would have less of it available for comprehension. So studies that directly compare age groups and use the same text will conflate decoding and comprehension.

Probably as a result of this, a research design that compares skilled and non-skilled comprehenders has been in the ascendancy in recent times. As noted earlier in this chapter with the work of Cain and Oakhill (1999), these studies typically match poor comprehenders with good comprehenders, and also match young good comprehenders with older poor comprehenders. Studies of this nature have found, as acknowledged above, that younger good comprehenders make more inferences than older poor comprehenders, and that poor comprehenders find it harder to answer inferential questions than literal ones (Oakhill, 1984). This provides evidence that the ability to make inferences is central to secure comprehension. However, the problem for the teacher of reading is that studies that compare poor comprehenders with good comprehenders are not able to locate which aspects of inference making should be taught, and at which point. For example, they may show that an 8-year-old good comprehender is better than a weak 10-year-old comprehender at making certain types of inferences, but this does not tell us what the profile of the 8-year-old comprehender looks like, or how it is different from that of the 10-year-old comprehender. It simply tells us that the younger skilled comprehender is better than an unskilled older comprehender at doing the same thing. It does not locate *how* inference making ability might be acquired over time or age.

A further complication to knowing how inference making skill develops over time is that it is difficult to measure. While some of the component processes of comprehension are relatively straightforward to measure – for example, being able to recall digits in a sequence (digit span) is an effective measure of working memory – inference making is not. There are a number of reasons for this. As we have hinted at already, there are many different types of inferences that we make for different purposes; and (as we shall see in the next chapter) many of these inferences are made in milliseconds. Added to this, some inferences require the application of prior knowledge, which we cannot assume will be the same for everyone. Finally, we must consider the text being read because, if decoding is a chore, it is likely that fewer inferences will be made. These issues make inference making a difficult process for researchers to isolate.

So while we accept that research should inform practice, in terms of giving teachers a detailed outline of how inference making skill is acquired, it has not been able do so as yet. As a result, the teacher of reading cannot (as yet) fully know how to sequence the learning and teaching to develop inference making skill, and thus it is difficult to be specific as to when discrete types of inference should be taught.

Problem 3: Inference making in research and inference making in schools – a worrying disconnect

Our third problem encompasses both the questions which the teacher of reading might ask, namely knowing which inferences to teach and when they should be taught. However, we cannot relate these solely to research; we need to consider them in the context of education.

Teachers teach a curriculum that provides guidance as to what should be taught; this in turn informs assessment practices. Sandwiched between the curriculum and assessment the teacher has to plan the content of learning and deliver it. The planning and delivery of learning will be informed (dictated?) by both the curriculum and assessment, to a greater or lesser extent. If we are working on the assumption that research can inform practice (which is a fair assumption, I think), then we would expect the findings of research to be explicit in the curriculum. This is not the case for inference making in reading comprehension, certainly in relation to the reading curriculum in England. Indeed, what emerges is an obvious and worrying disconnect between research and the curriculum.

The main thrust of research on the role of inference making in comprehension is about how readers attain a coherent understanding of written text. It is about word meanings; it is about how two sentences relate to each other; it is about how series of sentences relate to each other; it is about the accessing of relevant background knowledge to support this knitting together; it is about memory and how this limits processing capacity; most importantly, it is about the inferences made *during* the act of reading up to the instant at which the reading act ends. If we refer back to the Kintsch and Rawson (2005) conceptualisation, it is about the inferences we make *automatically* to achieve a coherent understanding of the text being read.

In contrast, the curriculum appears to view inference making as something more exploratory. It is something undertaken *after* the reading act has taken place. It is about characters and their motivation; it is about the influence of setting and how this impacts upon the characters; it is about the social and cultural context of the text; it is about inferring about the writer's motivation and their choice of words. As Kintsch and Rawson would describe it, it is about making *controlled* inferences. To give a brief example of this we can look at the summative assessment taken at the end of primary education at the age of 11, and just prior to secondary education in England (on the premise that this summative assessment should reflect the curriculum it purports to assess). This test, known as the Standard Assessment Test (SAT) for Reading, states explicitly that it measures two types of inference: simple inferences and complex inferences (You may note that these are not featured in the list of inferences above. They do not seem to appear in the literature related to inference making in reading, and they are not defined anywhere in the material associated with the test). However, Tennent et al. (2008) noted that a large number of questions require inferential responses even though they are not described as inference questions in the mark schemes. Specifically, these were all controlled inferences relating to the more exploratory aspects of reading.

In England, a new National Curriculum (DfE, 2014) became statutory in September 2014. A look at how inference making is described in the statutory requirements for English suggests that this focus on controlled inferences will continue. The statutory guidance states that in Year 1 (5–6-year-olds) and Year 2 (6–7-year-olds), children should be 'making inferences on the basis of what is being said and done' (pp. 21, 28). And children across the 7–11 age range should be 'drawing inferences such as inferring characters' feelings, thoughts and motives from their actions, and justifying inferences with evidence' (pp. 36, 44–5).

This disconnect between research and curriculum is neatly captured (though it appears not intentionally) by Cain (2010). She refers to two overarching inference categorisations: necessary inferences are the ones made to ensure textual coherence, that is, inferences the reader makes to ensure the text makes sense; elaborative inferences are those that 'enrich' (Cain, 2010: 56) our understanding of the text. In general, the focus of research appears to be on the former, and the focus of education appears to be on the latter. The implication of this is that it becomes difficult for research to inform classroom practice; or indeed for practitioners to expect research to be informative, because the curriculum mediates a separation between research and practice. So we may be able to choose the most relevant inference types that are likely to support children's reading development, but we have to be aware that these may not be the ones that the curriculum, even implicitly, is directing us towards.

Dialogue Point

Investigating inference in the curriculum

Read the reading curriculum you are most likely to implement. Make a note of:

- How often the term 'inference' is made
- In which year group(s) inference is mentioned
- The types of inference that are named or implied (automatic or controlled?)
- Any statements that imply inference making is required but where it is not explicitly stated (relating to character, setting, writer's intent etc.)

Share your findings with colleagues.

Working in association with colleagues, each person research a reading curriculum from a different country or state.

Complete the same analysis as you completed for your 'local' reading curriculum.

Come together and compare how inference is conceived in different reading curricula. Make judgements as to which might be the most effective and why. (Or maybe you will come to the conclusion that they are all good or all not!)

OVERCOMING THESE PROBLEMS

A bleak situation, then? Well, not really. The reading comprehension process in general is complex because it requires the application of different components that work interactively. Finding a developmental path to general reading comprehension is never going to be an easy task. As we have noted in this chapter, inference making is a centrally important component of comprehension, and as one might expect, therefore, it is a process that reflects the complexity of text comprehension generally. So rather than focus on what research has not told us, let's focus on what it has.

The first problem noted was that there are numerous types of inferences so care needs to be given to how these are organised and presented. The Kintsch and Rawson (2005) conceptualisation of inference making considered how inferences were made in relation to time – those that were made automatically (more or less) *during* the course of reading, and those that were made in a controlled manner *after* reading. Cain (2010) presented a bimodal categorisation of 'necessary' and 'elaborative' inferences, which also reflects this 'during' and 'after' reading link, and which was further evident in the studies of Casteel and Simpson (1991) and Barnes et al. (1996). This division of inference making into 'during' and 'after' reading might be a useful one to inform classroom practice.

The second problem we looked at related to the lack of a clear developmental sequence for inference making. As already noted, this is difficult to achieve; however, a number of studies have been described above that have investigated the acquisition of inference skill by age. While these studies have limitations, they do raise one interesting point: children of *all* ages in all these studies were able to make *all* types of inference. Indeed, making links back to some older but influential research supports this. Omanson et al. (1978) found that even 5-year-olds were able to make inferences about the characters' goals (though again not as many as the 8-year-old children in their study). So there is some evidence that younger readers can make controlled inferences. Also, Paris and Upton (1976) found that 6-year-olds were able to make inferences more obviously related to words (again not as well as the 10-year-olds in their study), which might suggest some ability to make automatic inferences. This would suggest that the teaching of inference making skill should be a feature across the primary age phase (as the new curriculum in England does indeed suggest) and that some thought needs to be given to making children aware of both automatic and controlled inferences.

The third problem related to the link between research and practice is perhaps a more difficult one to address. As we have noted, the focus of the curriculum is on the inferences made after reading – not during; and teachers are likely to act in response to a statutory curriculum because of a perceived lack of choice. However, if we want children to make these controlled inferences about characters, settings and the motivations of the writer, we need to ensure that those inferences made during the act of reading are established *first*, because it is these inferences that create the more literal understanding from which these more reflective inferences can be made. As suggested by the general categorisation given to them by Cain, they are necessary. The implication is that if we want to fulfil the curriculum requirements that relate to inference making, we cannot but make the link between research and practice.

DEVELOPING A FRAMEWORK TO SUPPORT THE TEACHING OF INFERENCE MAKING

Effectively then, if we accept, first, that children of all ages can make all types of inference (to a greater or lesser extent) and, second, that we need to ensure literal comprehension is established by way of making those 'necessary' inferences prior to making the more exploratory types of inferences, we have gone some way to addressing two of our three problems. The final problem to address is deciding which inferences need to be taught.

Now, as stated previously, there is some justification in arguing that all types need to be taught, but that presenting them as a long list to be addressed, and then teaching them as such, is unsound practice educationally. So, organising inferences into categories will provide a useful starting point. A bimodal categorisation suggests itself from the analysis so far, which relates to both the time at which the inference is made by the reader, and the purpose for making the inference. As such I am going to suggest the following categorisations as ones that will have relevance in the classroom context:

1. Coherence inferences: those inferences made which help the reader to achieve a coherent understanding of the text; and which are made automatically (more or less) during the course of reading.

2. Interrogative inferences: those inferences made which deepen understanding through text exploration; and which are made in a controlled manner after the reading episode is completed.

These two inference categories will be explored in depth in the following two chapters.

Within each category some specific inference types will be presented. Each inference type is described with reference to research, and implications for the teacher of reading will be discussed (indeed these implications have relevance for teachers generally as much learning is mediated through written texts).

The inference types presented within each category were not chosen randomly; rather, the choice was informed by taking two factors into account. The first factor relates to the theoretical background to inference making. Inferences were considered in relation to Kintsch and Rawson's conceptualisation of inference making, and so reflect the implications outlined earlier, such as that inferences can be made on-line (during the act of reading) or off-line (after the act of reading); and that they are made to support different levels of textual understanding (word, sentence and text levels). Alongside this, attention was paid to those inference types most commonly associated with research in the field of inferential processing. The second factor relates to classroom practice. The question to ask is which types of inference would it be useful for teachers to know more about to inform their teaching? To address this question links were made to common themes in curricula as this relates inference types to what teachers are expected to teach. This informs the chapter on interrogative inferences particularly. The six-word stories we began to investigate in this chapter hinted at these different types of inferences, and these will be picked up again in the next chapter.

CONCLUSION

In this chapter we have defined inference making as a process of filling the gaps in understanding created in written texts. We began to consider how these gaps might look different depending on the type of text we are engaged with. We considered this briefly with reference to some six-word stories and a six-word non-story. Here, we found that some texts create more gaps than others, and that these gaps are not all the same.

Our investigation into the role of inference making in reading comprehension raised a more general critical point: inference making is a centrally important component of the reading comprehension process, and an inability to make inferences means that written text will not be comprehended. As the purpose of reading texts *is* to comprehend, then the matter of how children (learn to) infer meaning from text becomes a central issue for the teacher of reading.

The problems in translating this to classroom practice include knowing which ones to teach (because there are many) and knowing when to teach them; while at the same time negotiating the demands of a curriculum that may not recognise the nature of inference making in comprehension. These are not easy problems to solve.

The next two chapters aim to present one approach to solving this by outlining a bi-modal classification of inference (coherence inferences and interrogative inferences), which draws together research findings and curricula expectations with reference to some specific inference types.

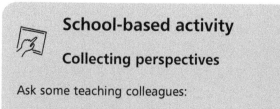

School-based activity

Collecting perspectives

Ask some teaching colleagues:

- How they define inference
- Whether they explicitly teach inference making

  o If so, how do they do it?

(Continued)

(Continued)

- o If they teach it implicitly, how do they do it?
- o If they don't teach it at all, why not?

- How effectively they think inference is presented in the curriculum

Try to choose colleagues from across the age range.
Share these findings with colleagues.

CHAPTER 6

COHERENCE INFERENCES

Chapter Overview

This chapter introduces the first of two categories of inferences: coherence inferences. Coherence inferences are defined as those that the reader has to make to ensure a coherent understanding of text is achieved; and which are made as the text is read. With reference to worked examples, three types of coherence inference are outlined: anaphors (those that involve the resolving of pronouns); bridging inferences (those that ensure coherence is maintained between sentences and statements); and predictive inferences (which acknowledge that the reader is likely to bring some prior knowledge to the act of reading). The point is made that these inference types work in an interactive manner, and the further point, that unless coherence is achieved, understanding cannot be deepened, is reasserted.

INTRODUCTION

Reading the opening pages to *The Sound and the Fury* (1929) by William Faulkner is a most disorientating experience. It's not that it is difficult to decode – in fact it is very easy. Readability formulae are a useful way to gauge the ease or difficulty of a text; for example, the Spache (1974) readability formula attempts to assess text readability by taking into account sentence length and the number of familiar words. Analysing the first 100 words of *The Sound and the Fury* reveals that it has a readability age of 7.3 years. Basically any child of 7 who is reading at, or near, their chronological age would have no problem decoding it. So why is it so disorientating?

Well, the reason is that the opening section of the book is narrated by a 33-year-old man who has the mental capacity of a child. It takes some time to establish this, as the narrator slips between relating one event and then another. The difficulty for the reader comes in trying to make sense of these movements in thought; but also in making sense of each individual thought. The sentences and statements do not follow one another easily. For example, a few lines into the first page the narrator states:

> They took the flag out, and they were hitting. Then they put the flag back and they went to the table, and he hit and the other hit. Then they went on and I went along the fence.

Eventually the reader can work out that in this scene the narrator is watching a game of golf from the boundary of the course. However, at least initially in this instance, the reader has to expend great effort in trying to make links between sentences while reading, which in turn makes the act of pulling the ideas carried in successive sentences together to ensure a general overall understanding, more difficult. For the reader then, the initial difficulty comes in trying to attain a coherent understanding of the text as they are reading it.

In the previous chapter we established that to achieve a coherent understanding of text required the reader to make inferences. We also noted a disconnect between the focus of research, which associates inference making with this process of creating coherence, and the curriculum, which appears to define the inference making process largely as a way of deepening understanding. This disconnect was negotiated by positing the idea that even if the aim of the curriculum is for children to develop inference making skills to deepen their understanding of text, this cannot be achieved without developing those inference skills that help to establish a general understanding in the first place. You cannot deepen an understanding of something if there is no understanding to deepen.

So as teachers we cannot but engage with the research and consider how inference making supports the acquisition of textual coherence for children learning to read. In this chapter we will investigate those inference types that help the reader to establish this.

COHERENCE INFERENCES

As stated, when initially engaging with text the reader's first aim is to achieve a coherent understanding of it. Cain (2010) suggests that readers aim to achieve this on two levels. Local coherence refers to the integration of information between adjacent sentences as each successive sentence is read. Global coherence relates to the sense the reader makes of a text as a whole. This may lead to the reader locating the general theme of the text and is likely to require the application of background knowledge in relation to this theme.

There are a number of inferences the reader is likely to have to make to achieve this coherence. These inferences are categorised as coherence inferences here. Cain (2010) notes that these types of inference are often given the categorisation of backwards inferences (backwards because you work from the statement that you have just read to previously read text), or necessary inferences (necessary because if they are not made coherence cannot be achieved). These terms have not been used here.

I have not categorised these inferences with the term 'backwards' because one of those presented in this section relates to prediction. Clearly, predictions do not work backwards from a just-read statement; rather, they work forwards from it. In fact, predictive inferences have been categorised as a type of forward inference (van den Broek et al., 1996). I have included predictive inferences here because I am conceiving coherence inferences as those that take place as we read. There is evidence to suggest that we do make predictions about the text as we read it. Also, I have not used the term 'necessary' because this may suggest that if any one of these (little and local) inferences that link sentences is not made then the reader's understanding is incoherent. This is not the case. The coherence may be impaired but the child is still likely to have made some sense of the text. This would mean that coherence, much like the Kintsch and Rawson (2005) conceptualisation of automatic–controlled inference making, can also work on a continuum: this time from complete incoherence to complete coherence. For the teacher, the important issue is *how* coherently the text has been understood, so the term 'coherence' provides both a useful categorisation of, and conceptualisation for, these inferences. The central purpose of making inferences in this category is to achieve coherence.

The key features of coherence inferences then are that they are made to achieve a general understanding of text and that they take place 'on-line' during the process of reading. They are made automatically, or at least they are the ones we may have to teach children to make so that they become automatic.

Before moving on from this point, it is worth noting that what actually constitutes 'on-line' inference making is a matter of much debate. Some theorists maintain that 'bottom–up' processing is central to ensuring a coherent understanding of text (Perfetti et al., 1996). These relate more closely to our knowledge of language; of words and how they function in sentences. For example, in the previous chapter, in the 'house' six-word story we began to consider how we might make sense of the word 'it'. However, other theorists suggest that we view texts in a more holistic manner and that we actively apply 'top–down' processes while reading to ensure the text is understood; that we cannot help but bring some aspects of prior knowledge to every act of reading. For instance, both Graesser et al. (1996) and Gernsbacher and Robertson (1992) suggest inferences can be made about characters as we read, if it is essential for understanding.

As we are focusing in this chapter on those inferences that are made while reading, it is not an argument we can entirely (or want to) avoid, nor necessarily solve, although I would argue that knowing whether children are making inferences about characters in stories while they read is likely to emerge by talking with them – and by talk, I mean purposeful, dialogic talk – and that teachers are some of the best placed people to work on this. Therefore the types of coherence inferences outlined below will acknowledge both perspectives.

TYPES OF COHERENCE INFERENCE

As much of the research on inference making has focused on how we attain meaning during reading, it is probably no surprise to learn that the majority of the inferences listed in the previous chapter in Table 5.1 could be outlined here. And as stated in the previous chapter, this is not necessarily helpful because this list has to be viewed in terms of its pedagogical application. The process of narrowing down this list was made by considering relevance to classroom practice; by subsuming some inferences into others; by noting which ones are addressed elsewhere in this book (inferences about words are covered in Chapter 3 but would certainly fit into the coherence categorisation); by choosing to leave some out entirely; and by acknowledging the point that reading is an active process that children bring something to. So for this reason, three types of inference labelled as coherence inferences will be presented here: anaphors, bridging inferences and predictive inferences. A rationale is provided for including each type, references to research are made and examples are presented to show how these inferences are made by readers.

Anaphors

'Anaphor' comes from the Greek and means to resolve something that has gone before. In relation to the study of reading it includes the resolving of pronouns. The resolution of pronouns is a form of inference making, although it is worth noting that pronouns also need to be considered as a cohesive device (Cain, 2010); they help to make the text more readable. Consider the following text:

> The children built a sandcastle. The children took a long time to build the sandcastle. The waves came near the sandcastle. The children tried to protect the sandcastle, but the waves went past the children. The waves hit the sandcastle and knocked over the sandcastle.

The passage has an odd feel to it because there is an absence of pronouns; it is the use of pronouns that help to make written text cohesive.

How does this relate to the making of inferences? Well, every time a pronoun is used, it means a noun has not been explicitly stated and the reader has to work out what the pronoun refers to. This creates a gap in the reader's understanding; although the information required to resolve who or what the pronoun refers to is likely to be given in the text, it may not be explicit to the reader – particularly the young reader. So the reader has to make a link within the text if coherence is to be maintained. This might be one of the reasons that Faulkner's opening to *The Sound and The Fury* is so difficult to make sense of. The short extract presented in the introduction to this chapter is laden with pronouns for the reader to resolve. It is for this reason that the study of anaphors is an extensive branch of study in the literature on reading comprehension. Pronoun resolution relates to the word and sentence levels.

As noted, we have encountered pronoun resolution already in the previous chapter. In the 'house' six-word story, for example, reference was made to the word 'it'. This involved resolving the meaning of a pronoun by assigning it to the correct noun; we related the word 'it' to the noun of 'house'. This seemed to be a straightforward task so why bother considering it? Well, as skilled readers – and making a link back to Kintsch and Rawson's (2005) conceptualisation of inference making – we did this automatically. But if we pause for a moment and consider how we resolved this, we were actually doing something cognitively complex. Look at the story again:

House built. The children destroyed it.

The bold arrowed line shows our normal course of reading – we work from left to right, word by word. However, when we get to the last word, 'it', we now need to resolve a pronoun. So *as* we are reading we look to make a link back to nouns that have gone before. This is shown by the dotted arrowed line. There are two nouns that we have held in memory as we have been reading (specifically our working memory); however, we skip past the first one because we have decided that 'it' cannot refer to 'children' (otherwise it would mean the children destroyed the children) because it doesn't make sense. Instead, we track further back and consider the noun at the start of the sentence: 'house'. 'The children destroyed the house' does make sense, and hence the pronoun in our six-word story is resolved. As skilled readers, we were able to remember the nouns introduced and to skip back far enough to choose the appropriate one. And we completed this task in milliseconds.

Children learning to read may not necessarily have either this ability to hold in their head words they have recently encountered (in their working memory), or have the automaticity to complete this task at speed. As with the making of predictive inferences, these issues may slow down a child's reading and use up more of their limited processing capacity, as they attempt to maintain a coherent understanding of the text – no matter how short.

Indeed there is evidence to suggest that this is the case. O'Brien et al. (1990) found that distance was crucial when resolving pronouns. If the pronoun in the text follows soon after the person or object being referred to, comprehension is made easier. In our 'house' example, the pronoun was five words away from the object it referred to – the house. If the text was longer and it was ten words away, for example, it would have been more difficult to make the link.

There is also evidence to suggest that readers slow down when they meet an anaphor because of this need to resolve meaning (Garrod and Sanford, 1990), particularly so when the pronoun resolution task becomes more complex. Garrod and Sanford provide an example that may demonstrate the point. When you have finished reading it consider whether the act of pronoun resolution is more demanding than in the 'house' example, and whether it took you longer (accepting the fact that we are working in incredibly short timescales):

Roger gave the ball to Barry and he ran off with it.

As skilled readers we understand that 'it' refers to the ball, and that 'he' refers to Barry. It must be Barry because he now has the ball. This example is more complex in terms of pronoun resolution because the reader has two pronouns to resolve and they have to infer which pronoun relates to which noun, almost simultaneously.

For the teacher of reading, pronoun resolution has significance for a number of reasons. At the word level it helps to support the attainment of literal comprehension. In this case linking a pronoun to a noun gives meaning to the pronoun itself. This in turn will help to give meaning to the sentence (or sentences) in which the noun and pronoun are held. If we link this back to the previous chapter, where we introduced Kintsch and Rawson's (2005) conceptualisation of inferences being on a continuum from automatic to controlled, the teacher of reading must be aware that for children learning to read, pronoun resolution is not something that will necessarily be automatic; and any difficulties experienced in relation to this could possibly disrupt their meaning making. Children will not necessarily be at the 'automatic' extreme, but rather somewhere along the continuum. Whereabouts any particular child is located on this continuum will be depend upon the complexity of the text itself, as well as whether the child is experiencing any working memory difficulties (commonly associated with dyslexia). If pronoun resolution becomes a controlled inference making activity (and this might mean that the child has finished a sentence and come to a complete and significant stop – it still represents an end point, if not the end of the whole text) then the teacher might need to take steps to support the child to develop pronoun resolution skills.

As children become more competent and skilled readers, making inferences related to pronouns is likely to become more automatic. What scenarios such as these also show, however, is that in the process of reading the child reader is aiming to make sense of the text. It is not a straightforward left-to-right journey across the page; rather, we seek to make connections between words. Furthermore this meaning making process can be undertaken by children in the earlier stages of reading, emphasising the point that the cognitive complexity involved in making meaning from text is not the preserve of older readers alone. In fact, it is essential for younger readers.

Bridging inferences

The six-word stories outlined above showed that to comprehend even extremely short pieces of text it is likely that the reader will have to make some sort inference. However, it is very rare that we ask children to engage with texts of this nature; instead we are more likely to ask them to engage with more extended text – even if this is in the form of a short reading scheme book with only one sentence on each double page. Working with text of this nature, no matter how extended, requires the reader to consider each new sentence in the context of the previously read ones. If single sentences require readers to make inferences (and we noted this to be the case in the six-word stories) it is perhaps no surprise to learn that this requirement is increased when reading sequences of sentences. As a new sentence is read, the reader has to comprehend it in two ways. It has to be understood as a stand-alone sentence (much in the same way as we made sense of the six-word stories), but also it has to be understood in relation to the previously read sentence (or sentences). To achieve this, the reader has to make connections between this just-read sentence and the previous one(s). This is achieved by making bridging inferences.

Bridging inferences are made to ensure coherence between two adjacent pieces of information and also to connect new information with previously read information that has been read earlier and might be some distance away (Lumbelli, 1996). These pieces of information can be connected – or bridged – by the reader's prior knowledge, through other information in the text, or both (Clark, 1977).

When making a bridging inference, the reader is aiming to find some kind of causal link between the two sentences. One sentence should explain the other. This is also known as causal bridging.

So, when generating bridging inferences the reader works backward from the current message in a text, linking it to a prior one in an attempt to achieve coherence. However, the nature of making links between a current 'just-read' clause and previous information is a complex one. This is because the reader has to locate the relevant piece of previous information first to achieve this coherence. As with the inferences made to resolve pronouns, this involves memory. As we have noted in Chapter 4, there are different memory bases (working, short-term and long-term memory) which have different storage capacities. Any one of these might be storing the piece of information that the reader is required to access depending upon the distance between the 'just-read' clause and the relevant information. Short-term memory is likely to be important when the information is adjacent or relatively close.

Now to be clear, 'bridging inferences' is a categorisation in itself, and a common one in the literature (so we could consider bridging inferences here to be a category within a category effectively). They can encompass specific types of inference, such as connecting inferences that relate to adjacent statements, and reinstatement inferences where the reader reinstates ideas that were introduced before. They might also include some aspects of reasoning. I have chosen to treat these generically to avoid the presentation of a long list of inferences presented en masse. As stated, these are tedious, descriptive, necessarily over-brief and are more likely to disorientate than help. The key point to bear in mind is that bridging inferences fill gaps in understanding by linking different parts of the text to create coherence. This is achieved with reference to previously read statements and the application of background knowledge. These inferences are made largely at the sentence level.

An example of a bridging inference can be seen with reference again to the 'house' six-word story presented in the previous chapter. This was presented as being a text of little literary interest but one that recounted events in a simple narrative:

House built. Then children destroyed it.

We did begin to unpack this story in the previous chapter, and one of the key factors for the reader to make sense of might have related to the size of the house. Reading the first sentence might have brought to mind a two-storey structure made of bricks (assuming that this is being viewed from the cultural perspective of someone living in England, of course). By the time the second sentence has been read, it is likely that the size of the house has shrunk significantly, and indeed may not now be conceived as a liveable dwelling – it is more likely to be a playhouse or den. In this way, a causal link has been made between these adjacent sentences. We have connected the idea of a house in the first sentence with further information about it in the second sentence and made an inference about the size and type of house featured in the story. This inference has been made with reference to our background knowledge: we assume the house is small because we would not expect children to destroy a full-size house. There is no information given in the text to suggest this.

It is rare, however, for reading episodes to encompass only two sentences or statements. It is when further successive sentences are read that things get really interesting. Extending our six-word story by adding another piece of information can show this:

House built. Then children destroyed it. Their parents were not happy.

The reader now has to consider this third statement in the light of the first two. It is difficult for readers to hold successive, separate pieces of information in their head at the same time, so the reader integrates the information they already have. This integration is supported by making bridging inferences. So far we have integrated information from the first two sentences in our story and the 'thought cloud' below shows what the narrative might look like now *in the reader's head*:

The children have destroyed a small house, probably a playhouse or den.

House built. Then children destroyed it. Their parents were not happy.

The reader can now access the integrated information that is in their head *instead* of the actual words in the story (the dashed underlined words). They will use the integrated information to then make another bridging inference (signified by the arrow) between this and the new information about the children's parents. The reader can make the link that the parents are not happy *because* the children destroyed the playhouse or den. The reader has made a causal link between the previously-read text and the just-read text. To make this second bridging inference the reader has been able to make the link from the information in the text.

This knowledge about the parents' unhappiness and the reason for it then itself becomes part of the integrated information, which can then be applied to any further following new sentences:

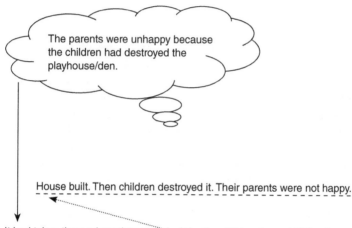

Once again, the thought cloud represents the new integrated information held in the reader's head; the dashed underlined text is the actual story that is beginning to become superseded by the integrated information; and the arrow represents another bridging inference that the reader is required to make. In this new sentence the first piece of new information that the reader learns is that the parents made the house. In this instance the reader is likely to first make a link to the text itself, specifically the first sentence. By way of a bridging inference the reader will make a causal link between the fact that the parents made the house and the fact that the house was built. It was the parents who caused the house to be built. This is an example of a reader having to make a bridging inference across distance in a text.

The information that the parents built the playhouse or den then becomes integrated into the information held in the reader's head as they make one final bridging inference:

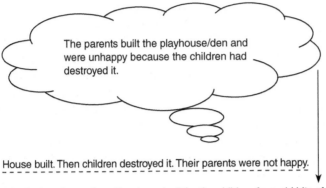

House built. Then children destroyed it. Their parents were not happy.

It had taken them a long time to make it for the children from old bits of wood.

The dashed underlined words are now part of the integrated information held in the reader's head (the thought cloud) and a bridging inference can be made in relation to the last new piece of information: that the house was made from wood. Here the reader makes a bridging inference between the integrated information held in their head gained from the text, their background knowledge and the new information, which states what the house was made from. The reader can then confirm that the house is likely to be some sort of den rather than some sort of playhouse (although this also assumes that the reader knows what a den actually is, highlighting the importance of the vocabulary knowledge we bring to the text). This information is then integrated and modifies what the reader previously thought.

So, by way of bridging inferences, the reader turns the actual written text –

House built. Then children destroyed it. Their parents were not happy. It had taken them a long time to make it for the children from old bits of wood.

– into a mental representation (held in the reader's head) which will look something like this:

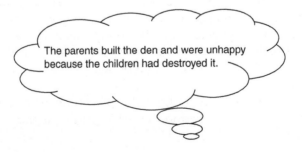

The mental representation held in the reader's head is starting to diverge from what is actually written on the page, and you can probably see how this is likely to change further as more information is encountered. What is retained in the reader's head is not the actual text (Bransford and Franks, 1971), but rather the representation of it. The ability to make bridging inferences is crucial in helping readers to achieve this.

Numerous studies have shown that bridging inferences are frequently drawn when reading texts (Bloom et al., 1990; McKoon and Ratcliff, 1992; Singer et al., 1992). This would suggest that for skilled readers this is something that is undertaken with relative automaticity. What cannot be assumed, however, is that children learning to read will make these bridging inferences automatically. Moreover, we noted in the example above that a reader is likely to make a sequence of these during the course of reading. We cannot be certain either that the child reader will make all the necessary required bridging inferences to create an adequately coherent understanding of the text. In the example above we made bridging inferences that required background knowledge to be accessed. If the child reader does not have this background knowledge, for example knowing what a den is, or does not have the appropriate background knowledge (remember the point made earlier about how the term 'house' can be conceived in different ways by different people – all texts are culturally located), then the bridging inference will not be made and a gap in understanding will remain. Also, we cannot assume that even if the information is explicitly available in the text, as when we linked the unhappiness of the parents to the destruction of the house, children make these connections. Skilled readers make these connections automatically, but children are still learning these skills. If children do not know that they need to make connections between different parts of the text, they may not do so. As a consequence, bridging inferences may not be made and the representation they develop of the text may be only weakly coherent. Actively making these connections is a metacognitive skill that involves understanding how text works, and is something that will need to be taught. Studies have shown that this is possible. Yuill and Oakhill (1988) trained groups of 7–8-year-old good and poor comprehenders to develop inference skills in this area and this was found to be beneficial, particularly so for the poor comprehenders.

Predictive inferences

So far we have investigated two types of coherence inference: anaphors (pronoun resolution) and bridging inferences. These relate to the knowledge of words and sentences and would be considered to relate to the 'bottom–up' processing we acknowledged earlier in the chapter. In contrast, predictive inferences relate to 'top–down' processes that involve bringing our prior knowledge to the text as we read it (Fincher-Kiefer and D'Agostino, 2004; Schmalhofer et al., 2002; Shears and Chiarello, 2004). Predictive inferences have been included here to acknowledge the 'bottom–up/top–down' online processing debate. This area of study is an interesting one because, unlike Graesser et al. (1996), who suggest we make 'top-down' inferences about characters and actions only when they are essential to maintain coherence, the act of making predictive inferences while reading would suggest that the act of applying prior knowledge is a continuous one. So while we can acknowledge that there is a range of thought as to how much 'top–down' processing takes place while reading, we will focus on predictive inference making, as it provides a more obvious counterpoint to the anaphors and bridging inferences previously investigated.

Predictive inferences are made at the text level. They address the future, but they are made specifically to help us engage with upcoming text *during* the process of reading. They involve anticipating future events. Predictive inferences are guesses made on the part of the reader as to what subsequent events might be. These guesses are based upon information in the prior text in relation to the new information in the current sentence. If a prediction made about a future event proves to be correct the predictive inference serves to integrate sentences and thoughts.

In the previous section we extended the 'house' six-word story to four sentences; and clearly we could extend this further. Up to the point at which we left the narrative, we had found out that the parents who had built a kind of den for their children were annoyed because the children had wrecked it. We may expect certain actions to follow: the children might be reprimanded; the children might be told to rebuild it; they might be expected to apologise; they might be sent to bed without any dinner; and there might be tears. All of these are logically plausible and based on our own life experiences and our knowledge of narrative. The point to be made here is that as we prepare to read any following text we would be alert to these types of events taking place. If the next line in the narrative read

> The children started to laugh and then ran back into the house, demanding their dinner,

we might be somewhat surprised because our prediction was not met.

Millis et al. (1990) investigated whether there was a relationship between predictive inferences (which they refer to as future-event inferences) and reading time. Interestingly, Millis et al. found that predictive inferences are generated *automatically* during the course of reading. They also found that the act of making these automatic inferences led to differences in how long it took for their participants to read the text; if the predictive inference was accurate then reading time was quicker. The authors suggested that if the future event is confirmed then the burden on processing capacity is likely to be reduced. Indeed, van den Broek (1994) also notes this but talks in terms of a 'trade-off' between accurate and erroneous predictions. If predictions are accurate, then it will be easier for the reader to gain an understanding of the text. If predictions are erroneous then it may result in the wasted use of limited processing capacity. It can also result in comprehension failure. This is probably not the case in the little addition to our 'house' story above.

We may think the outcome odd but we resolve it all the same. This may not always be the case, however. In Chapter 4, the work of Sanford and Garrod (1994) was noted, where they presented a scenario to university students of a plane crashing across the border of three countries. The problem they set students was to decide where to 'bury the survivors'. Twenty-five per cent of the students did not spot the anomaly in the scenario. It appears that as the text was read, these students had already made up their mind what was going to happen in the scenario and then did not attend closely enough to the text. The implication here is that although we have described predictive inferences as ones that support the development of coherence, making them has the potential to disrupt it entirely.

A further problem to consider with predictive inference making arises when the reader is faced with unfamiliar or unexpected discourse structures. Cook et al. (2001) found that the context of the text was important for readers. When the reader was able to relate to the context of the text (which suggests some sense of familiarity with the content, style of writing and structure) they were able to make predictive inferences rapidly. When presented with what the authors describe as 'low-context' text the readers in their study were not able to make predictive inferences as easily, and this impacted upon the speed at which they completed the task.

These findings have implications for the teacher of reading. To begin with, it is worth noting that that the Millis et al. (1990) and the Cook et al. (2001) studies were conducted with participants of university age. Given this, it is fair to assume that they were skilled readers. It seems, therefore, that one facet of a skilled reader is that they are able to, and will seek to, make predictive inferences during the course of reading to support their attempt to comprehend the text.

Of course, the making of predictive inferences is supported by the type and content of the text. When reading texts we are likely to do so with some sort of understanding (or schema) of the structure, and possibly the likely content, of the text we are dealing with. For children learning to read, this is likely to be related closely to knowledge of story structure. This would suggest that children with an impoverished knowledge of story structure are necessarily going to read the story more slowly, using more of their limited processing capacity in the attempt to make sense of it; more so if they are making erroneous predictions. The issue of text type has further implications. If the child reader is unfamiliar with a text type or the content of the text, it will be more difficult to make predictive inferences. This unfamiliarity with text type and content is likely to manifest itself in education systems where there is a transition point from generalist to subject specialist teaching, because children are likely to be asked to engage with texts that they have had little or no experience with. As a parallel to this point, I am assuming that most people reading this book will have completed studies at a Higher Education level, and probably based around a specific subject. Think about how long it took you to become familiar with the style of the reading material associated with this subject. This lack of experience will make it difficult for children to make these important predictive inferences, which help to support their comprehension by ensuring they are maintaining sense of what they are reading.

A final implication (and perhaps the most important one) to consider is that if predictive inferences are made automatically it locates the act of reading as an act undertaken *for* comprehension. It is as an active and on-going process. Active readers, and therefore effective comprehenders, are anticipating the upcoming text. We make predictive inferences automatically, when we can, to help us monitor our understanding as the text is read. Therefore, making meaning from text is not something we do only at the end of the reading act once every word has been decoded; encouraging children to view text in this manner is likely to impair comprehension.

CONCLUSION

In this chapter three types of coherence inference have been presented which are believed to take place on-line, during the act of reading. These are summarised in Table 6.1. Coherence inferences are made *while reading* and are made automatically to a greater or lesser extent.

Table 6.1   Coherence inferences

Inference type	Definition
Anaphoric	Inferences made to resolve pronouns.
Bridging	Inferences made to maintain coherence between two sentences and series of sentences. These are made by either by making links between different parts of the text or by activating prior knowledge.
Predictive	Inferences made about anticipated future events while a text is being read.

Viewed as a whole, they acknowledge the possible application of both 'bottom–up' and 'top-down' processes. And viewing them as a whole is important because although they are presented as three separate types, they are likely to operate interactively and simultaneously. Indeed, some theorists have begun to develop models of text comprehension that incorporate predictive and bridging inferences into one theory (Schmalhofer et al., 2002). This emphasises the point that when children engage with text, just to get a general, coherent understanding is a cognitively complex task.

This complexity was hinted at in the introduction to this chapter. We reflected upon some of the opening lines of William Faulkner's *The Sound and the Fury*, where the reader struggles to make sense of the action taking place. It is easily decodable but not easily understandable. As we noted, Faulkner gives a distinctive voice to his narrator, and also uses literary devices such as time-shifts triggered by specific words; and we can appreciate this (well after the text has been read and we have achieved some sort coherent understanding of it, of course). The point to pick up on here though is that Faulkner is able to disrupt the process by which the reader gains a coherent understanding of the text; and he disrupts this process in skilled readers. If it is possible for skilled readers to experience this disruption, then as teachers we need to be sensitive to the fact that this is also likely to happen to children learning to read, and with texts that are not deliberately designed to derail their attempt to create coherence. The implication to be drawn from this chapter is that if a child has not been able to develop a coherent understanding of text, or indeed if this understanding is only partially coherent, the likeliest reason is that they have not made the necessary coherence-creating inferences. And it would make sense to assume that if the understanding of a text is not coherent it becomes very difficult to deepen it (which it appears the curriculum requires teachers to do). This leads us on to the next chapter, which investigates interrogative inferences.

 Dialogue Point

Investigating coherence inferences

Read the text below.

The Boy and His Dog

Again, the dog carried back the useless, deflated ball and dropped it at the boy's feet. This time, in exasperation, the boy sent it spinning into the tennis courts. He started to walk home. It was nearly dinner time. The boy pulled his jacket around him tightly. It was getting cold. He was fed up having to walk the dog but his parents had bought it for him. It was his. The dog trotted alongside him.

1. With colleagues, work sentence by sentence and unpack the coherence inferences that have to be made by the reader. Refer to Table 6.1 to help you.
2. Think of some children you are working with and choose a text you think you might use with them. Locate points in this text where they might have difficulty filling the gaps in understanding. Share these with colleagues.
3. Think about your classroom practice. Consider how you would best support children to make coherence inferences. Discuss this with colleagues.

Note: The first of these three activities can be completed with any text. You can complete this as a 'think-aloud' activity where you stop after a few sentences and state how you are making sense of it *as you read*. Recording this on your own and then sharing it with colleagues who have also recorded themselves thinking through the same text is useful and revealing.

School-based activity

Select a child to work with one-to-one.

Select a text that they will be able decode with general accuracy.

Divide the text into short sections (3–5 sentences). Ask the child to read each section silently to themselves. After reading each section, ask them to stop and to think aloud about what they have read.

Ask them to:

- Say what's happening in the story
- Explain how they know this
- State what they think may happen next.

Note down what they say (ideally record it).

Repeat this over the series of short sections.

Help them to locate the point where they finished, if necessary.

Select two more children and complete the same process *using the same text*.

Note the connections each child made between sentences. Use the coherence inferences in Table 5.1 to help you with your analysis.

Compare the three children. Note similarities and differences, and locate areas that may need further support.

CHAPTER 7

INTERROGATIVE INFERENCES

Chapter Overview

This chapter introduces the second of two categories of inferences: interrogative inferences. Interrogative inferences are defined as those the reader has to make to deepen and enrich their understanding of text after the reading act has finished. With reference to worked examples, three types of interrogative inference are outlined. Elaborative inferences are presented as those that develop our representation – or picture – of the text and act as a conduit for the making of the other two types of interrogative inference – deductive inferences and inductive inferences. Interrogative inferences are acknowledged as having stemmed from curriculum expectations rather than the research in the area; however, a rationale for their importance is presented in relation to how they are necessary for helping readers to evaluate and appreciate texts.

INTRODUCTION

Where the Wild Things Are is a picturebook by Maurice Sendak, first published in 1963.

The book centres around a boy called Max. As a punishment, Max is sent to bed by his mother without any supper. After this, a forest grows in his bedroom; he goes on a journey where he meets and tames the wild things, and eventually becomes their king. When Max becomes bored of being king, he returns home on a boat and finds his supper waiting for him.

In the previous chapter the opening pages of William Faulkner's *The Sound and the Fury* were investigated. As with *The Sound and the Fury*, the written text that features in Sendak's book is easily decidable; but unlike *The Sound and the Fury*, there is little difficulty in linking this written text across pages, by way of coherence inference making. This ability to link the text across the pages allows the reader to develop a coherent understanding of the text. And the previous paragraph demonstrates one expression of this coherent understanding (yours might be slightly different but it would probably be similar).

Yet there is something missing. *Where the Wild Things Are* is a picturebook. Here's what Sendak himself has to say about the relationship between the illustrations and the text:

> You must never illustrate exactly what is written. You must find a space in the text so that the pictures can do the work. (Sendak, quoted in Lanes, 1980: 110)

It is worth reflecting on this quote for a moment. To begin with, Sendak reiterates the point that no text is ever completely explicit; he talks about 'spaces in the text' in the same way that we have discussed, in Chapter 5, the 'gaps' that need to be filled. Sendak then acknowledges that we need to infer from the written text. However, it is questionable whether the spaces or gaps Sendak is referring to are exactly the same ones we discussed in the previous chapter. These gaps are the ones that need to be addressed for general understanding and coherence purposes. In *Where the Wild Things Are* any gaps in the written text that need to be filled to ensure coherence are relatively straightforward for the reader to address (as shown by the simple outline of the story above). What Sendak appears to be referring to here is how the gaps in the text can lead the reader (with the support of the illustrations) to treat the text in a more exploratory manner, beyond a simple, generalised understanding. Of course, the reader will have to make coherent sense of the illustrations as well as the written text, but the purpose of the illustrations for Sendak appears to be about encouraging the reader to search for meanings beyond a coherent general understanding. So when we say Sendak acknowledges the need to infer from text, he is referring to those inferences that require us to explore and interpret the text, and in so doing, deepen our understanding. Haynes and Murris (2012) demonstrate this in a really interesting way by showing how texts such as Sendak's can be viewed on a philosophical level when time is taken to analyse them.

It is this element of time that is pivotal to the making of these exploratory inferences. As with the coherence inferences, we access both our knowledge of language and our prior knowledge to make them. The difference is that we make inferences that explore the text in a controlled manner, after the act of reading has been completed. And it is these inferences that will be the focus of our second categorisation of inferences, which we will refer to from now as interrogative inferences.

INTERROGATIVE INFERENCES

Interrogative inferences were not noted in the list of inference types presented in Chapter 5, and it is not a categorisation highlighted in any previous research. The categorisation has been devised in response to the disconnect between how research has approached inference making and how various reading curricula have viewed it. As noted in Chapter 5, the reading curriculum tends to view inference making as a way to deepen understanding through the exploration of text *after* the text has been read, whereas the focus of research has been to emphasise the contribution that inference making has to creating a coherent understanding of text *while* it is being read.

Of course, research does recognise that inferences are made after reading. This is clear in the Kintsch and Rawson (2005) conceptualisation of inference making, where they describe post-reading inference making as taking place in a controlled manner. These types of inference have been categorised generally as elaborative inferences (Cain, 2010; Garnham and Oakhill, 1996; Long et al., 1990). This term does have some descriptive merit, in that inferences made after reading inevitably must elaborate on the general understanding that has been developed (and to re-iterate, we are working from the premise that those inferences that deepen understanding can only be made *after* coherence has been established). They cannot repeat what has already been established, and it is possible to argue therefore that these inferences will 'enrich' (Cain, 2010: 56) our understanding of the text. However, this term will not be used here, and the reasons for this are twofold. The first is theoretical. In the literature, elaborative inferences are presented, it seems, as being of little purpose and of limited value. This is because they are not made while reading and thus do not, on the whole, contribute to the creation of coherence (which, as we know, has been the focus of research). This is discussed more fully below, where I am going to suggest that elaboration is actually a key factor in deepening understanding. As such, while accepting elaborative inferences as a specific type, I am going to focus on elaboration as a pedagogical process.

The second reason for not using elaborative inferences as a category is more explicitly pedagogical, and this is when the term 'interrogative' becomes relevant. Interrogation necessarily involves the asking of questions. This is important if we want children to engage with text more deeply. For this to happen we have to ask them questions, and if the children's reflections on, and perceptions of, the text are to be explored these questions need to provide a springboard for dialogic interaction (we will consider this in more detail in the Practices section of this book); otherwise we will not know what they are thinking, or why they are thinking it.

Now it might be argued, with some justification I think, that readers are asking themselves questions all the time as they attempt simply to achieve coherence. In the previous chapter as we read 'The boy and his dog' text presented in the Dialogue Point, we might have asked ourselves, 'What does "sent" mean?' and 'What did the boy throw into the tennis courts?'. These questions are likely to be made automatically, for skilled readers at least, during the act of reading, although teachers will probably pick up on them after the reading episode is over, and it is important to do so to ensure the children have achieved a coherent understanding. However, these questions are literal by nature, and they seek to address literal understanding. If the aim is to deepen this understanding (as the curriculum appears to want us to do) we need to go beyond the literal by asking questions which encourage the interrogation of text.

Thus, interrogative inferences are those made as a result of text interrogation.

A text from which to explore interrogative inferences

To support this investigation we will need to show how, once again, these inferences work with reference to text. The texts that we have used so far are rather brief, so we will consider the inference types in relation to the slightly longer text below, which was introduced as a Dialogue Point activity in the last chapter:

The Boy and His Dog

Again, the dog carried back the useless, deflated ball and dropped it at the boy's feet. This time, in exasperation, the boy sent it spinning into the tennis courts. He started to walk home. It was nearly dinner time. The boy pulled his jacket around him tightly. It was getting cold. He was fed up having to walk the dog but his parents had bought it for him. It was his. The dog trotted alongside him.

The Boy and His Dog: making inferences to create coherence

Before launching into the inferences that facilitate the interrogation of text and deepen our understanding of it, we will assume that a coherent understanding of the text has been achieved and that a number of inferences have already been understood while reading the text. We might have anticipated (or predicted) that the boy was 'fed up' with the dog by his actions at the start of the narrative, and this is confirmed. We would hopefully have resolved the pronoun relating to the statement 'the boy sent *it* spinning into the tennis courts'. We presume 'it' was the ball that was thrown over the fence and not the dog. That wouldn't be nice. We access our background knowledge about what is culturally appropriate (throwing dogs into tennis courts isn't) and also consider whether this would be feasible generally. However, the text does not actually say that he threw the ball into the tennis courts – the word used is 'sent'. We discount the idea that it was sent in the mail with a letter (Dear Tennis Court, Please find enclosed one useless, deflated ball …) because that wouldn't support the drive to create coherence. We decide instead that in this context that word 'sent' must mean thrown. So we make an inference about word meanings. We have also made a number of bridging inferences. We made a link between the boy's action of pulling the jacket closer to him and the weather. He 'pulled his jacket around him tightly' because it was getting cold. We also linked the fact that he was returning home with the specific time of day. He was returning home because it was dinner time. Thus, we made causal links between adjacent sentences. And in case we had any lingering doubts we can confirm that the boy did indeed throw the ball into the tennis courts and not the dog. We note at the end of the story that the dog was trotting beside him. This confirmation comes by way of a bridging inference – a connection that spans a distance of six sentences.

TYPES OF INTERROGATIVE INFERENCE

Textual coherence established, we can now consider inference types that support the interrogation of text and which are likely to deepen and enrich understanding. The difficulty we have here is that the making of inferences in a controlled manner after the reading episode has been completed is not an area with any real research base. As we have noted in the last two chapters, the focus of research has been on the making of automatic inferences to achieve a coherent understanding of text. So while these inferences (which, as stated above, are generally termed elaborative) are considered to enrich text understanding, there is no indication given as to how.

This creates a problem in terms of knowing which types of inferences children should be encouraged to make to assist the interrogation of text. However, this problem is not insurmountable, particularly if we view interrogative inferences in conjunction with, rather than separate from, the coherence inferences. There are a number of inferences that children can be encouraged to make to help them explore texts, and indeed we make these as part of the process of creating coherence by bridging and connecting ideas across adjacent and nearby sentences. Essentially what we are doing here is treating a few of these inference types in a more consciously controlled manner, rather than in an automatic manner.

We will consider three specifically: elaborative inferences, deductive inferences and inductive inferences. Each of these inference types will be explored in relation to the types of question they might raise. Elaborative inference making will be viewed here as an important conduit to the other two.

Elaborative inferences – a conduit to deduction and induction

Earlier, elaborative inferences were described as those that 'enrich' (Cain, 2010: 56) our understanding of the text, but which are not actually necessary for coherence. Cain provides the following example:

> Charlie dug a hole to plant a new fruit tree. He had always wanted to grow his own apples. (p. 56)

In this example we might infer that Charlie used a spade to dig the hole, even though this is not explicitly stated. (Do you remember our example of implied instrument inferences presented in Chapter 5? This is another one.) We could check whether this inference has been made by asking: 'What did Charlie use to dig the hole?' However, even if we do not make this inference, we can still make sense of the text, and we are able to maintain coherence across the two sentences. Thus, knowing that Charlie used a spade is not necessary for maintaining coherence.

Presumably because we do not need to make elaborative inferences to maintain coherence, Long et al. (1990) suggest that these are not made during the course of reading at all, but afterwards. As such, elaborative inferences are controlled inferences. In the words of Long et al., they 'merely embellish' the text representation.

But let's think about this for a moment. 'Merely embellish': it makes it sound as if making these inferences is a waste of time. Now, we have encountered the term 'mental representation' on several occasions, and indeed we attempted to create one in the previous chapter, in the section on bridging inferences about the parents who built the den. We used thought clouds to show how this was created. However, this representation showed how we ensured coherence was maintained during the reading of the text. It did not account for any elaborations we might have made after we had finished reading. With elaborations included, our final thought cloud might not have looked like this:

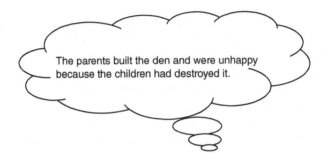

Instead, it might have looked more like this:

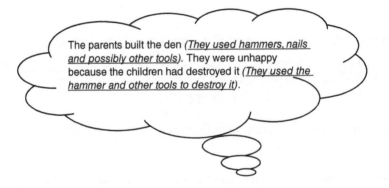

In this second thought cloud two elaborations have been added. They may have been added by the reader independently after reading; or at the instigation of the 'experimenter' (Garnham and Oakhill, 1996: 323), or the tester (Cain, 2010), or perhaps a teacher. Either way, they relate to two questions that might have triggered the elaboration: 'How did the parents build the den?', and 'How did the children destroy the den?'

So the issue is whether any of this extraneous information in our heads is unnecessary. Well, if the aim of reading is just to maintain coherence then, yes, it is unnecessary. However, we read texts for different purposes and different goals. Non-fiction texts, such as those where we are required to follow instructions, may not require much more than the maintenance of coherence. We need to take the first action, followed up by a second action, followed by a third one, and hey presto, you have a perfectly layered lasagne! Thinking back to the Hemingway six-word story featured in Chapter 5, if Snopes.com are correct and this was nothing more than an advert in a newspaper, we may be reading too much into it and there is no pathos to be had. However, for other text types, such as narrative texts and historical recounts, we are required to go beyond simply getting a coherent understanding of what has happened; we want to know *why* they happened.

And this is where elaborative inferences might be important because they give us a starting point from which to interrogate the text. The more elaborative inferences the reader makes, the more detailed will be their mental representation, and the more easily they will be able to interrogate the text. How many elaborative inferences a reader makes will depend on how easily it has been to create a coherent literal understanding of the text. As Cain (2010) notes, readers are likely to generate far more coherence inferences than elaborative ones. This emphasises the point that coherency is the starting point of comprehension. If coherence inferences have not been made, or have proved difficult to make, then the generation of elaborative inferences is likely to be minimal.

Assuming coherence has been established, the reader can make numerous elaborative inferences about the 'The Boy and His Dog' text, and these will be part of the mental representation that has been developed after having read the text. For example, the reader may have made an elaboration about the ball, by asking 'What type of ball was it?'. We might presume that this is a football – although it doesn't state this. It can't be a tennis ball because these don't deflate. We might have an idea of what type of jacket the boy is wearing. We could ask 'What kind of jacket is the boy wearing?'. It might be quite a light jacket as he had to wrap it close to keep warm. We might have decided what the boy looks like and how old he is; and we might have made some sort of assessment with regard to the size of the dog. And again we can frame questions to answer both of these: 'Can you describe the boy?' and 'What type of dog is it?'

There are two points for the teacher to consider here. First, we know that these mental representations do not have to be visual (Johnson-Laird, 1983), and the example we created with the bridging inferences in the previous chapter certainly is not dependent upon developing a visual image. However, I would argue that when we engage children with written text with the aim of deepening understanding, then asking them to create a visual representation is important. This is because we ask them to engage with linguistically interesting narrative texts featuring devices such as adjectives, adverbs, similes and metaphors. We also ask them to engage with picture books. The creation of an image becomes a point of reference to consider the content of the narrative. This might explain why visualisation is seen as an important aspect of teaching children how to read (Fountas and Pinnell, 1996). Making elaborative inferences is an important way of developing the visualisation of text.

A second point to consider relates to how elaborative inferences have been described as a starting point to the interrogation of text. Throughout this section each elaboration has been presented alongside a question that might have triggered it. These questions, such as the ones triggered when creating textual coherence, tend to be literal, although Gernsbacher and Robertson (1992) present some evidence to suggest that we can make elaborative inferences about characters' feelings if they are essential for coherence. However, the fact that these elaborations do tend towards the literal means that in themselves elaborative inferences are not going to allow for the interrogation of text. However, *the more the text is elaborated, the more detailed will be the text representation; and therefore the easier it will be to interrogate.* Whether this takes place independently or with teacher support (or both), the process of text elaboration is clearly important. It is at the point that teachers actively explore and develop this extra information that is not about creating coherence that text elaboration becomes a pedagogical process.

So elaborative inference making is a process in its own right that needs to be explored. While these inferences have been described as those that enrich understanding, they actually do not – not unless they are acknowledged and time is given over to explore and develop them. When this happens, elaborative inference making can be then viewed as a conduit through which inferences that actually do enrich text understanding can be made. These are deductive and inductive inferences.

Deductive inferences

The role of deduction in reading comprehension is one that needs some consideration, especially when we consider how deductive inferences are defined. In the field of reading research, deductive inferences are said to work from the general to the specific independently of content or context. These inferences are 100% certain as they provide a true conclusion. They are derived from rules of logic to produce a valid conclusion (Yekovich et al., 1990). As such they are also referred to as logical inferences (Singer, 1994). Deductive inferences do not require the use of prior knowledge.

Let's look more closely at the definition: '100% certain', and where we reach a 'true conclusion' with no recourse to prior knowledge. Certainly, this works in the context of mathematics and in the field of logic (Franks, 1998). However, the process of text comprehension does not necessarily require these criteria to be fulfilled. This was made explicit by Johnson-Laird (1983) in his 'mental models theory'. This theory has proved to be influential in shaping the direction of research in the field of reading comprehension. Mental models theory acknowledges that when a reader attempts to comprehend text a mental representation of the content as a whole is constructed, whether this is a sequence of events or a place (Garnham and Oakhill, 1996). As noted earlier, we developed such a mental representation in the section on bridging inferences as an exemplar in the previous chapter. However, if you were asked to develop your own mental representation about a different piece of text it wouldn't be the same as mine. Indeed, Johnson-Laird makes the point that mental representations will vary from one reader to the next. He explains this by noting a distinction between mental models and mental logic. Logic by its nature is finite and has to state whether a premise is correct or not; and this is where deduction comes in. Johnson-Laird begins by using syllogisms to show this. An example of a syllogism would be as follows:

All owls can talk.

Plop is an owl.

Therefore, Plop can talk.

The first two statements are the premises and the third statement is the conclusion. The conclusion is a logically necessary one because of the two premises. However, the logic is faulty here because at least one premise is wrong: owls don't talk. This shows that when we are talking about deduction we have to be sure all stated premises are true.

A simple syllogism described by Franks (1998) shows us an example where the premises are indeed true:

All horses are animals.

Nellie is a horse.

Therefore Nellie is an animal.

The first two premises lead us to the conclusion, and as Franks states, it is a logically necessary conclusion. The conclusion is valid because the two premises we can assume are true: we can accept that all horses are animals, and if someone took us to a stables and pointed to a neighing animal and said 'That's Nellie', we could accept this too.

However, this does not work in all cases. Take the following example:

All mammals have backbones.

All birds have backbones.

Therefore all birds are mammals.

Again, we can accept the two premises, but can we accept that birds are mammals as a valid conclusion?

The point Johnson-Laird makes is that text comprehension cannot work on logic exclusively. If it did then every reader would comprehend the *same* text in exactly the *same* way. This immediately makes us consider the role of deduction in comprehension more carefully. For Johnson-Laird, the construction of a mental model, in contrast to mental logic, involves a search of *retained knowledge* stored in memory for alternative conclusions. Therefore, the mental model that is constructed is not going to be a homogenous one, and the manner in which the reader has comprehended the text will vary.

So the construction of a mental model as part of the reading process means we will inevitably access prior knowledge, which in turn will lead us to investigate alternative possibilities. This has relevance to the extent to which we are likely to make deductive inferences and the purpose of making them. This can be shown by thinking about the questions we ask of the text, either in our heads as skilled readers, or the ones we ask children as teachers. For example, if we interrogate the text 'The Boy and His Dog' we might ask a question such as 'How do we know that the dog had brought the ball back to the boy before?'. A response to this would make reference to the word 'again'. This is the very first word in the text and it indicates that dog has brought the ball back before. We can be certain of this. So as teachers, we *might* ask this; but if we do, we would be looking for a highly specific answer, which we as the teacher also know.

Alternatively, we might ask a different question related to information in the text, such as 'Why do you think the boy is exasperated?'. This question might elicit a response that acknowledges that the dog kept bringing back the ball. Again, this would make sense logically. In this second instance the reader is once again using evidence from the text to arrive at this answer. The evidence states that the dog brought the ball back again, and that the boy was exasperated. These are the stated premises. So our child reader might reach the conclusion that two premises are linked.

The reader may choose not to make this link, however. The reader may state that the cause of the exasperation is not the fact that the dog kept on bringing the ball back, but rather that the ball was punctured and couldn't be used. The exasperation reflects the boy's feelings about the ball, not the dog. In this instance the reader may be accessing prior knowledge about how you feel when your ball bursts to explain the boy's feelings. Of course, we do not actually know who the ball belongs to in any case. The reader may assume it belongs to the boy. This is still a plausible response but this sees a movement away from deductive inference making because we have an alternative answer, rather than one only, and because prior knowledge has been accessed.

So while it is possible to make deductive inferences, the manner in which we question texts may mitigate against this, and lead us more towards inductive inference making, where we make inferences that are logically plausible rather than being based on certainty.

We will look at inductive inference making shortly. In the meantime it is interesting to note that there is little research that has tapped this type of deductive inference making in reading comprehension specifically, which is probably explained by the theoretical basis that ties deduction to logic and certainty. Moshman (1990) found that children of primary school age were less able than college students to reason deductively when the conclusion went against their prior knowledge. This is perhaps not surprising, because as teachers of reading we actually want children to apply their prior knowledge to text. Indeed, the 'owl' syllogism might resonate here. In Jill Tomlinson's (1988) book *The Owl Who Was Afraid of the Dark*, there is an owl called Plop who does speak. This raises the issue of whether adults and children are going to accept the same stated premise as being incorrect. A second issue to consider is that narrative texts are not designed with deductive inference making at their core; the work of Maurice Sendak outlined earlier shows that. The gaps in the text that Sendak talks about will not be filled in exactly the same way by all children, which is what deductive reasoning would require.

However, if we are viewing deductive inference making as one way of reaching a conclusion from clues explicitly stated in the text then this is of value to the teacher of reading, and developing this skill with children will be beneficial. It encourages the close analysis of texts and makes clear to the reader that the text they are reading has a meaning with which they need to engage. Therefore, we can make deductive inferences from text, though these might be more limited than one would think. As Franks (1998) notes, the focus of research on reading comprehension has centred on the making of probable inferences. For this reason, perhaps we should not be focusing so much on deduction, but rather on induction.

Inductive inferences

Inductive inferences differ from deductive inferences in that they require the use of background knowledge to enable the understander to arrive at a likely conclusion when all premises are not explicitly stated. Prior knowledge is used to connect the information in the text (Seifert, 1990). Moreover, there is an assumption that those premises that are stated are true. However, even when an inference is drawn from these premises they will not necessarily produce a logically valid conclusion (Yekovich et al., 1990). These inferences are 'invited' by the content and contexts of the statements (Hildyard, 1979).

There are many inductive inferences that can be made about the 'The Boy and His Dog' story and this is emphasised by the variety of questions that tap inductive inference making that can be asked about it. Most obviously we could ask the reader, 'Where does the story take place?'. The reader might say a public park. If we interrogated this response further the reader might add that it is common to walk a dog in a public place, and it is a likely place to find tennis courts. It does not state that the boy and the dog are in a park, but the reader is applying their background knowledge to create a plausible location. Alternatively, if the reader responded by stating the story took place on Mount Everest, then you would know that there is likely to have been a major misconception, because this really isn't plausible. The point to note here is that it would suggest that the reader has not developed a coherent understanding of the text. The making of appropriate interrogative inferences is dependent on this, so you would probably need to take a step back and find the source of this incoherence.

An understanding of character motivation is something readers are expected to achieve in many curricula. So another question that might be asked is, 'Why did the boy throw the ball into the tennis courts?'. Again, the reader cannot answer this by accessing evidence in the text that is explicitly stated in its entirety, and so may have to apply their prior knowledge as well. In this instance, the reader may link the textual evidence that is provided about the boy's exasperation with the dog continually returning the deflated ball with, once again, their knowledge about public parks. In public parks tennis courts are often separated by wire mesh fencing that is very high.

By accessing and applying this knowledge the reader may make the response that the boy threw the ball into the tennis courts so that the dog would no longer be able to get to it and bring it back. In this statement the reader is also showing background knowledge about how structures such as fences are used to keep things in or out.

Explaining character emotions also features in reading curricula. So developing the previous question further, a follow up to this might be 'How did the people playing tennis feel about the boy throwing the ball onto the tennis courts?'. One response to this, which relies entirely on background knowledge, might be that the people on the tennis courts would have been angry because the boy's action might have disrupted their game. This is a plausible response. An alternative response, which links the reader's background knowledge to evidence in the text, is that probably no one was playing tennis. The reader may have noted that it was nearing dinner time and that it was cold. Therefore it might be an autumn or winter evening; it was certainly getting towards the end of the day. The reader might apply their background knowledge and note that there was probably no one playing tennis because people do not usually play tennis in the winter time in the dark in public parks. This of course depends on where you live – other people may know of where this scenario is more common; this is why background knowledge is so important. This second response to this question is as plausible as the first one. You might argue that the second response is more sophisticated, but the point is that both are logically plausible and there may be no one 'correct' answer when asking readers to think inductively. We can refer back here to John Manchester's six-word story introduced in Chapter 5:

'It was a dark, stormy ... aaaaargggh!'

The interpretation outlined initially was that the cry of terror was elicited by the monster or vampire (or whatever we constructed in our heads – or as part of our mental representation) who entered the story really early. This is plausible. Equally plausible is the idea that this wasn't a cry of terror but the cry of a frustrated teacher assessing some children's writing and having to read this story opening for the umpteenth time, despite all those wonderful lessons on how to write story openings.

A final point to consider with inductive inference making is that the reader can make these types of inference even if you want them to think deductively. The reader may not refer to the evidence presented in the text at all. Does this mean the reader is 'wrong'? Well, I believe if we think in terms of simple 'right or wrong', we are treating comprehension as though it were about logic. Moreover, we are giving precedence to our own interpretations and not the children's. A more useful way to look at this is to consider some other perspectives. For example, is it that the child cannot make these inferences at all? Or is it that they have just missed this particular clue in the text? Either way, this should be investigated. Again, it may be that the child hasn't made all the necessary inferences to establish coherence, and this should be investigated too. However, what is of interest is that they are obviously seeking meaning from the text, and they have been able to come up with a plausible response that needs to be explored. And it should it be.

CONCLUSION

The need to teach interrogative inferences stems from how inference making has been conceived in the curriculum. This conception views inference making as a process that deepens understanding, and there is little explicit attention paid to the role inference making has in ensuring coherence. Of course, this creates a paradox: the (loaded) curriculum requires teachers to teach inference making skills to deepen understanding, without having made explicit (or provided time to teach) the inference making skills that ensure coherent understandings of text are developed in the first place. Added to this, there is a paucity of research that has investigated inference making explicitly beyond the level of coherence acquisition. This raises the issue of whether we should be teaching inference making to deepen understanding.

I would argue the analysis of Maurice Sendak's thoughts and work provide a resounding 'yes' to this. We do not read texts just to establish coherence. If we did there would be no point to texts such as *Where the Wild Things Are*, and we might as well stop reading fiction. Narrative has been central to the development of writing, and as a consequence, reading. Of course, it may be argued that Sendak's work relies on the pictures to drive forward the analysis at a level beyond coherence. There is something in this, but it is not the whole story. I would point you back to the Hemingway six-word story introduced in Chapter 5. Many readers assume that there is some pathos to be had in this story; and this assumption highlights the fact that we seek meaning from the texts we engage with.

And it is this meaning that allows us to enjoy (or hate) particular texts. In this sense then, the making of interrogative inferences is itself a conduit for readers making more evaluative judgements about texts. In the same way that we cannot deepen understanding without having attained coherence in the first place; it is difficult to make a judgement without having achieved a deepened understanding through the making of interrogative inferences.

Table 7.1 Interrogative inferences: types and definitions

Inference type	Definition
Elaborative	Inferences that are made as part of developing our mental representation – or our picture – of the text. They are extra bits of information that we have gathered but which we don't need for coherence. They may support deductive and inductive inference making.
Deductive	Inferences that are made when we question the text. These inferences are made from evidence directly available in the text.
Inductive	Inferences that are also made when we question the text. These inferences are made when prior knowledge is accessed to arrive at a logically plausible answer.

Dialogue Point

Investigating interrogative inferences

1. Think of some children you are working with and choose a text you think you might use with them. (You may want to use the same text you used to complete the task relating to the investigating coherence inferences Dialogue Point.)

   o Locate some elaborative inferences that you might expect them to make. Share these with colleagues.
   o Generate some deductive and inductive inference questions you might ask them. Share (and refine) these with colleagues.

2. Think about your classroom practice. Consider how you would best support children to make interrogative inferences. Discuss this with colleagues.

School-based activity

Select a child to work with one-to-one.

Select a text (or part of a text) that they will be able decode with general accuracy. (You may want to use the text that you investigated in the Dialogue Point activity.)

Ask the child to read the text silently in its entirety.

Ask the child some questions to ensure they have developed a coherent understanding of the text.

Ask the child some deductive and inductive inference questions.

Ideally, record this.

Select two more children and complete the same process *using the same text and questions.*

Note the answers each child gave. Compare the three children. Note similarities and differences, and locate areas that may need further support.

CHAPTER 8

TEXT COMPREHENSION: UNITING THE SEPARATE COMPONENTS

Chapter Overview

This chapter aims to show how the components of comprehension work interactively. It does so by relating these components to models of text comprehension. However, rather than just outline a vast number of models (there are many), specific ones have been selected because they tell us something very important about the comprehension process. From these selected models we learn that comprehension is a constructive, cumulative process that requires information to be activated at different times. These models also establish inference making as being centrally important, and perhaps most importantly, the point is made that the same text can be comprehended differently. The implications for teaching are investigated and these include the points that inference making needs to be explicitly taught, and that dialogic teaching approaches are necessary.

Colin Thompson's (1995) *How to Live Forever* is a picture book set in a library. At night, when the general public have left, the characters in the books come alive. One of these characters is a boy called Peter. Peter lives in one of the books on a shelf. He hears about another book called 'How to live forever', which, just by reading it, gives eternal life. He goes on a quest to find the book. He eventually finds the Ancient Child, the only person to have read the book and who is still in possession of it. Peter is startled to see the Ancient Child is a grey, sad character of 10 years of age who wishes he had never read the book; he has no friends (they had all grown up, fallen in love and had children) and no new experiences. In the Ancient Child's words,

'Now I am frozen in time. I keep saying that I had everything, but all I had was endless tomorrows. To live forever is not to live at all ...'

I have used this book with children on many occasions in guided reading sessions and always found that it generates much engagement and some quite profound debates. One group that particularly stands out was a class of 10–11-year-olds in an inner-city London school, none of whom had an anglicised first name like Peter. However, all of the children either had first-hand experience of being in one of the world's contemporary zones of (adult) conflict, or had been touched by it through the experiences of family and relatives. Their responses to this text were deep, thought-provoking and, I would say, philosophical (I would also add, humbling); indeed one of the key ideas to emerge from their analysis of this book was that death gives meaning to life. It could be described as one of those 'Why I became a teacher' moments.

All well and good, but it still takes us back to our central question: How have the children comprehended this?

As a teacher, I need to know what it tells me about their comprehension abilities. Up to this point we have treated comprehension as set of discrete and separate components; while we have hinted at their inter-relatedness, what we have not done as yet is to consider how these components fit into the larger construct of 'comprehension'. To investigate this it would be useful to refer to some theories and models of text comprehension.

THEORIES AND MODELS OF TEXT COMPREHENSION: WHAT CAN THEY TELL TEACHERS OF READING COMPREHENSION?

Various theories and models have been developed to show how the reading comprehension process takes place. These theories and models were developed from studies based in psychology. As we have already noted, the focus of psychology-based research is concerned with how text is understood as it is being read to the point at which the reading act finishes. It is less concerned with the more interpretative and affective aspects, as it would be argued that these do not reflect actual text comprehension *per se*, but are rather responses made once the text *has been* comprehended. To reiterate my own position on this, it is important that children evaluate and appreciate what they read, but they cannot do these things unless they have some sort of general understanding of the text in the first place. These models and theories of text comprehension go some way to explain how text is understood and therefore are of direct relevance to the teacher of reading.

It is not possible to describe all the theories and models of text comprehension – there are many of them and we are left with the issue of deciding what to include and what to omit. It would also require us to engage with a number of academic debates; and while these are interesting, of greater importance for the teacher of reading is how they inform teaching. So instead we will focus on some key issues raised by these models and theories. We will touch upon some theories and models themselves to show the key issues that arise, and then focus on drawing out some of the direct implications for teaching.

So what do we know?

1. The components of comprehension need to work interactively and simultaneously

Historically speaking, the work of Kintsch and van Dijk (Kintsch and van Dijk, 1978; van Dijk and Kintsch, 1983) has been influential in creating a theoretical basis for the development of text comprehension models. One a psychologist, the other a linguist, they noted that prior to the 1970s the study of text comprehension in both fields tended to focus on individual words and sentences while ignoring the fact these words and sentences occurred in the context of wider discourses (van Dijk and Kintsch, 1983). Their model attempted to address this and suggested that, as we read, text is represented (or we could perhaps say, engaged with in our heads) at three levels: the *surface structure*, the *textbase* and the *situation model*. These are outlined below, and in these descriptions we can begin to see how they relate to components we have looked at in the previous chapters.

Surface structure

The surface structure relates to the actual words and sentences coming into our heads as we read them. Bransford and colleagues (Bransford and Franks, 1971; Bransford et al., 1972) showed that it is very unusual for the exact wording and sentence structure to be recalled verbatim. We may on occasion learn things 'by heart'. You may remember learning the chemistry periodic table, or quotes from Thomas Hardy novels for examinations, but this involves much active re-reading of the same information for a very specific purpose. Generally the surface structure is transient. We noted this when we investigated cohesive inferences. To reinforce the point, without looking back, can you recall the scenario that opened this chapter word for word? Or can you just recall the gist of it?

Textbase

It is likely that you can remember the gist of that opening scenario but not the exact wording. To do this you constructed what is known as a textbase. As we read successive pieces of information we need to organise them into some coherent form. The textbase is a network of all the pieces of information or ideas that is developed in our heads from the words and sentences we have read in the surface structure. Again, we made a nod towards this in the chapter on cohesive inferences and when we investigated working memory in Chapter 4. Each new piece of information that we read is viewed in relation to the network that has already been developed from previous information. The new piece of information might relate strongly to a network already constructed and simply add to it. Alternatively, the new information might conflict with the network we have developed and cause us to reconstruct it. In both scenarios the network is modified to a greater or lesser extent by the new information.

At the textbase level, inference making is critical.

Situation model

The situation model puts the network, or networks, of propositions or ideas generated in the textbase into a context. Basically, the reader has to relate these propositions or ideas to an actual situation. This is critical because unless the reader does so they will not understand the text (van Dijk and Kintsch, 1983). To relate what has been read to an actual situation requires the reader to access their background knowledge stored in long-term memory.

How the levels of text representation work interactively

A brief example might help to explain how these three representation levels operate, and to do this we will use another very contrived story. This one is called 'The Sultan and the Gado Gado':

> The Sultan left his throne and went to the table. He was about to start his meal. The gado gado was on the table. He was feeling very hungry. Savagely, he bit into his dinner. The Sultan fell to the floor, poisoned.

Let's take this story sentence by sentence and see how these three levels of text representation might play out in our heads. We will assume that there are no difficulties with decoding. This is the first sentence:

> The Sultan left his throne and went to the table.

There are possibly three important pieces of information in this sentence: 'Sultan', 'left – throne' and 'table'. Do we know what these words mean? Well, referring to our background knowledge we might know sultans are similar to kings and are (or were) likely to be found in Islamic countries in the Middle East or South-East Asia. And we know that kings sit on thrones; a throne is a special chair. So we have a context; we are developing our situation model. We are likely to be in a palace somewhere in Asia. We know what a table is and given the fact it probably belongs to the Sultan we might assume it is quite a nice one. We could even begin to think about what the Sultan may be wearing and what his throne could look like. We are also developing our textbase network. The network developed here may not look exactly like ones we develop in real life. There are a number of researchers working on developing detailed computational models. We will develop a very simplified version to give us a starting point:

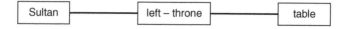

However, while we are developing this network of information and making sense of it by creating a situation model as a context, we might also have to deal with new information. We are back to the surface structure, as more words and sentences are presented in the second sentence:

The Sultan left his throne and went to the table. He was about to start his meal.

As far as the surface structure is concerned we might still have the first sentence in our working memory because it is adjacent. We have new information to add from this second sentence (just one piece probably): 'start – meal'. We can add this to our network in relation to the Sultan by resolving the pronoun 'he' (obviously we would not expect the throne or the table to eat a meal – they are not people, so these pieces of information, or concepts, will not join together).

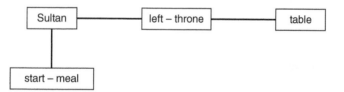

Out network is becoming more detailed, as is our situation model. But again, here comes some more information. Let's add another sentence to the previous ones:

The Sultan left his throne and went to the table. He was about to start his meal. The gado gado was already on the table.

The first thing to notice here relates to the surface structure. We have some more information to deal with held in the third sentence. As we deal with this new information the first sentence may begin to fade from our working memory (to show this I've put the first sentence in italics), but that's OK because we have the important information in our textbase network. But who or what is a gado gado? It's an Indonesian salad made from boiled vegetables served with a peanut sauce, but maybe you knew that anyway. So we might have some background knowledge about what a gado gado is; and given the context of the Sultan in Asia, this seems to fit. We are developing our context further as well as our network, which may begin to look like this:

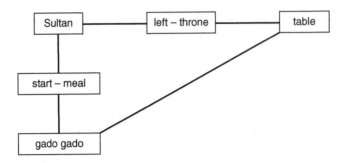

We can link the gado gado to the table. Anyway, here comes some more information. Let's add another sentence:

> *The Sultan left his throne and went to the table. He was about to start his
> meal.* The gado gado was already on the table. He was feeling very hungry.

Again, as we read further on through the text more of the surface structure will
start to fade (again shown in italics) because we do not retain it. In this fourth
sentence the information we need to add is about 'feeling hungry'. We are likely to
have an understanding of this feeling. So now we can join up our network further:

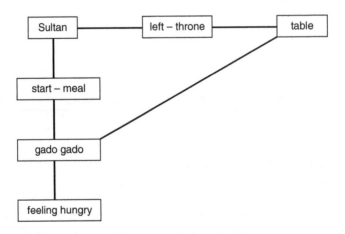

Maybe we won't join up 'table' to the new information in the network – it doesn't
seem that important to the central thrust of what's going on. It's still in our heads
though. Let's add some more information:

> *He was about to start his meal. The gado gado was on the table.* He was feel-
> ing very hungry. Savagely, he tore into his dinner.

By this time the surface structure of the first sentence may actually already have disappeared (Look! It's gone!), and other sentences that we have read more recently will start to fade (*again in italics*). We have more information to add: 'tore' and 'dinner'. Presuming we have this in our background knowledge, we know that if someone tears into their food they are likely to be eating quickly and aggressively; more so, if we know what 'savagely' means. So we can place the Sultan's action in a context, thus developing our situation model. We can develop our network and we may choose to link to both the manner in which he ate the food and the fact that it was his dinner. They both seem important. So our network might look like this:

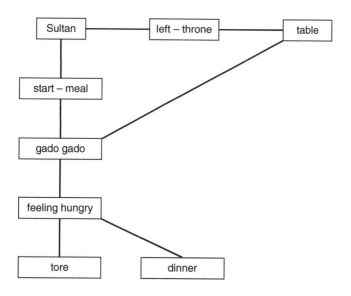

Let's add the last sentence:

> *The gado gado was on the table. He was feeling very hungry.* Savagely, he tore into his dinner. The Sultan fell to the floor, poisoned.

More of the earlier surface structure will fade away completely (the first two sentences have gone now!) and more of the later part of the story will begin to fade (*again, in italics*). We have two new pieces of information to add to our network. We may now decide that the more important piece of information to join the new pieces of information to is the fact that the Sultan was having his dinner.

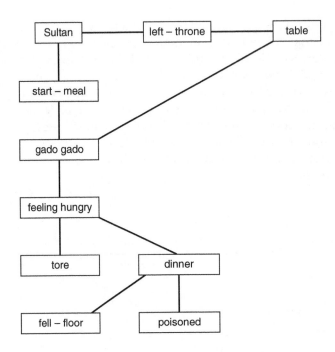

Can you see a pathway developing? It is this pathway that carries **the main idea of the text** so far. In this instance we know the following:

> The Sultan, who is feeling hungry, has gado gado for dinner and is poisoned by it.

This is a very simplified and contrived network. In reality the networks we create as we read are very complex. This is because we have to deal with numerous characters and numerous actions. But what does this simplified network show us?

The words coming into our head *as we read* will mean nothing unless we can organise them into some sort of network at the textbase level. It is important that readers construct networks of this nature because *as we read* successive pieces of text, we will not recall the exact wording of previously read text. However, creating this network *as we read* also requires us to place the network into a real-life, or known, context which we achieve by making links to our background knowledge. The point to be made here is that these levels of text representation (and thus the components of comprehension) work interactively and simultaneously.

Implications for teachers of reading

The first port of call in comprehension is to identify the main idea of the text

All children, of whatever age, are required to apply these component skills interactively and simultaneously if they are going to make sense of written texts. The central purpose of applying these components is initially to identify the main idea of the text.

Identifying the main idea of the text can be made difficult
because the components work interactively – preparation and planning are
crucial

Another important implication for the teacher is that because the comprehension processes work interactively, they are likely to impact upon one another. For example, if my objective relates to improving children's inference making skills, and if I make the assessment that a child is poor in this area, how certain am I in my judgement? Am I sure that this wasn't caused by an inability to engage with the surface structure of the text I gave the child? Perhaps the child had trouble decoding it. If this was the case, I have to question why I chose a text that was difficult to decode when my objective was inference making. To use an analogy, we don't ask children to play football on full-size pitches for a reason: they would spend most of their time trying to cover the ground rather engaging with the ball. Perhaps the issue is not decoding, but rather about knowing what the words on the page mean, or indeed the wider context that is described in the text. So, have I considered the background knowledge the reader needs to bring to the text if they are to understand it?

2. Comprehension is a constructive, cumulative and integrative process, and as we read our understanding changes in the light of new information

In the previous section you will have noticed that we accumulated information as we progressed through the text. You may also have begun to notice that as we construct some sort of understanding from these pieces of information, we do not treat them as separate lumps. Readers actively try to make links between these bits of information and in the process integrate them together. Kintsch and van Dijk (1978) explain how we do this by outlining the concept of the reading cycle.

A reading cycle takes place when a reader encounters a statement or sentence in the text. So imagine that we have read just a statement or sentence, which we will call 'Reading Cycle 1'. As we read the sentence, it triggered some related information and associated knowledge (Linderholm et al., 2004) in our heads. In this instance, let's take the first sentence of 'The Sultan and the Gado Gado' and call it Reading Cycle 1. If we refer back to our first diagram, it reaffirms the idea that when we read the story three pieces of new information were triggered in our mind: 'Sultan', 'left – throne' and 'table' (see Figure 8.1).

When a new statement or sentence is encountered, a new reading cycle begins. We can call this 'Reading Cycle 2'. Again, this reading cycle will trigger information and associated knowledge in the reader's mind. Now, what is interesting here is that the information and knowledge in Reading Cycle 1 gets *carried over* to Reading Cycle 2. What happens next is that if the reader can make links between the information and knowledge in Reading Cycle 2 and the previous information and knowledge in Reading Cycle 1, this will be *combined* and *integrated*. In 'The Sultan and the Gado Gado' story, let's say the second sentence is Reading Cycle 2. As the right-angled arrow in Figure 8.2 shows, the information from Reading Cycle 1 ('Sultan', 'left – throne' and 'table') gets carried over in our heads and linked to the new information in Reading Cycle 2 ('start – meal'). So we are holding two lots

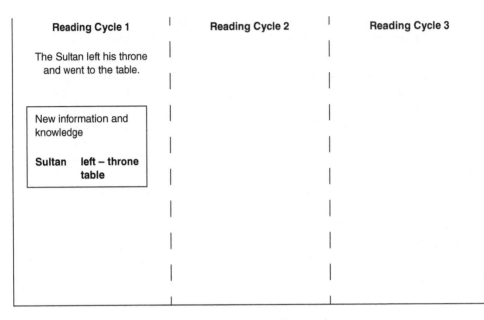

Figure 8.1 'The Sultan and the Gado Gado' – Reading Cycle 1

of information in our heads. What we do then is to **seek links** between the two sets. If we follow the straight arrow down in Figure 8.2 we can see the information we have decided to combine and integrate. We didn't integrate all the information from Reading Cycle 1; we only integrated 'Sultan' into the new information. You will notice there is another box underneath which shows other information ('left – throne' and 'table') that has not been integrated – at this stage.

If a new sentence or statement is then encountered, which we may call Reading Cycle 3, yet more information and knowledge will be triggered. The information and knowledge that was combined and integrated from Reading Cycles 1 and 2 will then be carried over into Reading Cycle 3 and recombined and reintegrated with the new information and knowledge here. So if we refer back to 'The Sultan and the Gado Gado', let's describe the third sentence as Reading Cycle 3. If we follow the second right-angled arrow in Figure 8.3 we see that this time it is the integrated information in Reading Cycle 2 ('Sultan' and 'start – meal') which gets carried over in our heads and linked to the new information in Reading Cycle 3 ('gado gado' and 'table'). If we follow the second straight arrow down we can again see the information we have decided to combine and integrate ('Sultan', 'start – meal', 'gado gado'). Again, you will notice there is another box underneath which shows other information ('table') that has not been integrated – at this stage.

This process of combination and integration continues as further reading cycles are completed. You can work how what the remaining reading cycles in this story might look like.

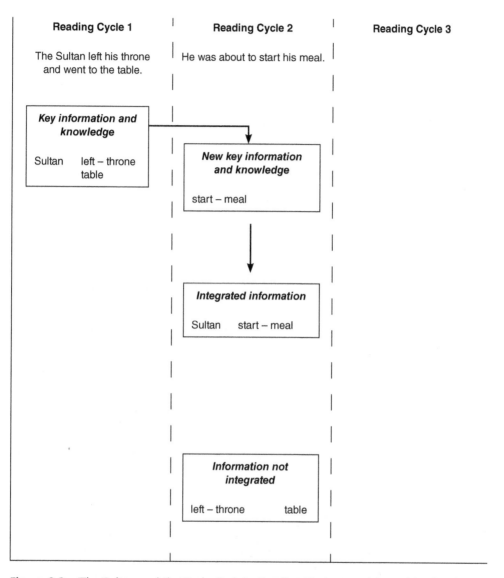

Figure 8.2 'The Sultan and the Gado Gado' – Reading Cycles 1 and 2 combined and integrated

You will also have noticed that the new information presented in each reading cycle was the same information that we included in our textbase network. So you will also see how, then, the textbase network we develop is a lot more complex than the one we looked at above.

The concept of the reading cycle shows us that the comprehension process is a constructive one. As more information is gained from succeeding sentences or statements, the concepts activated from the text are developed and reformed.

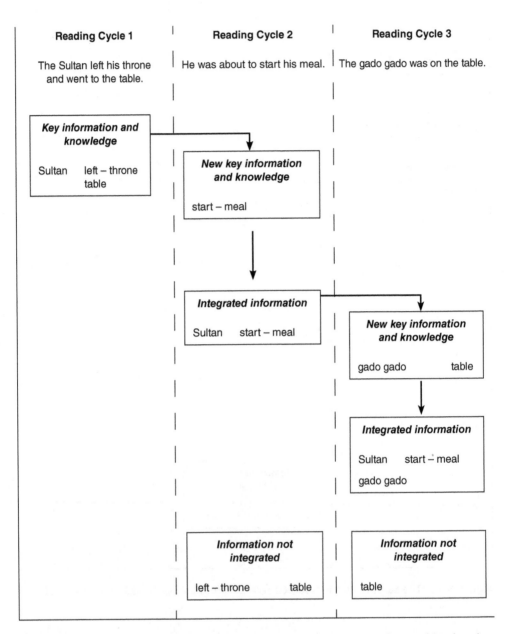

Figure 8.3   'The Sultan and the Gado Gado' – Reading Cycles 1, 2 and 3 combined and integrated

As this development and reformation takes place we also understand that the comprehension process is cumulative; we build our understanding by gathering information and knowledge from across different reading cycles. Our interpretation of the sentence we are currently reading is conditional upon the sentences that have preceded it (Garnham and Oakhill, 1992). To give some structure to the numerous pieces of information and knowledge we have accessed in order to give meaning to the text we read, we integrate them.

Implications for teachers of reading

You are asking children to undertake something very complex when you ask them to read

The teacher of reading has to be aware that this process of integrating information is a cognitively complex one for children learning to read. Moreover, if a reader has poor working memory it makes it more difficult for this information to be carried over and integrated from one reading cycle to the next. With adjacent reading cycles this process of recombination and integration happens very quickly, which explains why working memory is so important.

Make children aware that their understanding of the text is likely to change as they read

The implications for teaching also extend to the metacognitive aspects of children's comprehension of text. For example, are children aware that as they read text, their understanding of it is likely to change? Or do they develop a 'pathway', which they initially believe to be correct, and then cease to integrate new information if it does not fit with what they believe the text to be about? This relates closely to comprehension monitoring, which we investigated in Chapter 4.

3. Information from any part of the text might prove to be important to ensure understanding

We have noted that not all the information in a particular reading cycle may be carried forward to the next one. This may be because there is no clear link between that particular piece of information and what is presented in the new reading cycle. Another reason is that readers can only process a limited amount of information as they read (Kintsch and van Dijk, 1978). In 'The Sultan and the Gado Gado' we have a story that requires six reading cycles to be processed. In an extended piece of text the reader would have to process many more reading cycles; this is a lot of information to keep active in your head as you take in yet more information.

It is this issue of activation we will turn to next. In their 'landscape' view of reading, van den Broek et al. (1996) present a model that emphasises the importance of activation. As we read a text we know that new information is activated; we also know that some information gets reactivated. In 'The Sultan and the Gado Gado', we saw how the 'table' was introduced in the first sentence, disappeared in the second sentence, and returned in the third sentence. The van den Broek et al. landscape model also considers the strength of the activation; they have developed 3-D computational models that list the concepts in a story on one axis; the sentences (or reading cycles) of the story on another; and the measured strength of the activation on the vertical access. It really does look like a landscape. We do not need to investigate the concept of activation in such a detailed manner. However, let's take three concepts or ideas that are introduced in 'The Sultan and the Gado Gado' story:

Sultan   table   throne

Which of these do you think is activated most strongly? Well clearly, it is the Sultan; he appears in every sentence in one way or another apart from the third one. The least strongly activated is 'throne'. Now imagine this story is not complete; it is just the beginning and there are another 30 reading cycles to go through until we get to this final one:

The Sultan's brother now sat where the dead Sultan once sat.

Well, where did the Sultan's brother now sit? Presumably on the throne. So the reader may not have considered this to be information that was really important to the main idea of the story, but they would still have had to keep the concept of 'throne' in their head as they were reading, and it is not until the final sentence that this becomes reactivated. However, if the reader cannot recall it, they can still activate background knowledge of sultans and thrones from long-term memory, or re-read the text.

The point to make here is that even if a text is easily decodable, and even if the reader can apply background knowledge, they are likely to have to hold a large number of related concepts in their head at the same time, and if one concept needs to be reactivated it is not necessarily a straightforward process.

Implications for the teacher of reading
We must consider text complexity

One implication of this is that we need to consider the complexity of the text we introduce to children. It is not simply about whether they can decode the text, it is also about how many concepts or characters are involved. A text may be easy to decode, but how many concepts are being introduced? It is important therefore that teachers know the texts they use with children and read widely.

4. Inference making is central to text comprehension

Interestingly, there is a general consensus across all models of text comprehension which suggests that text is represented at the three levels proposed by Kintsch and van Dijk (1978) and which were analysed earlier in the chapter. Their model has been used as the basis for the numerous other models that followed, although these models are not all the same. Historically, two schools of thought have developed in terms of text comprehension models: those that subscribe to memory-based models, and those that subscribe to explanation-based ones. The essential difference between the two relates to the amount of inference making that is believed to take place during the reading process.

Memory-based models of text comprehension relate to what has been termed by McKoon and Ratcliff (1992) as the minimalist hypothesis: we make only a minimal amount of inferences when we read. This is because the comprehension process relies upon automatic memory processes that appear to take very little thought. The reader constructs inferences of only two types while reading:

those that help to establish local coherence between just-read information and information still active in memory, and those that access readily available information from general knowledge and explicit statements in the text. Advocates of these types of model are considered to focus on the 'bottom–up' aspects of comprehension.

Explanation-based models, such as the constructionist model (Graesser et al., 1994), agree that these automatic inferences are made but they also suggest that alongside this, the reader constantly attempts to make causal links between what they are reading and their world knowledge. The reader attempts to explain such things as actions and events during the process of reading and attain a more global coherence. So, explanation models suggest that further inferences are made as the text is being read. Advocates of these types of model are considered to focus on the 'top–down' aspects of comprehension.

We have already noted the 'bottom–up' and 'top–down' issue, in the chapter on cohesive inferences. It is not a debate that we need to engage with at this point (though it is an interesting one and in the long run will have implications for teaching). The important point to note is the cause of the debate: inference making. By making it the focal point of the discussion, these two schools of thought go some way in explaining the central role of inference making in comprehension. We have looked at inference making as an isolated concept and considered how we might view it as a process that helps to create a cohesive understanding of the text, or one that allows us to interrogate text in depth. However, we need to be aware that inference making itself takes place in the context of the comprehension components. We can show this by referring once again to our Sultan. Let's take the first three reading cycles from 'The Sultan and the Gado Gado':

> The Sultan sat on his throne. The gado gado was on the table. He was feeling hungry.

At the beginning of this chapter I assumed you knew what gado gado was (and if you didn't I filled in this piece of background knowledge for you anyway). But what would happen if you didn't know this? In this situation you would have to make an inference to achieve any coherent understanding of the text. We know the Sultan is hungry and so we might infer (correctly) that gado gado is a type of food. But what if we inferred incorrectly? What if we thought that the gado gado was actually a small creature, perhaps like a lizard? This could potentially change the whole meaning of the text because the reader suddenly has an important issue to resolve: Who is hungry? The Sultan or the gado gado lizard? The implications of this potential mix-up are explored in more detail in Figure 8.4.

Implications for the teacher of comprehension
Inference making needs to be explicitly taught

The implication of this for teachers is to ensure that inference making is explicitly taught. As part of this we need to know which inference types to teach. The chapters on inference making can provide a starting point on this.

5. Readers comprehend the same text differently

The model proposed by Kinstch and van Dijk builds upon studies undertaken by Bransford and his colleagues (cited earlier). The work of these theorists initially helped to establish that the components of reading work interactively and simultaneously, and that meaning is constructed by accumulating and integrating information and knowledge over successive reading cycles. We also know that typically we do not retain the exact wording of the texts we read. This last point is an important one because it raises the question: What do we retain? Bransford and colleagues pointed out that we do not retain a linguistic representation of text when we read it (if we did, we would remember the exact wording). Rather, they suggest that we create a mental representation of the text.

What do they mean by this? One way to think about this is if I asked you to think about what the perfect classroom looks like, and then asked you to capture this in a drawing (a visual representation), this might go some way to explaining it. It might feature particular important objects; or perhaps there is a teacher (Is she smiling? What does that tell you? And why is the teacher a 'she'?). Johnson-Laird (1983) states that a mental representation does not have to be visual, but I believe it is a good way for beginning to think about it.

Nation (2005) notes that there is a consensus across many different mental models of text comprehension that readers build up a mental representation of a text (Garnham, 2001; Gernsbacher, 1990; Kintsch, 1998). If this is the case (and there is much evidence to support it) then this has one important implication: the mental representation that is created is unlikely to be the same between different readers. This is because each reader comes to a text with unique stores of general (or world) knowledge and linguistic ability.

At this point it is worth acknowledging another theory of text comprehension: mental models theory. We began to explore mental models theory, as proposed by Johnson-Laird (1983), in our exploration of interrogative inferences, where we investigated the role of deduction in reading. This builds upon the work of Bransford and his colleagues (Bransford and Franks, 1971; Bransford et al., 1972). It acknowledges that text comprehension is an integrative and constructive process, and also that when a reader attempts to comprehend text a mental representation of the content as a whole is constructed, whether this is a sequence of events or a place (Garnham and Oakhill, 1996). It is also explicit in its belief that the mental representation that is developed from a text will vary from reader to reader. The fact that this constructed mental representation will vary from one reader to the next is explained by noting a distinction we have already encountered in Chapter 7 between mental models and mental logic. Logic by its nature is finite and has to state whether something is correct or not. We noted how Johnson-Laird (1983) used the example of syllogisms to explain this.

Let's take this distinction between mental models and mental logic beyond the issue of deduction and apply it more globally to the concept of comprehension.

If text comprehension were based on logic then every reader would comprehend the same text in exactly the same way. The construction of a mental model (or mental representation), on the other hand, involves a search for alternative conclusions. Therefore, the mental model that is constructed is not going to be a homogenous one, and the manner in which the reader has comprehended the text will vary.

Figure 8.4 attempts to show this. It presents the (hypothetical) thoughts of five children as they engage with 'The Sultan and the Gado Gado' story. I am going to assume that there are no working memory issues and that decoding is not a problem.

	Child 1	Child 2	Child 3	Child 4	Child 5
First sentence	The Sultan left his throne and went to the table.				
Ongoing thinking	I can read this. Bark!	OK, Sultan is like a king. I saw one in a film once. It was in a far away country.	Sultan? Must be some kind of a king. He's got a throne. Probably an old story set somewhere far away. Why has he gone to the table?	Sultan? There was one in Aladdin I think. So this is an old story. What's on the table?	A Sultan is like a king. Probably has a palace with minarets, like in Aladdin.
Second sentence	The Sultan left his throne and went to the table. He was about to start his meal.				
Ongoing thinking	I can read this. Bark! Bark!	OK, he's gone to the table to eat.	OK, he's left his throne because it's time for his dinner.	OK, his dinner is ready.	He's gone to eat at the table.
Third sentence	The Sultan left his throne and went to the table. He was about to start his meal. The gado gado was on the table.				
Ongoing thinking	I can read this. Bark! Bark! Bark!	What's a gado gado? Seems important. Can't make sense of this now.	I have no idea what a gado gado is. It's on the table. ... Could be an animal ... Must be small ... a lizard?	What's a gado gado? Is it his dinner? Or is it a special food? Or is it something else? What does the next sentence say?	Gado gado? That's like a salad. I had one at a restaurant once. And I read about it in a book about Indonesia.

(Continued)

Figure 8.4 (Continued)

Fourth sentence	The Sultan left his throne and went to the table. He was about to start his meal. The gado gado was on the table. He was feeling very hungry.				
Ongoing thinking	I can read this. Bark! Bark! Bark! Bark!	What's a gado gado? I hope she doesn't ask me about this! I'll answer the first question – it's bound to be about the Sultan. Feeling a bit hungry myself.	Yes! A gado gado is a lizard and he's hungry. He might eat the Sultan's food.	OK, the Sultan is hungry so I think he's going to eat the gado gado. It is a food. Still don't know what it is though.	So he's going to eat the gado gado if he's feeling hungry.
Fifth sentence	The Sultan left his throne and went to the table. He was about to start his meal. The gado gado was on the table. He was feeling very hungry. Savagely, he bit into his dinner.				
Ongoing thinking	I can read this. Bark! Bark! Bark! Bark! Bark!	Actually it must be dinner time soon. What's a gado gado?	Hold on … The gado gado has got his own dinner. Is he the Sultan's pet? What does 'savargely' mean?	Savagely? Must have something to with him being really hungry. He's eating the gado gado though; whatever that is.	Wow, he must be really hungry. The Sultan is eating like an animal!
Final sentence	The Sultan left his throne and went to the table. He was about to start his meal. The gado gado was on the table. He was feeling very hungry. Savagely, he bit into his dinner. The Sultan fell to the floor, poisoned.				
Ongoing thinking	Finished! Got to the end! Bark! Bark! Bark! Bark! Bark!	So he's fallen over near the table.	Oh wow! The Sultan is the gado gado's dinner! The gado gado bit the Sultan and killed him with his poison!	Wow! The food is poisoned! Is he dead?	Oh, there must have been poison in the salad. Who did it?

Figure 8.4 'The Sultan and the Gado Gado': five hypothetical children making different meanings from the same text

Dialogue Point

Analysing texts to see the load they place on working memory

Working with colleagues, analyse how each of the hypothetical children in Figure 8.4 makes sense of the text as they progress through the story.

Consider how they engage with the following components of comprehension as they read:

- Prior knowledge
- Vocabulary
- Grammatical structures
- Inference making
- Comprehension monitoring

What assessments could you make from this as to their comprehension abilities? And is it clear cut as to who is the best comprehender?

IMPLICATIONS FOR THE TEACHER OF READING COMPREHENSION

To understand whether a child has comprehended a text, dialogue is important

The meaning we, as individuals, make from text is unique, and texts are likely to be understood in different ways; so if two readers are presented with the same text we would expect them to create two different mental models. They will have a different understanding of the text; it may be similar but it will not be exactly the same. If we transfer this to the classroom context where we have multiple children, it is obvious to see how this might create difficulty for the teacher. How do we know whether the child has understood the text? How do we know whether they are right or wrong? Can we assume there is only one answer? These questions cause us to question the manner in which we teach and assess comprehension. Perhaps we need to accept that, as Rasinksi and Padak (2008) suggest, readers are capable of establishing different 'shades' of meaning, and that we cannot assume that a child has misunderstood a text because they arrived at a different understanding than the one that we might have expected; especially as this 'expected' understanding relates to what is going on in *our* heads. It would suggest that trying to understand what's going on in the child's head might be a bit more important than what we have already established in our own heads. The best way to do this is by talking to them and listening to them.

CONCLUSION

We began this chapter by thinking about how a group of children engaged deeply with Colin Thompson's text *How to Live Forever*. If we make some links back to the previous chapters, we can begin to see how this moment came about. Clearly, the children in this scenario are bringing elements of general knowledge to the book. They have a concept of what it is to be a child, and they all had some personal experience of death. This knowledge was different from their teacher's, reiterating Mercer's (1995) point that knowledge is created by sharing.

From a linguistic perspective, the written text is not difficult to decode and the sentence structures are largely predictable. There is challenge presented in some aspects of idiomatic language. The visual text is also challenging and, as one would expect from an effective picture book, it does significantly more than just support the writing. The children appear to have been able to negotiate these challenges. This would suggest that, for this group, working memory was not an issue and they were able to make the necessary coherence-type inferences as they were reading. This then supported them in making the interrogative inferences after they had finished reading, which allowed them to interpret, evaluate and justify.

In this chapter we have seen how these components worked interactively in a constructive and cumulative manner. Moreover, we can now see that each member of the group reading *How to Live Forever* applied these components from a unique perspective; as such they made sense of the text in different ways (although there was evidence of individuals rethinking their sense of the text through discussion). The point to be made here is that each member of the group accessed the same components of comprehension and these components were seen to work interactively.

SECTION 2
PRACTICES

In the introduction to the 'Processes' section of this book, reference was made to Vygotsky (1978) and his belief that learning involved the psychological (the 'intramental') and the social (the 'intermental'). In this vision of learning, all knowledge that learners acquire happens in the context of the social and cultural world around them. Reference has been made previously to Mercer's (1995) comment that knowledge is socially constructed.

With this in mind, the following section focuses on the 'intermental', and the fact that learning takes place in a social setting – and in this instance, school classrooms specifically.

This section on Practices outlines the issues that teachers need to consider to explicitly teach reading comprehension. The chapters take us on a journey from text, to talk, to teaching.

Chapter 9 outlines an important issue that must be considered before the act of teaching; and this relates to how we choose texts and indeed what we consider text to be. Chapter 10 places the act of teaching comprehension into a broader pedagogical structure and in particular makes a case for implementing dialogic teaching approaches. It suggests shaping the dialogic interactions in three ways: through exposition, exploration and expansion. Chapter 11 investigates specific teaching practices related to comprehension.

CHAPTER 9

SELECTING TEXTS

Chapter Overview

This chapter investigates the important role that texts play in supporting the development of comprehension. Discussions on teaching and learning tend to focus on the actual interaction between the teacher and the learner; however, when thinking about comprehension it is essential to consider the text as well. Text is defined here in its broadest sense to include not only written words, but also such things as pictures, moving images and sounds. All these different types of texts can support the development of comprehension skills. However, written text has a dominant role in current conceptions of comprehension, so this chapter presents a discussion on how suitable written texts might be chosen. The issue of text readability is explored with reference to the Spache (1974) readability formula, and a 'ready reckoner', which might be simpler to use. Examples of both are given to demonstrate how teachers might choose whether a text is suitable. This is followed by a discussion about what to consider when using non-fiction texts.

Tony Blundell's (1993) *Beware of Boys* tells the story of a boy who has been captured by a wolf and is about to be eaten. Immediately we can see a link to traditional folk tales, such as 'Hansel and Gretel' and 'Little Red Riding Hood', both of which feature children in danger from wolves. This link to traditional tales is further evident in the plot of *Beware of Boys*, which references a story sometimes known as 'Stone Soup'.

For those of you who are unfamiliar with 'Stone Soup', this is a story of trickery set in the distant past. A vagabond traveller knocks on the door of an old lady's house and asks if he can boil up some water so he can make some stone soup. The curious old lady agrees. The traveller places a large stone in the bottom of a pan and proceeds to boil the water. He tastes the soup at regular intervals and notes what the soup is lacking in flavour: salt, pepper, chicken. Each time he makes these judgements he asks the old lady if she has these ingredients; and each time the old lady goes away and finds the ingredient. This then gets added to the soup and before you know it, the traveller has a full meal when all he had initially was a stone.

In Blundell's story, the boy is in total control of the situation. Unlike the child characters in the traditional folk tales, the boy in *Beware of Boys* shows no fear of the wolf – if anything the boy considers the wolf to be rather stupid. In an interesting parallel to the 'Stone Soup' story, the boy sends the wolf off to find ingredients for a 'boy soup' recipe, although in *Beware of Boys* this turns into a series of dangerous escapades. Eventually, the boy escapes and the wolf becomes a psychological wreck. Beware of boys – not wolves – indeed.

What is interesting with *Beware of Boys* is that children of different ages and experiences are likely to comprehend it (or not) in different ways. For example, when the issue of how the wolf is going to eat the boy is initially introduced in the story, the following interaction takes place:

'What are you going to do with me?' asked the boy. The wolf licked his lips.

'Why, eat you, of course,' he replied.

'Raw?' said the boy.

The wolf roared.

'No,' sighed the boy, 'I mean, aren't you even going to cook me first?'

This is a funny moment in the book (one of many actually), and one that the written text and illustrations, working in conjunction, cleverly build up to deliver. It is also one that a group of 'averagely' attaining (whatever that means) Year 3 children (7–8-year-olds) I was working with only partially understood. Why?

Dialogue Point

Uncovering the link between the text and the reader

In the vignette above, I haven't told you in what way the text from *Beware of Boys* was partially understood, and I haven't told you anything about the group apart from their age and the fact that they were 'average' attainers. Regardless, look closely at the text.

Working with colleagues, consider why the group didn't see the humour in this piece of writing (this is quite straightforward actually), but also consider other potential stumbling blocks this short piece of text presents.

Think about the issue of decoding, but also refer to the components of comprehension outlined in previous chapters:

- Prior world knowledge
- Knowledge of language
- Memory
- Monitoring
- Inference making (cohesive and interrogative)

Again, working with colleagues think of a group of children you have worked with (it doesn't matter what age). How would they cope with this text? If the answer is 'easily', then explain why. If there are potential stumbling blocks, how could they be addressed?

The reason for this partial understanding could be attributed to many sources. In the previous chapters we have noted that comprehension is composed of a number of components, any one (or indeed any combination) of which could impact upon how well the text is comprehended. What this example does show is that we cannot view the reader in isolation from the text, or the text in isolation from the reader. There is an interaction between the two. The implication of this is that teachers have to be mindful of the texts they present to children *before* they begin teaching. Text choice is something that needs careful consideration, and must be done with the reader in mind.

WHAT CONSTITUTES A TEXT?

Of course this raises the question as to what constitutes a text. Intuitively perhaps, when we think of developing children's reading comprehension we think of this in relation to written texts; of how effectively they are able to get sequences of written words off a page and to understand them. This makes sense when we consider the point that children from a very young age are surrounded by written text to which they have to assign meaning. In Chapter 1 we noted Frith's (1995) logographic stage of reading development where meaning is assigned to symbols, and gave the example of the 'golden arches' that signify a McDonald's restaurant. This of course forms the letter 'm', but is only one small example of how children interact with written text on a day-to-day basis. There is the on/off button on a television remote control; the advertisements on billboards; the apps on an iPad; the instructions related to a computer game. Children are surrounded by written text; and understanding this text plays an important part in helping them to understand the world around them. It is unsurprising then that when we think of text comprehension, engagement with written words is likely to be the dominant mode.

Yet by highlighting the fact that children are using iPads, playing computer games and watching television (amongst other things of this nature), it makes clear that written text is not the only mode they are engaging with. Actually, Wyse et al. (2013) note four different modes:

- Written mode – such things as meaning of words, font and layout
- Visual mode – such things as composition, movement and colour
- Sound mode – such things as tone, pitch and pauses
- Gestural mode – such things as facial expression and posture

And this leads us to the idea that to view text only as written words is to take a very narrow view of what constitutes a text. If we take these other modes into account we can begin to take a broader view and start to engage with texts that work multimodally. Wyse et al. (2013) state that multimodal texts include such things as picture books (*Beware of Boys* is a multimodal text), comics, graphic novels, computer games, podcasts and films. Indeed, in the context of film these authors explicitly state that 'Just as we teach children to read written words, so we need to teach them to "read" moving images' (2013: 290). Presumably this can be extended to teaching them to 'read' static images (paintings, pictures and illustrations) and sounds (probably including songs).

Of course, this raises the question of whether there is any value in taking this broader view of text. Written text is still the dominant mode in schooling – and the assessment of schooling – so why bother addressing these other modalities of text?

To address this I would like to take the statement by Wyse et al. noted above, and for the purposes of this book substitute the word 'read' with 'comprehend'; and I want to make clear the following very important point: To comprehend a film, or a painting, or a picture book illustration, the comprehender needs to access the *same* components of comprehension as those required to comprehend written text.

Take the book *Beware of Boys* described at the beginning of this chapter. This is an example of a multimodal text in that the words work in conjunction with the illustrations; the reader uses both to make sense of it. To do this successfully, the reader has to access the components of comprehension outlined in the previous chapters. For example, background knowledge is accessed (probably about the role of wolves in traditional stories, and for some perhaps an understanding of the 'Stone Soup' story); previous action or events are held in memory and viewed in the context of new information carried in both the words and the pictures (as we see the wolf sent on another dangerous errand to find a new ingredient for the boy soup recipe, we keep in mind the affect that finding previous ingredients has had); and, importantly, inferences are made (we know the boy is not scared of the wolf by the way he talks to him, but also by his gestures in the illustrations, both of which inform us about the boy's character).

If you refer back to the scenario in which this text was presented, it was being shared with a group of 'average' 7–8-year-olds. As such, these children would still be in the process of developing their decoding abilities; they were not fluent decoders. Advocates of the simple view of reading note that there is a 'trade-off' between decoding and comprehension during the course of learning to read (Perfetti et al., 1996). If this group only engaged with written texts, their opportunities to develop their comprehension abilities could potentially be limited by the decoding burden – and as we shall see later in this chapter, the written text of *Beware of Boys* when taken in isolation has a readability age just about commensurate with their chronological age. Using this multimodal text supported the development of their comprehension skills.

Can the same be said of films? Yes, think of any film you have seen recently. What background knowledge did you bring to the text (and yes, I will refer to it as a text)? How did you keep track of the text as it progressed? Through short-term memory. How did you make judgements about characters? By making inferences based on what they said and what they did.

Viewing text in its broadest terms allows teachers to support comprehension by developing the underlying components such as inference making, the application of prior knowledge and monitoring skills. Young readers will then be in the position to apply this broader understanding of how components are required in the context of written texts; although they will be need to be taught how to do this still.

CHOOSING TEXTS

Young readers (as with adult readers) are more likely to want to read something that interests them. They are more likely to be motivated to read it and they will be more likely to engage with it. In this context, exposing children to quality texts is important. They need to see what good writers do and this will help to instil an enjoyment of reading.

And at this point, I should imagine, you are thinking of the number of times you have heard this before. It's obvious, isn't it? Of course, we need to engage young readers with interesting texts by good writers so that they enjoy reading. Why would we want to do otherwise? But I think it's obvious to the point that statements such as these are in danger of becoming slightly banal, 'throwaway' remarks.

Let's try and look at this in a slightly different way because what matters here is how we might go about ensuring this happens. We can do this by considering two questions. The first question to ask is who decides what interesting and engaging literature looks like? As adults we make this choice for ourselves, by and large. We may be given recommendations by friends, or by things we see or read in the media, but the final choice is essentially individual. In contrast, how much choice do children get over the material they read, particularly in schools? The responsibility for choosing texts through which to teach reading falls to teachers largely. And rightly so, I think. Certainly we want the children we teach to be independent readers who can express preferences and make choices, but teachers play an important role in supporting this. So when it is stated that teachers need to have a wide knowledge of children's literature, it is an important point. This is something that teachers can build up over time – although working collaboratively with colleagues helps.

The second question to ask is critical: How does this book support the learning of particular children and at particular times? Now, enjoyment of reading is something we should strive to achieve; however, to enjoy reading generally requires an understanding that texts need to be comprehended – and not just superficially. By and large most texts with which young readers engage will require engagement with written texts, even picture books. In this section, therefore, I would like to focus on what teachers might look to keep in mind when choosing texts.

TEXT READABILITY

In Chapter 6 a brief reference was made to the concept of text readability. At this point it is appropriate to consider this in more depth. Readability is an area that has been somewhat overlooked, and that can be of great benefit to the teacher of reading, as it provides a basis for deciding which texts might be suitable for specific children.

Just to be clear, readability is not the same as comprehension; as Harrison (1980) points out, the two concepts are fundamentally different. Comprehension relates to the ability of the reader to understand a text, whereas readability relates to the text itself and how *likely* it is to be understood. Readability is concerned with features within the text that are likely to make it easy or difficult for the reader to understand it. These include such things as the number of syllables in each word, the number of nouns in a passage, the number of 'commonly' used words and sentence length.

Bentley (1985) suggests conducting readability studies is a valuable process because judgements can be made as to whether the reading level of the written material matches the reader's likely ability to understand it. So by considering features such as sentence length we are more able to make a prediction as to whether a reader will comprehend it. This is important when we think back to how we defined comprehension in Chapter 2. Yes, comprehension is about understanding what has been read, but we also noted that the teacher of reading cannot stop at this point. The onus is on the teacher of reading to ensure that the children make judgements, express preferences, evaluate the writer's effectiveness and engage with the affective aspects of reading. Indeed, statements such as these are common in reading curricula across the English-speaking world. However, we cannot support children's learning in these (important and essential) areas unless the text has been comprehended.

The readability of a text is measured using a formula, of which there are a number to choose from. These formulae attempt to arrive at a readability score by measuring the features of the text that are likely to affect comprehension.

As noted above, there are a number of readability measures, each with a different formula. Harrison (1980) makes clear that the choice of formula needs to be considered carefully as some are more sensitive to particular age ranges. He suggests that for testing the readability of texts in the primary years, the Spache formula (1974) is the most reliable, so let's focus on that one. The Spache formula takes into account both sentence length and the difficulty of the vocabulary used, based on a familiar word list that was developed through the analysis of words commonly found in school reading books and textbooks. A difficult word is thus described as a word that does not appear on this list.

The formula itself is:

(0.121 × average sentence length)

+ (0.082 × number of difficult words)

+ 0.659

= US grade + 5 = UK readability age

The Spache formula provides a score that relates to the US school grades starting from Grade 1. When applied in the UK, 5 is added to the US grade to give a readability age in years and months. So, if the formula is applied and the text is found to have a US grade of 2.3, for example, 5 is added and a readability age of 7 years and 3 months is scored.

How did Spache arrive at the numbers for this formula? I have absolutely no idea, but it seems to work. Below is an analysis completed on the first 100 words of Tony Blundell's *Beware of Boys* prior to teaching the 7–8-year-olds in the vignette outlined earlier. All the vocabulary that might present difficulty (those words not on the word list that accompanies the Spache formula and which can be found in Harrison (1980)) is underlined. As we can see, there are twelve possibly unfamiliar words – in other words 12% of the 100-word text. We can count 10.5 different sentences (the last one would take us over 100 words so we cut it off and see what proportion of the sentence is left; in this case it is a half), and on average each sentence has 9.52 words. We can now apply the formula. What we find is that this text has a readability level of 7 years and 8 months – so we can say that the text should be just about within the range of our averagely attaining Year 3 children. They should be able to comprehend it, but it might present some challenge (which indeed it did).

🗁 Readability analysis: *Beware of Boys* by Tony Blundell

Once upon a time, not so very long ago, nor so very far away, a small boy took a short cut through the <u>forest</u> … and was <u>captured</u> by a <u>hungry</u> wolf.
  '<u>Silly</u> boy,' smiled the wolf, and carried him back to his <u>cave</u>.
  'What are you going to do with me?' asked the boy. The wolf <u>licked</u> his lips.
  'Why, eat you, of course,' he <u>replied</u>.
  '<u>Raw</u>?' said the boy.
  The wolf <u>roared</u>.

(Continued)

(Continued)

'No,' <u>sighed</u> the boy, 'I mean, <u>aren't</u> you even going to cook me first?'
The wolf thought about it.
'Go on, then,' he said. 'What do

Number of sentences = 10.5

Average sentence length = 100/10.5 = 9.52

Percentage of unfamiliar words = 12%

(0.121 x wds/sen) = 0.121 x 9.52 = 1.1519

+ (0.082 x % ufmwds) 0.082 x 12 = 0.984

+ (0.659)

+ 5 = 7.7949 = 7.8 years

Below is a second example, which I used with a group of Year 5 (9–10-year-old) children who were considered to be attaining slightly 'below average'. It is taken from the first 100 words of *The Eye of the Cyclops* as re-told by Anthony Horowitz. It is one of a number of short stories that appear in his excellent book (read it!) entitled *Myths and Legends* (2007). As we can see from the underlined words, there are 28 possibly unfamiliar words, in other words 28% of the 100 word text. We can count seven different sentences, and on average each sentence has 14.28 words. Applying the formula we find that this text has a readability level of 9 years and 7 months. Now, I have a dilemma. How readable will this text be for my group of 'below average' 9–10-year-olds? It is a brilliantly entertaining text after all, and I know the group would enjoy it. The decision I have to make is whether to use it.

Readability analysis: *The Eye of the Cyclops* by Anthony Horowitz

The Cyclops was <u>certainly</u> a <u>terrifying</u> <u>creature</u>. It was about the <u>height</u> of a <u>two-storey</u> house, with thick, <u>curly</u> hair, a <u>matted</u> (and <u>usually</u> <u>filthy</u>) <u>beard</u> and only one eye set square in the middle of its <u>forehead</u>. It was <u>grotesquely</u> <u>ugly</u>, <u>extremely</u> <u>bad-tempered</u>, <u>inordinately</u> <u>violent</u> and <u>generally</u> <u>worth</u> going a long way to <u>avoid</u>. All this, any good book of Greek <u>myths</u> will tell you. But what is <u>less</u> often <u>mentioned</u> is the <u>fact</u> that the Cyclops was also <u>incredibly</u> <u>stupid</u>. It was <u>probably</u> one of the most stupid <u>monsters</u> that ever lived. There were a great many Cyclopes.

Number of sentences 7

Average sentence length = 100/7 = 14.28

Percentage of unfamiliar words = 28%

(0.121 x wds/sen) = 0.121 x 14.28 = 1.727

+ (0.082 x % ufmwds) 0.082 x 28 = 2.296

+ (0.659)

+ 5 = 9.682 = **9.7 years**

THE LIMITATIONS OF READABILITY STUDIES

Readability analyses can be informative, but we must be aware of their limitations. For example, as Bentley (1985) notes, we must consider aspects that relate to how the written text is presented. The style and size of font might be important. Readability analyses cannot measure the effect of these. Neither can they measure the effect that illustrations might have in supporting (or not) comprehension. In Chapter 7 we noted how Maurice Sendak made links between the words and the illustrations, and how even then these created 'gaps' in the text which the reader has to fill (through inference making). This would certainly be the case with the *Beware of Boys* text that we have investigated in this chapter. It does not ask the reader to construct meaning through the singular mode of the written word; the illustrations are important. We have focused very much on the written text, abstracting it from the context of the illustrations. Perhaps the illustrations will make it more readable for the groups we choose to use it with.

There is another aspect we need to consider with readability analyses, and this relates to its practicality. Applying a readability formula takes time. Some word processing programs can complete a readability analysis for you, but you cannot be sure the formulae available are the most appropriate ones to use; and you will probably have to type the text in anyway. If you opt to do this 'manually' you will find yourself referring to lists of words constantly and having to make a number of calculations as part of each one. This process does become more efficient with practice, and I would recommend investigating Harrison's (1980) book to see how readability formulae work. However, schools are very busy places and there might be occasions where you just need to make a quick assessment of a text's suitability. To walk around a school with a word list and a calculator about your person on the off-chance that you will need to make a readability analysis is most peculiar behaviour (which is why I stopped doing it). However, we can still make a reasonably accurate readability analysis by way of a 'ready reckoner'.

CHOOSING TEXTS – A QUICK 'READY RECKONER'

Some time ago a colleague in New Zealand showed me a really quick and accessible way of deciding whether a text is appropriate to use for teaching. First, reflect on the reading capabilities of the class, group or individuals you are selecting it for. After this, analyse the texts against three criteria:

1. Difficult words – Are there words in the text that they are not going to be able to decode?

2. Language features – This could include such things as punctuation, which they may have had limited experience of, possibly ellipsis. It could include unusual grammatical structures, and it could include such things as figurative language, similes and metaphors.

3. Concepts – this works on the same principle as using the word list related to the Spache formula – but without a word list. You know the children; it is highly likely that you can anticipate the words that they will have difficulty conceptualising.

As with our Spache analysis, we again count 100 words, but this time keeping the criteria of difficult words, language features and concepts in mind. We could code them like this:

Difficult words

(Language features)

[Concepts]

Using this coding we can revisit the first 100 words of *Beware of Boys* and reanalyse it using these three 'ready reckoner' criteria. Working on the premise that I am familiar with the 7–8-year-old children in the earlier vignette, I think there is only one word they might struggle to decode. This is the word 'captured'. If you look in the following box, I have underlined this word. In terms of language features, I could think of three that might present difficulty. The wolf says, 'Why, eat you, of course'. This is an unusual grammatical structure. It begins with a question word but it is not a question and the whole statement relates to a very particular type of speech pattern. I think this group will stumble over this; so I have circled it. I also note there is a pun in this piece of text, when the boy says 'raw' and the wolf roars. I think they might miss this (and indeed this lack of experience of puns was the cause of their partial understanding in the vignette presented earlier). I have circled this too. I have also circled 'licked his lips' as I thought this might cause some confusion. In terms of concepts, I'm not sure whether all of the group will understand what 'raw' means. I have noted this as a second potential difficulty by putting a box around it.

So, I have found five possible areas of difficulty presented by this text: one difficult word; three language features; and one concept. This is where I have to do some maths again but this time it is really easy. I have found five areas of difficulty in a 100 word text. If I subtract the five from the 100 I am left with ninety-five: ninety-five is the readability level of *this* text for *this* group. If I had found ten areas of difficulty or more I would have been worried because it means the text is likely to be too difficult, as shown in Table 9.1. With a readability of ninety-five the text will be challenging but can still be used. I just need to make sure I explain the language features, ensure they understand what raw means (the best way is to ask them of course), and clarify the word 'captured' with them. Then, and only then, can I launch into exploring the text in greater depth.

📁   **Readability analysis of *Beware of Boys* by Tony Blundell using the 'ready reckoner' criteria**

Once upon a time, not so very long ago, nor so very far away, a small boy took a short cut.

through the forest … and was <u>captured</u> by a hungry wolf.

'Silly boy,' smiled the wolf, and carried him back to his cave.

'What are you going to do with me?' asked the boy. The wolf (licked his lips.)

('Why, eat you, of course,') he replied.

'Raw?' said the boy.
The wolf roared.

'No,' sighed the boy, 'I mean, aren't you even going to cook me first?'

The wolf thought about it.

'Go on, then,' he said. 'What do

Difficult words = 1

Language features = 3

Concepts = 1

5 difficult features

100 – 5 = 95

I can repeat the same process for Anthony Horowitz's *The Eye of the Cyclops*. If you remember, this was a text I had in mind to use with a group of Year 5 (9–10-year-old) children who were considered to be attaining slightly 'below average'. The Spache readability test showed a readability age of 9.7 years, which suggests that I need to think carefully as to whether it might be too difficult. As with *Beware of Boys* I can take a 100-word sample of text, and again analyse it using the three criteria of difficult words, language features and concepts. This analysis is shown below. As we can see, *for the group of children I have in mind* this text presents a number of difficult words (four to be exact), which have been underlined: 'creature', 'grotesquely', 'inordinately' and 'violent'. As I cast my over the text, I can see three language features that might inhibit comprehension. I know this group of readers are not sure of how brackets work so I have circled the section of text that uses these. I'm not sure they will understand the idea of 'going a long way to avoid' something, so I have circled this too. Finally, I have circled the word 'Cyclopes'. This is a pluralisation of Cyclops, which I only found out by checking in a dictionary; I am sure they won't know this either. In terms of concepts that I think this group would find difficult, the first was the Cyclops itself. If they had seen a film featuring the Cyclops then I might be lucky, but I cannot be sure and so I have put a box around it. I am fairly sure some of them will not understand the concept of a 'two-storey house'. 'Storey' is an unusual word for this group and anyway they all live in flats; again, boxing the word seems appropriate. Boxing the word 'matted' and the phrase 'set square' also seems appropriate as I'm sure they will not have a conceptual understanding of these. I have also boxed the word 'myths' as we have not covered this on the curriculum yet.

In this instance, I have found twelve possible areas of difficulty which this text presents to this group of 'below average' 9–10-year-olds: four   difficult words, three language features and five concepts. Again, we can complete the same simple maths. I have found twelve areas of difficulty in a 100-word text. If I subtract

Table 9.1 Deciding whether to use a text

Readability level	Number of areas of difficulty	Implication	Options
Less than 90	10 or more	Too difficult for the children to read independently	Choose a different text OR If the objective is based around comprehension, read it to them
90–95	5–10	The text will present a reasonable amount of challenge	Children can read this independently or in pairs. Spend time establishing that the text has been comprehended
95–100	5 or less	The text is not difficult in terms of comprehending it	You can still use this text but you will need to reconsider your questioning approach. A long series of questions focused on assessing literal comprehension would not be appropriate

the twelve from the 100, I am left with eighty-eight. Eighty-eight is the readability level of *this* text for *this* group. Now I have to consider whether I can use this text because it is going to be very challenging. I will need to ensure that all the areas of difficulty that I highlighted in my readability analysis are explained, and this could take some time. I may have to choose another text. If I do decide to use it, I may ask the children to read it in pairs, or I may have to read the text to them. This is fine if my objective is related to comprehension and not decoding.

📁 ## Readability analysis of *The Eye of the Cyclops* by Anthony Horowitz using the 'ready reckoner' criteria

The │ Cyclops │ was certainly a terrifying <u>creature</u>. It was about the height of a │ two-storey house │

with thick, curly hair, a │ matted │ (and usually filthy) beard and only one eye

│ set square │ in the middle of its forehead. It was <u>grotesquely</u> ugly, extremely bad-tempered,

<u>inordinately</u> <u>violent</u> and generally worth (going a long way to avoid.). All this, any

good book of Greek │ myths │ will tell you. But what is less often mentioned is the fact that the

Cyclops was also incredibly stupid. It was probably one of the most stupid monsters that ever lived.

There were a great many (Cyclopes).

Difficult words = 4

Language features = 3

Concepts = 5

12 difficult features
100 − 12 = 88

🖼 ## School-based activity

Assessing the suitability of a written text by way of a 'ready reckoner'

Choose a guided reading group that you are currently working with. With this group in mind, select a range of texts (three should be enough) that are available in your school. Choose 100-word sections from two or three parts of each text.

(Continued)

(Continued)

If this not possible because the story is short then choose one section. If the story is really short, then count to 50 words and double everything (remember, all you are trying to achieve is a rough estimate of the text readability).

Complete a 'ready reckoner' analysis to see whether these texts are suitable for the group you have in mind.

Plan and teach some lessons using these texts.

Through observation and by asking the children, consider:

- How accurate your assessment of the text readability was
- How the children responded to the different texts
- If the children in the group responded differently to each text and see if you can explain why

At some point, share your findings with colleagues.

CHOOSING NON-FICTION TEXTS

The examples we have looked at so far have all been related to fiction texts. Non-fiction texts can present a different set of challenges to young readers. There are reasons for this which can be traced back to the components of comprehension in the previous chapters. To begin, non-fiction texts often present readers with new knowledge, and this knowledge will be related to particular (and often highly specific) domains; for example, if a class is undertaking a topic on 'The Sea' they may choose to look closely at great white sharks. Personally, I know very little about them; I assume that they are great and white, and I know that I wouldn't want to be swimming in close proximity to one. Beyond this, I have an impoverished knowledge base. In contrast, stories tend to be reflective of everyday life and experience (Britton et al., 1990), and for this reason we can more readily apply our knowledge of the world to fiction. As Black (1985) explains, stories tend to vary around themes that the reader has experienced extensively, whereas non-fiction describes new information, topics and themes.

Added to this, Graesser (1981) suggests that as many as nine times more inferences are generated when engaging with narrative texts than with non-fiction texts. One reason for this might of course be the fact that we learn to read through stories primarily, but it is also likely to be because we are dealing with new vocabulary and new concepts. This relates to Kintsch and Rawson's (2005) conception of inference making taking place on a continuum from automatic to controlled. Automatic inferences are made very quickly and with little apparent thought, while controlled ones take time; for example, we might pause in a piece of text to make sense of what we have just read.

So teachers using non-fiction texts have to bear in mind that these types of texts are likely to be read more slowly than fiction texts; that it might take longer to process, thus increasing the load on working memory; and that it might be more difficult to maintain coherence if the reader has to check for coherence regularly (Britton et al., 1990).

Thus, when we choose a non-fiction text for children we need to keep in mind why we are asking them to read it. When we engage with text, we do so for a purpose: we read for meaning; we read to know. Reading goals relate to an understanding of what is to be achieved by reading a particular text. Knowing this is important because this informs the reader about which aspect of their prior knowledge, if any, is likely to be relevant. In all likelihood, a reader reading this particular book does so with the goal of finding out something specific about how children understand text. (You wouldn't read it for enjoyment, after all.)

🗁 Solving text choice dilemmas with non-fiction

A cluster of five schools in North-East London is working together to develop children's reading. Two representatives from each of the schools are designated reading champions and the group meets regularly to develop and share practice. An issue that emerged through discussion was how to engage children with non-fiction texts. Two problems were located. The first point related to the purposes of reading non-fiction. When we read non-fiction we usually have a very clear focus in mind. For example, you might be reading this chapter of this book because you want to investigate issues related to choosing texts; you may not look at any other chapters. You have approached this text with a specific purpose. This comparison is important because when we work with children on non-fiction texts it is all too easy to choose a text without asking them what they want to find out. As a result, they may learn some strategies to use when dealing with non-fiction texts, but not in the context of what they might want to find out. Related to this, a second problem was raised and this related to readability. It is often difficult to find non-fiction texts that are at the appropriate readability level, in relation to topics being taught in classrooms. We visited one of the school libraries and selected books related to topics being taught and this seemed to prove the point.

To get around this, Teacher D started using film as a way into his topic on the sea. He asked one of his guided reading groups to decide what they wanted to find out about the sea. They decided on great white sharks. In the lesson, using laptops and headphones, Teacher D got the children to look at some YouTube clips (which he had carefully chosen) of great white sharks which had a commentary as part of the film. The children watched the clips several times and made notes about what they had heard and seen. They then, through discussion, shared their notes and developed some key facts related to great white sharks. Following this, the teacher then set them a really interesting question: 'Do you think great white sharks get a bad press?' This formed the basis of an in-depth discussion that encompassed such issues as food chains, how species survive and conservation. The children also developed some age-appropriate texts which they could then share with peers.

IMPLICATIONS FOR THE TEACHER OF READING

View text as a multimodal concept

There is a tendency to view written text as the dominant mode, over such things as visual texts. However, visual texts can support comprehension because they require the 'reader' to access the same processes and knowledge bases.

Don't forget the reader(s)

Harrison (1980) states that 'The child's own interests, and the kind of material he or she has read previously will be at least as important as the prose difficulty level in helping to decide what to choose' (p. 120). This once again highlights the point that when considering which texts to choose, the reader has to come first. You may find a text that matches a particular group or individual very well in terms of its difficulty, but if it is not interesting to the reader, engagement will be limited. And this is why exposing young readers to quality literature is so important. Teachers have to make a judgement of this.

Read widely

The flipside of knowing what interests the children you teach is in knowing which texts they might actually like. This requires some knowledge of children's literature.

Think of the learning you want to take place and the stumbling blocks in the way

Enjoyment of reading is an important affective outcome, but when you look at a text it is not enough to think 'yes, they will like this one'. It may have (what you consider to be) funny jokes and events, or it may be about a particular topic of interest, but how easily accessible are they to the children? That same text may have numerous potential difficulties. Readability analyses may bring these to the surface.

Dialogue Point

Widening knowledge of children's literature

A visit to any good bookshop or library will confirm the fact that there is a vast number of children's books available. The only way to know whether these books might be suitable for the children we teach is to read them. One way around this is to pool the reading burden.

Find three children's books that you think children will enjoy. Read them and consider the following:

Readability – who will be able to read it independently?

Language features – what do these books present in terms of challenge, difficulty and interest?

Share your findings with colleagues.

CONCLUSION

At the beginning of this chapter a scenario was outlined where a group of 7–8-year-olds missed a clever and funny pun over the words 'roar'/'raw' in Tony Blundell's book *Beware of Boys*. The question was raised as to why they missed it. To answer this, we must begin by considering what the group were bringing to the text. They had some experience of working with traditional tales, such as 'Little Red Riding Hood', so the idea of wolves eating children wasn't a new one. They also knew the 'Stone Soup' story. In relation to the specific piece of text above, what became clear was that this group of children didn't understand the purpose of some specific language features – in this case, a pun. It also emerged that they had limited experience of dealing with texts which attempt to subvert specific story genres. In this instance it took them a while to realise that the boy was not scared, and that this was unusual. Of course, another explanation for this is perhaps they had experienced stories that subvert specific story genres but were not explicitly aware that this is what was going on. So this raises an important question: Was this an appropriate text to have given this group? The answer to this is 'yes' – for a number of reasons. First, the text is appropriate in terms of readability, as we saw using the Spache readability formula. The 'ready reckoner' also showed that it was a text which this particular group of children could engage with. Second, we know that good literature has different layers that need to be unpacked, and as Zwaan (1996) points out, many literary texts are written in a style that is meant to be 'inconsiderate' (p. 241) to the reader; and we ask children to engage with texts that are often inconsiderate because they are more interesting to read. This is important if we want to develop children who are interested in reading. Third, it provides a great formative assessment opportunity. If we know that these children have missed something specific, we can begin to address next steps in learning; in this instance it could be about the use of puns, or developing a wider understanding of how story genres could be subverted – *whichever the teacher thinks is more appropriate.*

This chapter has focused on the choice of text to use when teaching comprehension. As teachers, we develop a feeling for how texts can support learning. The next step of course is to consider how we actually use these texts with children.

CHAPTER 10

TEACHING COMPREHENSION: PEDAGOGICAL PRINCIPLES

Chapter Overview

This chapter suggests some pedagogical principles to underpin comprehension teaching. It does so by considering what the teacher must consider in a teaching and learning interaction, based on Alexander's (2008a) three teacher repertoires: how the interaction is organised; the type of talk used by the teacher; and the type of talk used by the learner. A pedagogy for comprehension must take into account what we already know about text comprehension, which includes such things as our knowledge of language and life and the crucial role of inference making. With this in mind it is suggested that a pedagogy for comprehension should encompass scaffolded learning that encourages discussion and dialogue. This will allow for the teaching and learning interaction to be shaped in three possible ways: exposition, which requires the learner to demonstrate a literal understanding of the text; exploration, where the learner deepens this understanding by finding evidence in the text itself; and expansion, where understanding is deepened by making links to the learners' knowledge, understanding and values.

Posh Watson (1995) is a short story written by Gillian Cross in which the smooth running of a boring and uninspiring school is disrupted by the arrival of new a boy: the eponymous Posh Watson. Posh is brash, bold and noisy. He appears to be from an affluent family and comes into school wearing different clothes every day. These clothes are loud and garish and none of them conform to the regulation school uniform. Much to the exasperation of Mrs Juniper, the head teacher, all the children in the school imitate Posh's behaviour and copy his various styles of dress. The school is in disarray and Mrs Juniper seems powerless to do anything about it.

The only child who is not happy is Natalie. Natalie lives next door to Posh and is in the same class. Natalie likes the school as it was before Posh arrived. She likes to learn. For Natalie, this involves completing lots of maths sheets on her own. When the school receives notice of an inspection, it is Natalie who swings into action.

A teacher used this short story with a group of Year 5 (9–10-year-old) children. The group had a range of decoding ability; and with this in mind the text was chosen because it presents few difficulties in terms of readability. The teacher could have taken a section of the text, worked out a series of questions (say, perhaps ten), asked the children to provide a written response for each (perhaps in full sentences) and then marked it. This might have provided some sort of formative assessment where the information gathered could be used to inform future teaching (and indeed, if the teacher does not do this then this activity is pointless). But this, what we might call, traditional approach to comprehension in the classroom is not teaching – because teaching requires an interaction (Alexander, 2012) between the teacher and the learner.

Instead, the teacher used the *Posh Watson* text in a group reading context. The teacher asked the group to make a prediction as to what the story might be about prior to reading the first part of it. From Chapter 5 we know that predictions can support the inference making process (for example, if I write 'The boy opened a new loaf of bread, and looked over to the toaster' you might make a predictive inference as to what is likely to happen in the next sentence or two), so this is a justifiable teaching decision. The discussion centred on the word 'posh' initially as the teacher wanted to ensure the children understood the meaning of this word. Again, we know that vocabulary knowledge is important for comprehension so this is also a justifiable teaching decision. To support this, the teacher asked whether the group would describe him as 'posh', to which some members of the group said not. The following interaction took place:

Pupil 1: You don't talk posh. You don't sit posh. Ah….

Teacher: OK, so you act in a particular way. But what makes somebody posh? What have they got a lot of that …

Pupil 2: They … They sit all straight, like…. and they act all like …

Teacher: OK, what have they got a lot of that I probably haven't?

Pupil 3: Money!

 ## Dialogue Point

Looking at learning, looking at interactions

In the text above, an outline was given of the beginning of *Posh Watson* – a short story by Gillian Cross – and a brief transcript was presented to show how one teacher introduced it to a group of pupils.

There are two points to consider:

1. Natalie is a fictional character but she does present us with a view of learning. In her case it involves completing as many maths sheets as she can without being disturbed. Reflect on this in relation to these questions:
   o What are your thoughts on this as a picture of learning?
   o Do you think learning is taking place?
   o What does effective learning look like?
   o What does effective teaching look like in the light of your response to the previous question?

2. I would argue that the transcription shows an example of very poor teaching, which does not inform the teacher about the pupils' comprehension or support it in any way. Decide whether you think this to be the case. Refer to the following components of comprehension to support your thinking:
   o Prior world knowledge
   o Knowledge of language (vocabulary and syntax)
   o Memory
   o Inference making (cohesive and interrogative)

Also consider where the line of questioning could (or perhaps should) have gone.
   Share your thinking with colleagues in relation to both points.

In the *Posh Watson* story, Gillian Cross presents us with one child's (albeit a fictional one) perception of what learning looks like. This in itself would be interesting to explore, but for now it is useful to focus on the short interaction presented earlier (which lasted all of 19 seconds). The rationale for this relates to a statement made by Robin Alexander (2012), and which I have already alluded to. Alexander, whose work I will reference frequently in this chapter, stated the following at a Department for Education seminar on oracy:

> In teaching, however it is organised, it's the quality of the *interaction* that makes the difference.

The interaction transcribed earlier is precisely the kind that needs to be avoided when teaching comprehension. If you have undertaken the task at the dialogue point entitled 'Looking at learning, looking at interactions' you may have come to a similar conclusion, or perhaps not. Regardless, to reach a conclusion on this point requires us to first consider what might constitute a 'quality' interaction.

DIALOGIC TEACHING: THE TEACHERS' REPERTOIRE AS THE BASIS FOR TEACHING INTERACTIONS

Alexander's statement on the quality of teaching interactions is linked to his wider pedagogical concept of dialogic teaching (Alexander, 2008a). This concept is centred on the idea that regardless of what is being taught, it is the nature of the talk that provides 'the foundation of learning' (p. 9).

Alexander (2008a) suggests there are three main considerations to a classroom interaction, which he describes as forming the teacher's repertoire. By repertoire, he means the approach we take to an interaction that best suits the needs of the learner, the content being taught and the context in which the learning takes place. First, the teacher must consider how the interaction is organised, for example whether it takes place in a whole-class setting, within a group (mixed-ability or otherwise), or in a one-to-one context.

The second repertoire is the type of talk used by the teacher. Alexander (2008a) locates five types of teacher talk and the situations in which they are likely to be used:

- Rote: drilling of facts and ideas through repetition
- Recitation: asking questions for recall or to cue pupil answers
- Instruction/exposition: giving pupils information or explanations
- Discussion: sharing ideas and information and solving problems
- Dialogue: building a common understanding through structured questions and purposeful discussion

The third repertoire the teacher must consider is the type of learner talk they want to promote in an interaction. Alexander (2008a: 39) outlines the following types:

- Narrate
- Explain
- Instruct
- Ask different kinds of question
- Receive, act and build upon answers
- Analyse and solve problems
- Speculate and imagine
- Explore and evaluate ideas
- Discuss
- Argue, reason and justify
- Negotiate

On one level, these three repertoires are intuitive. We know that classrooms are organised in specific ways; teaching for comprehension, for example, is likely to take place in the context of shared reading or guided reading (both of which we will investigate later in this chapter), but how often do we consider the rationale for these? We know that talk is an obvious feature of classrooms, but how often do we reflect on the type of talk we use as teachers, and in turn the type of talk that this elicits from learners? It might be argued that when the interaction involves both teacher and learner, learner talk is dependent upon teacher talk; it is generally the teacher who instigates the interaction, after all. It is likely that different types of teacher talk will be used as we teach, most obviously your talk may aim to recount previous learning (recitation) before introducing some new learning (instruction/exposition). What is interesting though is that Alexander's (2001) own research based on classroom observation suggested that most classroom interactions in the English school context were centred on the first three, and there was very little time given to discussion or dialogue. This leads to the question of whether it matters. Should teacher talk seek to instigate discussion and dialogue? I am going to argue that for effective comprehension teaching, discussion and dialogue are not optional, but necessary. To support this we will need to consider how what we know about the comprehension process relates to classroom practice. This requires us to engage with the term 'pedagogy'.

Dialogue Point

Teachers' repertoires

Alexander (2008a) locates three different repertoires that teachers need to consider when organising an interaction with learners: the organisation, types of teacher talk and types of learner talk.

Look back at these and, with colleagues, clarify what you think each of them means.

Now consider the relationship between these repertoires:

- Which types of teacher talk facilitate specific types of learner talk?
- How might the different types of learner talk look different in different organisational settings?

Share your thinking with colleagues in relation to both points.

PEDAGOGY

Alexander (2008b) notes that pedagogy is a term that has been viewed with suspicion in England historically, as relating to some sort of 'chalk and talk' direct instruction model where the learners are passive in the process. Freire (1973), who originally developed adult literacy programmes in Brazil, describes this approach as the 'banking' model where knowledge is deposited. In both instances knowledge is transmitted from teacher to learner without being questioned. This is akin to behaviourist models of learning where the teacher aims to achieve correct and rapid responses from learners, and where information is memorised (James, 2004). Intuitively, and perhaps emotionally, this is an approach that many teachers rail against. However, it is wrong to associate pedagogy with transmission type models of teaching alone; as Alexander notes, pedagogy is considered in a much wider context in continental Europe and Russia, where it includes justifying *why* we teach what we teach, and *how* we teach it. As such, Alexander (2008b) presents the following definition:

> Pedagogy is the act of teaching together with its attendant discourse of educational theories, values, evidence and justifications. It is what one needs to know, and the skills one needs to command in order to and justify the many different kinds of decision of which teaching is constituted. (p. 47)

However, we cannot take a 'one size fits all' approach to pedagogy. We will need to take different pedagogical approaches depending on what is being taught. Let's look at an example to clarify this point.

THE PEDAGOGY OF PHONICS TEACHING

If you walk into many classrooms in England and observe phonics lessons it is likely that you will see a very clear, structured approach to how it is taught. As noted in Chapter 1, this seems to link closely to the concept of 'learning to read, reading to learn' (Chall et al., 1990), which suggests that the focus of learning to read in the earlier primary years of schooling should be on decoding, and the focus on the middle to later primary years (from about 8 years of age onwards) should be on comprehension. It might be argued that the 'learning to read, reading to learn' conceptualisation of reading development provides a rationale that underpins the act of phonics teaching; alongside this, studies in the field have suggested that synthetic phonics taught systematically is the most efficient approach to take (Johnston and Watson, 2005). Together, these provide the evidence and justification for why phonics should be emphasised and how it should be taught.

This then informs the interaction that takes place. Organisationally, phonics is taught in whole class contexts, groups and ability groups depending on the scheme being used. Teacher talk is likely to centre on introducing new phonemes (instruction/exposition), making links to phonemes learnt previously (recitation) and leading the learners through a series of repetitious drills to practise the phoneme (rote). There is likely to be limited discussion or dialogue to be had (because that's not the point); and the learner talk is centred largely on using the phonemes, in both isolation and the context of words (because that *is* the point).

So there is a pedagogy related to phonics teaching, and talk is central to this. As Alexander (2012) states, 'Where would phonics be in the reading curriculum without talk? In the teaching of reading the relationship between grapheme and phoneme, between what is written and spoken, is fundamental'.

All well and good, but I would argue that what works (or what is considered to work) pedagogically for phonics will not work for comprehension. Phonics instruction requires the teaching and learning of 44 phonemes – it is a finite skill (Houck and Ross, 2012). There is an end point, which can result in an assessment sheet with 44 ticked boxes relating to 44 learning objectives. In contrast, comprehension is not a finite skill; it is something that learners bring to school (certainly in terms of language comprehension) and which then develops through life. For this reason, a different pedagogy is required.

A PEDAGOGY FOR COMPREHENSION

So which theories and discourses might inform a pedagogy for comprehension? At this point I will suggest three factors we might want to consider: what we already know about the comprehension process; the role of talk in the teaching interaction; and the importance of scaffolded learning in the interaction itself.

What we know about comprehension

Our understanding of comprehension has been outlined in the previous chapters. A few points are worth recapping. To begin with, we will want to consider our definition of comprehension. In Chapter 2 we noted that comprehension in its simplest sense means being able to describe or relate text that has just been read to demonstrate a literal understanding. However, we noted that developing a literal comprehension of text alone is not enough. As readers we need to interpret, evaluate and critique, as well as express more affective responses. We need to achieve both a literal and a deeper comprehension of text.

We also know that the knowledge readers bring to the text will go some way in shaping how it has been comprehended, because, as Mercer (1995) reminds us, this knowledge is socially constructed within a cultural context. This in itself goes a long way to explain why the same text can be comprehended differently. As we noted in our hypothetical example in Chapter 8, children are likely to understand texts in different ways (indeed, so are adults). Moreover, how we understand written text (and more broadly the world around us) changes with age and experience.

Yet knowledge and age are only two factors that impact upon comprehension. We know that the comprehension of written text is a cumulative, integrative process, again as we saw in Chapter 8, and our understanding of text changes as we read it, necessarily because we are encountering new information. However, we also know that comprehension is not a 'unitary construct' (Duke, 2005: 93), but rather is composed of separate (and separable) components that work in an interactive manner. These include such things as vocabulary knowledge, grammatical knowledge, the role of memory (working, short-term and long-term) and inference making. The knowledge we bring to a text and the extent to which we are able to comprehend it (literally or more deeply) are mediated by these various components. So our pedagogy needs to be informed by these various components, particularly inference making, as this provides the 'conduit' that takes us from meaning to interpretation (Perfetti et al., 1996).

Discussion and dialogue in teacher talk to facilitate a variety of learner talk

Bringing what we know about comprehension and applying it to the classroom means the first issue for the teacher of comprehension is to understand how learners have made sense of text. The most obvious way is to ask them. This brings us back to the nature of the interaction between teacher and learner, and once again locates the role of talk as being centrally important. However, the type of teacher talk, and the type of learner talk elicited in comprehension teaching, will not be the same as that which is more obviously noticeable in interactions in phonics lessons described previously. Of course, there will be a need for recitation and instruction or exposition, but this alone will not be enough. For example, Mercer and Littleton (2007) describe some studies they completed with colleagues which noted that those teachers whose children did better on tests of reading comprehension had qualitatively different classroom interactions than those teachers whose children did less well. Here are some of the features that these successful teachers displayed:

- Their sequences of questions didn't simply test knowledge, but guided the development of understanding

- They asked 'why' questions which allowed for reasoning and reflection

- They encouraged pupils to talk through their thought processes

- They encouraged pupils to give reasons for their views

- They encouraged pupils to exchange and build upon each other's ideas

These features were not observed in comprehension lessons specifically, but were seen to lead to an improvement on a measure of comprehension (interestingly, the pupils taught by these teachers also improved in maths). *This would suggest that teacher talk which supports the 'discussion' and 'dialogue' types outlined by Alexander are likely to support comprehension.* Actually, this makes sense. If teacher talk is focused on recitation and exposition, it does not allow the dialogic space for discussion; for arguing, reasoning and justifying; for speculation and imagination. Without providing the space for learners to undertake these types of talk they will not have the chance to make those inferences that support text exploration, or those that allow them to expand their understanding to issues which are outside the text but have a direct link to it, such as questions of morality.

Scaffolded learning and the social constructivist perspective

Of course, just because a dialogic space has been created by the focus of teacher talk being on discussion and dialogue, it does not mean that learners are necessarily going to be able to fill this space. It would be wrong to assume that learners know, for example, how to reason, justify and argue in relation to the text they have been reading – they are likely to need to be shown. Teachers need to do something. Indeed, Mercer and Littleton (2007) also noted that those teachers who used dialogue effectively in classrooms demonstrated the use of problem-solving strategies, for example.

At this point we need to proceed carefully because, as Mercer and Littleton note, we are not talking about simply showing – or modelling – how to do something. It also involves allowing learners to explore and experiment with what they have been shown. This in turn requires us to refine how we might structure the teaching and learning interaction. This entails taking a closer inspection of the process of scaffolded learning.

Scaffolded learning is closely associated with the social constructivist theory of learning. Social constructivism has its roots in constructivist theory. As described by Pritchard (2009), constructivist theory is based on the belief that learning involves mental construction where learners build on what they already know. Social constructivism accepts this premise but places importance on the social interaction that takes place as part of this. For social constructivist the interaction, and the dialogue this entails, is crucially important for learning. (At this point, you may want to consider Natalie, our fictional learner in the *Posh Watson* story, and how she views learning. Where's the dialogue? Where's the interaction?)

This is most obvious in the work of Vygotsky. Vygotsky's (1978) approach to guided learning takes account of what he describes as the zone of proximal development (ZPD). This theory states there are two developmental levels that can be located in novice learners: their actual developmental level (where they are now) and the potential developmental level they could attain if given support (where they might get to with help). The ZPD is the area between these two levels and the area where instruction takes place. The expert learner guides the novice through a task by initially assuming responsibility for most of the cognitive work. The expert learner gradually passes this responsibility to the novice learner as they become more skilled at the task. This continues until the novice becomes fully skilled at the task, at which point the expert learner withdraws their support. Wood et al. (1976) described this process as scaffolding the learning. This is an appropriate metaphor because scaffolds are temporary structures that provide support and which are removed when they are no longer needed. For Wood et al. a central feature of scaffolded learning is the concept of 'handover'. Unless the teacher passes over responsibility to the learner and allows them to explore and experiment with what the 'more able other' has shown them, the learning will not become embedded.

In outlining their concept of assisted learning, Tharp and Gallimore (1988) explain this as a series of stages, which it might be helpful to describe. Stage 1 is the first part of the ZPD and is where 'performance is assisted by more capable others' (p. 33). This is perhaps the most recognised element of Vygotsky's concept, in that at this stage the child is unable to work independently through a task without support because it is beyond their current abilities. The support given by the 'more capable other' is likely to include modelling. Through the gradual release of support the child then reaches Stage 2 – the second part of the ZPD – as performance becomes self-assisted. The skills being learnt are not fully automatised at this stage, but the learner is beginning 'to direct or guide behaviour with their own speech' (p. 37). Stage 3 lies outside the ZPD and is the point at which performance has become automatised and where teacher intervention is likely to be disruptive. Tharp and Gallimore also note a fourth stage, where de-automatisation takes place and recursion to the previous stages is required because what has been learnt needs to be reconstituted, because it has been forgotten.

For our purposes, it is enough to focus on the first three stages of Tharp and Gallimore's model, and the first implication for the teacher of comprehension is that simply modelling something is not enough. Learners need to be given space to explore and experiment with the matter being taught. I have referred to this previously as a dialogic space, and this links to what Mercer (2000) has described as the Intermental Developmental Zone (IDZ). Mercer and Littleton (2007) describe the IDZ as 'a shared communicative space' (p. 21) created and negotiated through talk and joint activity. This broadly fits into Stage 2 of the Tharp and Gallimore model and is where the teacher can shape the dialogue to include discussion and dialogue. This is essential if we want to develop understanding beyond the literal.

ORGANISING THE INTERACTION TO TEACH COMPREHENSION

Of course, how these features of a pedagogy for comprehension are manifested in practice will depend upon how the teaching and learning interaction has been organised. This takes us back to the first of Alexander's (2008a) teacher repertoires, and the one we have not investigated up to this point. Interactions that aim to support reading comprehension are organised in two ways typically: shared reading and guided reading. Both shared and guided reading are pedagogical approaches that have historical roots firmly linked to supporting children in comprehending text, but they were both developed with beginning and early developing readers in mind. This creates a potential problem because they have been applied across the primary age phase. Intuitively, we know that the needs of beginning and early developing readers are not the same as older developing readers. Unsurprisingly, the pedagogical structures of both shared and guided reading have changed since their conception.

Shared reading

Shared reading relates to Holdaway's (1979) concept of the 'shared book experience' and this sharing was designed to take place in groups or in a one-to-one interaction. Shared reading now describes a whole-class interaction that involves a text which is shared by the class, such as a big book or an e-book, with the aim of teaching reading strategies explicitly (Perkins, 2012). The teacher models a particular strategy, sometimes with a text that is of greater complexity than the ability of the class members. The rationale for this is that the text is read by the teacher who is modelling 'expert' reading. It also allows the learners to be exposed to a variety of texts and have an idea of the types of text they are likely to engage with in the future. The focus for early readers is still on such things as applying decoding skills and developing vocabulary (Primary National Strategy, 2006), but for older readers Wyse et al. (2013) note that the focus turns towards comprehension, through the teaching of strategies such as visualisation and inference making.

Perkins (2012) presents some interesting examples of shared reading interactions that use big books at Key Stage 1 (5–7-year-olds), and Wyse et al. (2013) present some useful follow-up activities for Jez Alborough's *Where's My Teddy?* (1992), which would support the scaffolding process, again at Key Stage 1.

It is unsurprising that both Perkins (2012) and Wyse et al. (2013) locate examples of good shared reading practice that relate to Key Stage 1; after all, shared reading was designed with beginning and early developing readers in mind, and the only thing that has changed is essentially the number of learners involved (it now involves a whole class). At Key Stage 2 (7–11-year-olds) some further thought needs to be given to shared reading. Examples of shared reading I have observed in this phase of learning have included teaching about such things as similes and metaphors. These are important, but as Perkins reminded us above, the purpose of shared reading is to teach reading strategies to support understanding. Similes and metaphors are language features, not reading strategies. The issue then is not simply to teach the language feature, but also to give learners strategies to make sense of them (for similes and metaphors visualisation would be a useful strategy to encourage). This is important because otherwise it just becomes a decontextualised teaching point.

Guided reading

Guided reading was developed in New Zealand as a method of small-group reading instruction for beginning readers (Simpson, 1966). The rationale for working in small groups was grounded in the belief that the skills needed for fluent reading were more easily acquired through discussion. In particular, the importance of what Simpson termed as '*guiding silent reading*' (p. 94) was emphasised. Teachers were to encourage the silent reading of text after some 'general discussion', and after some questions had been posed that required the children to search the text for implicit meanings. The importance of reading for meaning was emphasised, and the focus was placed on encouraging the early reader to use '... all the clues in his [sic] possession – the picture, his understanding of the situation in the story, the context in which the word occurs, and its phonetic elements' (Simpson, 1966: 48).

Guided reading still takes place in small groups. In its current incarnation it usually takes place in groups of about six. The rationale for this number appears to be managerial rather than educational. Classes in primary schools in England tend to have around 30 members, and presumably this allows every learner to be seen once in a five-day week. The texts used in these sessions should be challenging, but within the decoding ability of the children. For this reason the members of each group are usually of similar decoding ability. The teacher reminds the children to use specific strategies when reading. These relate to using the context of the sentence to work out unknown words, the application of phonic knowledge and their understanding of the story. The children read the text to themselves, although it is common for the teacher to intervene with individuals during the individual reading stage as they 'listen in' to the learners (which of course ceases to make it a silent act). This seems to relate to the work of Fountas and Pinnell (1996), which has been influential in this area. Their format to guided reading is closely akin to the one most obviously visible in classrooms in England and one that Wyse et al. (2013) describe in some detail. They still emphasise the importance of promoting cueing strategies such as meaning cues, structure or syntax, and visual information (Clay, 1993), and which again are considered to be of particular importance for early readers. In later work they state that the teaching of inference making, of analysing and of evaluating (to name but three) should take place in guided reading (Fountas and Pinnell, 2010), and again this seems to relate to older developing readers.

The issue for the teacher of comprehension is where to fit this in, given the formats for guided reading currently in common use. There is certainly room for discussion in guided reading in any suggested format, both prior to and after the independent reading part of the lesson. The task here would appear to be to move away from just the cueing strategies alone, and view such things as inference making as another strategy that needs to be taught.

RECIPROCAL TEACHING: AN ALTERNATIVE GROUP READING APPROACH

An alternative approach to group reading is reciprocal teaching. It is worth looking at this approach in some depth because it was designed to support reading comprehension specifically. Reciprocal teaching was devised by Palincsar and Brown (1984) as a method of reading instruction that aimed to foster and monitor the comprehension of text. By fostering comprehension they mean providing the reader with strategies to achieve an enhanced understanding of text; by monitoring comprehension they mean providing the reader with strategies to know whether they have comprehended the text. Thus, reciprocal teaching is designed to provide instruction that promotes both cognitive and metacognitive awareness.

This is achieved through engaging with four specific strategies:

- Predicting
- Questioning
- Seeking clarification
- Summarising

These strategies build upon the cueing strategies related to early reading development. Moreover these strategies support processes that readers actively undertake to ensure effective comprehension. The authors note six of these processes, which are outlined in Brown et al. (1984: 263):

- Clarifying the purposes of reading, that is., understanding the demands of the task, both explicit and implicit
- Activating relevant background knowledge
- Allocating attention so that concentration can be focused on the major content at the expense of trivia
- Critical evaluation of content for internal consistency, and compatibility with prior knowledge and common sense
- Monitoring ongoing activities to see whether comprehension is occurring, by engaging in such activities as periodic review and self-interrogation
- Drawing and testing inferences of many kinds, including interpretations, predictions and conclusions

Many of these processes have been referred to in earlier chapters.

Interestingly from the perspective of our analysis in this chapter, in a later paper Brown and Palincsar (1989) relate the reciprocal teaching process to Vygotsky's zone of proximal development (ZPD) (Vygotsky, 1978) explicitly. This link to Vygotsky is appropriate because the idea is that after being shown how to use the four strategies by the teacher, the pupils use them and, in effect, run the sessions themselves. This could be described as scaffolded because there is a sense of 'handover'. However, the most common criticism of Palincsar and Brown's initial study (and indeed in subsequent studies) is the speed at which this 'handover' took place. Pressley and Wharton-McDonald (1997), for example, suggested that there is a lack of direct teaching and that adult control is reduced too quickly.

Nevertheless, Palincsar and Brown found that the 12–13-year-old poor comprehenders in their study who experienced the reciprocal teaching approach made significant gains in comprehension compared to comprehenders who did not. Qualitative data were also presented to show that the quality of the dialogue improved dramatically for the reciprocal teaching group. The authors note particularly how the language used by the subjects came to resemble that modelled by the adult teacher. Since then, numerous studies have been undertaken in reciprocal teaching which give further grounds for considering it to be an effective pedagogical approach for promoting comprehension with different groups of learners. These include the following:

- 14–15-year-old poor comprehenders (Alfassi, 1998)
- Year 6 poor comprehenders (Greenway, 2002)
- Year 4/5 average comprehenders (Kelly et al., 1994)
- Science teaching with 10-year-olds (King and Johnson, 1999)
- Year 7/8 English as a Second Language students (Fung et al., 2003)
- Narrative teaching with 6-year-olds (Hacker and Tenent, 2002)

What is particularly interesting with the last of these studies is that Hacker and Tenent (2002) highlight how reciprocal teaching has been adapted in the different classrooms they observed and particularly the way teachers were extensively scaffolding the dialogue. This shows that reciprocal teaching itself is an evolving pedagogical practice, but also that there is an awareness of the need for teachers to consider how this 'handover' takes place.

A number of schools, including the cluster of five schools in North-East London mentioned in the previous chapter, have been using a teacher-led version of reciprocal teaching. The question making involves addressing inference-type questions that seek to focus and develop dialogue.

A procedure for teacher-led reciprocal teaching sessions

Before reading

Teacher reminds children of the reciprocal teaching structure (this is visible on a laminated sheet). Teacher briefly introduces the text.

Prediction. Pupils predict, using the title and illustrations, what the text is going to be about and explain why.

Question making. Teacher introduces three questions to focus the pupils' reading: one literal (Exposition), one text-based inference (Exploration), one inference that requires background knowledge (Expansion).

Silent reading component

Children read the text silently and without interruption. They make a note of any words they are not sure of, or any interesting words/language features.

(Continued)

(Continued)

The questions are visible throughout and the children are encouraged to think of answers to these focus questions as they read, and when they have finished reading.

After reading – the key dialogic space

Clarification. Unknown words and phrases related to specific language features are clarified with peer support, and teacher support if necessary. Viewing the unknown words in the context of the sentence is encouraged, as is thinking of synonyms that might have been used. Idiomatic and figurative language examples can be explored.

Answering questions. The three questions posed by the teacher before reading are answered and further questions posed, as follows:

Literal (Exposition): The key literal question is answered. This is followed by further questions related to the first which establish that the text has been comprehended.

Text-based inference (Exploration): The key text-based inference question is answered. This is followed by further questions related to the first text-based inference question and which might explore further evidence in the text.

Wider inference (Expansion): The key wider inference question is answered. This is followed by further questions related to the first wider inference question and which might explore wider issues raised in the text. This presents the opportunity for evaluation, justification etc.

Summarisation. Children are given time to 'run the film' of the action in their heads and then to describe it in a few sentences.

SHAPING THE DIALOGIC INTERACTION WHEN TEACHING COMPREHENSION

So far we have suggested that a pedagogy for teaching comprehension should include talk that instigates discussion and dialogue; talk that creates a dialogic space for learners to explore and experiment with the types of learner talk that discussion and dialogue facilitate; and it should acknowledge the components of comprehension, particularly inference making. So how can we shape the dialogue to encompass all this? Well to some extent it depends on what we want the learners to gain from the texts they are engaging with.

With this in mind, we can begin to consider how the dialogic interaction between the teacher and the learner can support the comprehension of text in three ways: by exposing the text; by exploring it; and by expanding upon it. To be clear, these are not being presented as a three-part lesson for the teaching of comprehension. It is not being suggested that you start from exposition, then move onto exploration, and then onto expansion. Rather, these three are being presented as a focus for shaping the dialogic interaction. The point to consider is how you might (or indeed if you can) shape the dialogue to encompass exposition, exploration or expansion (or a combination of these) into the organisational structures presented by shared reading, guided reading, reciprocal teaching, or indeed in one-to-one and paired interactions involving the teacher.

Exposition

Exposition relates to the literal comprehension of text. The aim here is to expose the learners' understanding of the text soon after having read it: basically, what can they tell you about it?

In the dialogic space, which Mercer (2000) refers to as the interdevelopment zone (IDZ), the interaction should focus on ensuring a literal understanding has been established; or for readers who do not know how to do this (those readers who 'bark' at text), this will need to be modelled. Vocabulary, if not pre-taught, and any language features, such as similes or metaphors, might need to be clarified as part of the interaction (in the reciprocal teaching procedure noted earlier this would be completed in the clarification section). The interaction might seek to teach how, or to ensure that, inferences that support coherence are being made. This would include bridging inferences, which help to make links across sentences. For example, in Chapter 6 we noted that the children in the story destroyed a den. The next sentence stated that the parents were not happy. We cannot assume that the learners will make the link that the parents were unhappy *because* the den was destroyed. Also, we need to establish that a coherent understanding of the text is not being affected by difficulties associated with resolving pronouns. This is particularly so for young readers.

In interactions of exposition, teacher talk is more likely to feature recitation and instruction or exposition, although some discussion may be appropriate. Learner talk is likely to seek to explain or narrate. The exposition of text is critical. If learners cannot attain a literal comprehension of text, they will not be able to explore it more deeply or expand upon it by relating it to their knowledge and experience.

Exploration

Exploration relates to an engagement with text that seeks to deepen understanding. It assumes that the text has been exposed and a literal comprehension established. It is unlikely that exploration will take place immediately after the text has been read, as the teacher will want to ensure that the text has indeed been understood. In the dialogic space the attention will turn to exploring the text itself. It is about searching the text for clues.

This can be supported by focusing on what were described in Chapter 7 as interrogative inferences. In the dialogic space, the teacher may want to help learners to develop a more detailed mental representation of the text. The text representation, we have said previously, does not have to be visual (Johnson-Laird,

1983), but it might help us to think of it as the picture the learner has developed 'in their head'. Encouraging elaborative inferences would support this. For example, in Chapter 7 we looked at a short piece of text that began, 'Again, the dog carried back the useless, deflated ball and dropped it at the boy's feet'. We may want to ask about the type and size of both the dog and the ball. These inferences do not necessarily add to understanding, but they may become relevant as future text is read. As we know, text comprehension is cumulative; it changes sentence by sentence. Establishing a more detailed representation may help the teacher to find areas of misunderstanding, and also help to explain the learner's thinking.

Exploration will also encompass the making of deductive and inductive inferences. It is about finding evidence in the text. The evidence might relate to such thing as characters and settings. It involves making links across the text.

In interactions of exploration, teacher talk will be based on discussion and dialogue. Learner talk may feature such things as analysis, evaluation, problem solving, reasoning and justification, all with reference to evidence from the text. Teachers should expect children to build upon each other's answers, which will elicit learner talk based on negotiation and argumentation.

Expansion

Expansion also relates to deepening understanding, but the focus here is on bringing the learners' knowledge, experience and values to the text more explicitly. Once again, it assumes that the text has been exposed and a literal comprehension established.

Expansion is also supported by interrogative inferences and the teacher may, once again, want to ensure that the text representation has been deepened through elaborative inferences. The focus can then switch to the making of inductive inferences largely. These inferences are those that are logically plausible given the content of the text but are not certain. Learners might be asked to consider character motivations that are not based on evidence in the text; consider alternative actions (for example, what should the character have done instead?); to make judgements (for example, is the character's behaviour acceptable?); and to evaluate the text as a whole.

In interactions of expansion, teacher talk will again be based on discussion and dialogue. Learner talk may feature such things as evaluation, speculation and justification. Once again, teachers should expect children to build upon each other's answers, which will elicit learner talk based on negotiation and argumentation.

CONCLUSION

In this chapter we have investigated what might make an effective interaction when teaching comprehension. With this in mind, we can see that there is much wrong with the interaction described at the beginning of this chapter. The interaction presents the teacher with an exposition opportunity. The teacher can find out what the children understand by the word 'posh', but this opportunity is wasted.

To begin with, the definition of posh equating with wealth is not strictly true. In the context of the story there is an element of this, which is why the teacher made this link, but as both Pupil 1 and Pupil 2 note, we can equate being 'posh' with a set of particular behaviours, such as how a person might sit and how they might talk. The teacher does not acknowledge this. This is where the central problem with this interaction begins to emerge. The teacher jumps in and does not let Pupil 1 or Pupil 2 finish what they were trying to say and does not offer support (through really obvious questions such as 'How do posh people talk?' or 'Who might talk like that?', which would expose their understanding). Essentially, the teacher is not listening to what the children are saying, but is rather listening out for what they are *not* saying.

In this situation the dialogue has been closed down and what we get is a situation of the teacher giving the message 'What's the word in my head?'. Worse still, Pupil 3 says one word in the dialogue – 'money' – which apparently gives the 'right' answer. This sends the message that Pupils 1 and 2 are wrong based simply on the fact that Pupil 3 has guessed (or reasoned) what's in the teacher's head. Indeed, the teacher could go away from this interaction and put a tick in a box against Pupil 3's name, but not those of Pupils 1 and 2.

Nystrand et al. (1997) would describe Pupil 3 as simply reporting what someone else is thinking (in this case, the teacher) and not being allowed to think for themselves. Indeed, Alexander (2012) would describe Pupil 3's response as a 'guess-what-the-teacher-is-thinking' answer. In this case it would have been better to have just told the pupils that the word 'posh' might relate to having money.

This interaction is the antithesis of what comprehension teaching should be about. As a teacher of comprehension, you need to know *what* the young reader has understood and *how* they have understood it (whether it be a word or an extended piece of text). It is not about what is in the teacher's head, *per se*. This example of an appalling piece of teaching – to which I have to own up and apologise, particularly to the children – hopefully shows you why recording and analysing your interactions with children can be beneficial to your practice in the longer term. (I'll certainly try really hard never to repeat it!)

In the next chapter we will investigate some dialogic interactions that do support comprehension and how teachers have shaped the dialogue in a way that allows for text exposition, exploration and expansion.

School-based activity

Analysing teacher talk and learner talk

Record a guided group reading situation that you are leading. Group situations are easier to record than whole class situations.

Following the session, play it back and locate two dialogic interactions with the following characteristics:

(Continued)

- One where the interaction went well and where the learning was obvious
- One where the interaction could have been better

In your analysis consider the following:

- Did the interaction feature exposition, exploration or expansion (or any combination of these)?
- What types of teacher talk and learner talk were noticeable?
- Was there evidence of scaffolding?
- Which types of teacher talk facilitate specific types of learner talk?
- How might the different types of learner talk look different in different organisational settings?

Share your findings with colleagues.

CHAPTER 11

TEACHING COMPREHENSION: PEDAGOGY IN PRACTICE

Chapter Overview

This chapter aims to show how the pedagogical principles outlined in the previous chapter can be translated into practice. This is achieved by considering three extended examples. The first example describes how a nursery teacher used famous paintings from the National Gallery in London as a stimulus for developing spoken language comprehension. The second example is taken from a guided reading session in Year 1 (children aged 5–6 years) that used an adapted version of reciprocal teaching. The third example is also taken from a guided reading session, but this time in a Year 5 class (children aged 9–10 years). Reciprocal teaching was also used in this example. In all three examples the dialogic interactions between the teacher and the learners are investigated. Particular attention is given to how the teachers shape the interaction to ensure exposition, where the learners demonstrate a literal understanding of the text; exploration, where the learners deepen their understanding by finding evidence in the text itself; and expansion, where learners deepen their understanding by making links to their prior knowledge, understanding and values.

TEACHER A: NURSERY

Restor(y)ing Paintings was an action research project funded by the United Kingdom Literacy Association (UKLA) and undertaken by Teacher A in a nursery in East London. This project aimed to use paintings from the National Gallery as a way into story writing. The interesting idea behind this project was that rather than listen to the 'accepted' stories associated with the paintings, the children in the nursery, the vast majority of whom had English as an Additional Language, were to be encouraged to develop their own interpretations. What became apparent in the course of the project was the central role of comprehension (in this case language comprehension). For the writing to take place it required the children having to make sense of the pictures they were engaging with.

Investigating the interactions between Teacher A and one child, 'Y', we can see how the elements of exposition, exploration and expansion were apparent. 'Y', who was 3 years old at the start of the project, began to engage with the paintings in greater depth as the project developed.

Exposition

In one interaction that took place at the beginning of the project, Teacher A invited 'Y' to look at Saint George and the Dragon by the fifteenth-century Italian painter Paolo Uccello. The painting depicts a scene where a dragon is slain outside a cave by a knight on a horse. The dragon is held by a queen, who holds the dragon on something resembling a leash, as if it were a pet.

Teacher:	Point to your favourite bit of the picture. [*Waits for some time.*] There's a white horse, and a green dragon, and a woman wearing a pink dress, and there's a big cave, and there's some, some blood, and some big sharp teeth.
Child:	What's that b … [*inaudible*] on his nose?
Teacher:	What's that?
Child:	What's that b … [*inaudible*] on his nose? [*Points to the leash on the dragon's nose.*]
Teacher:	I don't know. What do you think it is?
Child:	It looks like … A funny w … [*inaudible*]
Teacher:	A funny …?
Child:	A funny w … [*inaudible*]
Teacher:	Does it?
Child:	Yeah.
Teacher:	Well, what's that there, look? [*Tracks the leash back to the queen's hand where it is being held.*] See, she's got it in her hand. What's that there?
Child:	Eeeeh! [*Screeches*]

In this interaction Teacher A begins by asking 'Y' which is her favourite part of the picture. 'Y' does not respond, probably because she's not had any experience of dealing with paintings of this type. Teacher 'A' draws her attention to different parts of the painting, using naming words and colours. Teacher 'A' is modelling how to look at a visual text (in this case a painting) to attain a literal understanding of what's going on in the picture. He is assisting her in exposing the text. 'Y' asks a number of questions, most of which are inaudible, which reflects her confusion as to what to make of the painting. Teacher 'A' attempts to build on the aspect that interests 'Y', which appears to be the leash, and in doing so he is beginning to model the making of links between different parts of the 'text'. 'Y', at this stage, is not really able to name the things she sees or to make connections between them.

Teacher 'A' modelled this process further, however, by looking at various paintings in following interactions. One of these was 'Tobias and the Angel' by Verrocchio. In this painting we see a young man carrying a fish he has just caught. There is a river in the distance behind him. Teacher A asks 'Y' what she can see and in this instance she is able to name and make links.

Child:	He's holding a fish. Look! Look! A fish. He's holding a fish.
Teacher A:	Why's he holding a fish?
Child:	Because he's going to put him in the water.
Teacher A:	He's going to put him in the water?
Child:	[*Nods her head.*] And splash over.
Teacher A:	Where's the water?
Child:	Er. It's behind her.
Teacher A:	Where's the water?
Child:	It's far away. When you see a water you put the fish – when I hold with a robind [possibly means ribbon] and I can put him in the water and he can swim.

In this example 'Y' is beginning to lead the discussion and is attending to the picture in the way Teacher A had modelled it to her previously. She names different things in the painting – such as the character (which she defines as 'she', probably because of the way the character is dressed), the fish and the river (which she refers to as water) and then begins to make connections between them. In her mind, the character in the painting is going to put the fish in the river. Connective inference making supports this process in that she finds a causal link between the things she names. The character is carrying the fish *because* he is going to put it in the river. By linking these different parts she is beginning to achieve a coherent understanding.

Exploration

Teacher 'A' was also able to support 'Y' in expressing a deeper understanding of the text by encouraging a deeper exploration of the paintings. Work that focused on 'The Stonemason's Yard' by Canaletto provides an example of this. This is a very detailed painting of a busy scene. There is a sky featuring shades of blue and also a canal tucked away towards the bottom of the painting. Teacher 'A' continued to explore the idea of the fish and the water which 'Y' had been developing through these different pictures.

Teacher:	Well, we were talking about the fish, weren't we? And about the fish having to be in blue water not orange water. [This relates to a previous interaction relating to Turner's 'The Fighting Temeraire' which we will explore shortly.] I was wondering whether there was any water in this picture.
Child:	This looks like blue [*points to the sky*].
Teacher:	It looks like blue. Is that water?
Child:	It looks like the sky water.
Teacher:	It looks like the sky water?
Child:	It's melting all the way to the floor.
Teacher:	It's melting all the way to the floor? [*Laughs.*]
Child:	All the way down. [*Pauses to look investigate the picture further.*] Can you see these childrens? [The children are near the bottom of the painting, very small, and surrounded closely by buildings.]
Teacher:	What are the children doing?
Child:	There's a tiny bit of childrens in here. Cos they can't see the sky, they're so far away. They can't see them.

This interaction shows that 'Y' is taking an active part once again in making sense of the text. She responds to Teacher A's prompt about blue water and locates some in the picture. However, she quickly establishes it is not water but sky (and if you look at the painting, her description of the sky melting down is not only rather beautiful, it is actually very appropriate). What is interesting here is that 'Y' then directs her attention to the children in the painting. This involves a close attention to detail because they are small in the painting and hemmed in by surrounding buildings and numerous people undertaking various tasks. She then makes a link between the children and the sky. The children, who are small and towards the bottom of the painting, can't see the sky, which is at the top of the painting, because they are too far away. 'Y' reaches this conclusion through reasoning about the evidence available to her in the (visual) text.

Expansion

Teacher A was also able to encourage 'Y' to express such things as her knowledge, understanding and values in relation to the paintings. At one point Teacher A presented two paintings together: 'Tobias and the Angel' by Verrocchio, which was outlined in the exposition section, and also 'The Fighting Temeraire' by Turner. This painting presents a scene of a ship on the sea with a sun setting in the distance. This has the effect of turning the sea in the painting different colours and at one point it is particularly orange. Teacher A directed 'Y' to this second painting.

Teacher A: So where are we going to put the fish?

Child: Umm. In the water.

Teacher A: In that water. Do you think the fish would be happy in that water?

Child: No. He needs blue not orange. He doesn't like sea.

Teacher A: So he won't be happy in that water.

Child: Umm. He gets all – all orange. The – this fish (points to the fish in Verrocchio's 'Tobias and the Angel' painting) will get all orange in this (points to Turner's 'The Fighting Temeraire') orange water.

Teacher A: Oh, the fish will go orange in that water.

Child: [*Nods her head.*] I know! Blue. Blue doesn't make this fish orange. It makes him – er – grey.

Teacher A: It makes him grey?

Child: Yes, because he likes grey.

Teacher A: He likes grey. So the fish has to be in blue water.

The direction of this interaction was instigated by Teacher A's question as to whether the fish from Verrocchio's 'Tobias and the Angel' would be happy in the sea water in Turner's 'The Fighting Temeraire'. 'Y's response basically states that fish are grey and live in blue water; and if you put a fish into orange water it will change colour and it won't be happy. Teacher A has invited 'Y' to speculate. Her speculation is based on her knowledge from outside of this (visual) text about fish. In this context it is a logically plausible speculation based on the knowledge she is bringing to it.

'Y''s engagement with these texts grew with her experience of them, to the extent that she was able to make evaluated judgements. The following interaction took place after the exposition of 'The Stonemason's Yard' by Canaletto:

Child: How come there's yellow clouds? We don't like yellow clouds. I don't have yellow clouds.

Teacher A: You don't have yellow clouds?

Child: No, I don't like yellow. Do you want yellow?

Teacher A: I don't know. Yellow clouds? What colour should clouds be? What colour should they be?

Child: They should be blue?

Teacher A:	What does it mean if all that's blue?
Child:	Ahhh. I got …
Teacher A:	How does that make you feel? If all that was blue. How would that make you—?
Child:	[*interrupts Teacher A*] You need – you need blue, white skies in here OK?
Teacher A:	OK.
Child:	We don't like it <u>all</u> blue.

In this instance, the 3-year-old 'Y' has made a critical comment about Canaletto's painting – she thinks the sky is wrong. Later in the interaction she actually suggests getting some paint and re-painting the large print. Once again she is bringing her knowledge, understanding and values to the text.

TEACHER B: YEAR 1

The Dog from Outer Space by Nick Abadzis (2002) tells the story of an alien boy called Veeb. Veeb's father likes to visit other planets so they take a trip to planet Earth. Veeb wants to bring his new dog, Speezy, on the trip but his father won't let him. However, Veeb hides Speezy in his bag. When they get to Earth, Speezy runs off and Veeb has to look for him on his own. This book is from a reading scheme (or a basal reader in the United States) and is designed for early developing readers. As such it is written with decoding in mind and with a particular emphasis on high frequency words.

Teacher B used this text with a group of Year 1 children (5–6-year-olds). All group members were boys who were considered to be decoding well for their age, and all were native English speakers.

Teacher B chose this text in part because of resourcing issues. There were multiple copies of all books in the reading scheme in the school, including this one. As such, each of the group members had a copy to read. Teacher B chose this particular text because she knew that it was within the decoding abilities of the children in the group and this allowed her to focus on comprehension specifically. The teacher used an adapted form of reciprocal teaching. Before reading each double-page spread the children were asked to predict what was going to happen. These predictions were based on their analysis of the front and back covers initially, and then on the action and events that took place in each double-page spread. The children were then given a question to consider before reading the double-page spread. These questions were planned carefully prior to the session by the teacher and aimed to develop literal comprehension and to develop inference making skills. After reading the text any unknown words were clarified and the children were then given the opportunity to answer the question they kept in mind while reading. Answering this question was not an end in itself, but formed the basis for a discussion. Following this discussion the children were encouraged to summarise the text.

Exposition

Before launching into the text, Teacher B asked the children to scan the front cover to see if they could work out what the story was about. They knew it was about a dog because it was in the title. The children were invited to talk in pairs to see if they could find out any more information. They then shared the fact that there was an alien (hiding in the background) and a boy. The discussion initially focused on the boy.

Pupil 3:	I think that's his dog and he's escaped. And then he's so sad that he hasn't got him any more.
Pupil 4:	I think that's what might be happening.
Teacher:	Now, I saw 'S' [Pupil 2] turning to the back of the book. What were you reading at the back of the book?
Pupil 2:	I read the blurb.
Teacher:	Well done, that bit on the back is called the blurb, isn't it?
Pupil 2:	It tells you a bit of the story.
Teacher:	That's right.
Pupil 2:	Not the whole story.

[*Pupil 2 is invited to read out the blurb.*]

Teacher:	So what does that tell you then about – that gives us more information doesn't it? Who does the dog belong to?
Pupil 2:	The alien, so the alien lost him and then the boy found him and played with him and kept him.
Teacher:	And do you know the name of the alien?
Pupil 2:	Veeb.
Teacher:	OK, do you know the name of the dog?
Pupil 2:	Yeah, Speezy.
Teacher:	Speezy, it says on the back. So actually we haven't even opened the book, have we? And we've found out loads of information.

In this interaction we can see evidence of scaffolding, in that reading strategies that must have been previously modelled by the teacher are being accessed in the context of this text. The teacher notices Pupil 2's reading behaviour and asks him to explain why he was looking at the back of the book. Pupil 2 makes an explicit reference to the book blurb and knows its purpose. What Pupil 2 finds out from reading the blurb is that the dog is owned by the alien – not the boy. This is of importance for Pupil 3 and Pupil 4, because their initial prediction was that the dog was owned by the boy. This erroneous prediction might have made it more difficult for them to attain a literal comprehension of the text. It is also interesting to note how the teacher sustains the interaction with Pupil 2 through a series of questions that allow him to share further information from the blurb. In this way, before the group comes to begin the actual story they are well prepared to expose the text. They are coming to the reading with an idea about the purpose of the book.

Once they had finished reading the teacher and the group exposed the text further by clarifying the action of the story. They also looked at language features such as commas and apostrophes because it was raised as a point of interest by Pupil 3. At the conclusion of the discussion, Pupil 5 was asked to summarise the story to that point. He began by simply re-reading the exact words from the page aloud. This led to the following interaction:

Teacher: Hang on, Hang on, you're reading it! [*Laughs.*] You're not supposed to read it. You're supposed to tell me roughly what's just happened. Don't read it. Just tell me what we've just read about.

Pupil 5:   [*Looks away from the page and thinks.*] Veeb's dad liked to find out about other planets. Then they were going to planet Earth. And they – and dad said 'no' to take Speezy but the alien put it in his bag.

This is a very clear summarisation, which has been made without depending on the text alone. Pupil 5 has re-formulated the action into his own words and identified the main idea of the text read up to that point. Thus the text has been clearly exposed for the group through summarisation.

Exploration

Teacher B also created opportunities for the group to explore the text through careful questioning. For example, she asked the group, 'How do you know that Veeb didn't listen to his dad?'.

The group then discussed their ideas in pairs and then shared them. The following interaction took place:

Pupil 3:   He brang the dog. Because he brang the dog.

Teacher: He <u>brought</u> the dog.

Pupil 3:   He brought the dog and hid it in his sack.

Pupil 4:   He brought the dog and his dad told him not too.

Pupil 3:   Because his dad said what he if he ran off. And then they couldn't find him.

Teacher:	Does it say that in the book that he hid him in his sack?
Pupil 5:	Yes, it says 'He hid Speezy in his bag'.
Teacher:	[*talking to Pupil 3*] Right you used a different word there for 'bag'. What word did you use?
Pupil 3:	Sack.

In this example Pupil 3 makes an inference based from evidence in the text. He can show that Veeb doesn't listen to his dad because he ignores his instruction to leave the dog behind. To further support this, Teacher B asks if they can locate the evidence specifically in the text, which Pupil 5 is able to do.

At a later point in the lesson the teacher refers to one of the illustrations of Veeb which shows him looking for Speezy. Speezy has run off.

Teacher:	Why does Veeb look worried?
Pupil 2:	Because he's lost and he's lost his new dog, and he's going to get told off.
Teacher:	How would you be feeling if that was you?
Pupil 3:	Scared.
Teacher:	Scared? Why would you be scared?
Pupil 3:	Because I wouldn't be with any grown-ups.
Teacher:	OK, so he's on his own and not even with a grown up.

Here, Teacher B follows up Pupil 3's initial one-word response, allowing him the opportunity to develop his thinking. What is interesting here is that Teacher B links the character's feelings to Pupil 3; in effect the teacher is attempting to encourage Pupil 3 to empathise with Veeb. Pupil 3 says he would be feeling scared because there are no adults; at which point Teacher B makes a link to the text where we see Veeb on his own.

This dialogue develops further when Teacher B makes a reference to the feelings of the absent Speezy.

Teacher:	Do you think Speezy would be scared? We can't actually see Speezy in that picture, can we? But do you think Speezy will be scared?
Pupils 3 and 4:	[together] No.
Pupil 2:	Ye – maybe. Yeah a bit scared maybe.

At this point it is interesting to note that there is a difference of opinion as Pupil 2 tentatively suggests that Speezy might be scared. Teacher B follows up on this and provides Pupil 2 with a prompt related to the text.

Teacher: What does the forest feel like to you? What does it look like?

Pupil 2: It looks like a deep, dark wood.

Teacher: Very good. Good adjectives.

Pupil 3: Like Little Red Riding Hood.

Teacher: Yes, well done, we've been doing traditional tales haven't we?

Pupil 2: It looks creepy and a bit spooky.

So by using the visual clue of the setting, Pupil 2 makes an inference about Speezy's feelings from evidence in the text. This was supported by Pupil 3, who made the link to the Little Red Riding Hood story, which shows that between them they are able to make links between stories.

Another interesting development occurred as a direct result of this interaction when Pupil 5 questioned whether Speezy was indeed lost. The illustration shows Veeb walking along a winding pathway through the woods.

Pupil 5: Excuse me, I don't think he's lost because I think he might have followed that path.

Teacher: Have you ever taken a dog for a walk? Do they always follow the path?

Pupil 5: [*Thinks and shakes his head.*] No.

Teacher: No they don't always follow the path do they, dogs? Sometimes they go off into the undergrowth and go and smell out lots of different smells.

Pupil 1: And sometimes they go off to try and find things that they can do or eat.

Pupil 3: Maybe, maybe, he smelt something or saw, like, a ball or something, so then he went after the ball or what he smelt.

Teacher: Maybe

Pupil 5: Or what if he saw a bone?

Although his idea wasn't agreed with, Pupil 5 also makes an inference from evidence presented in the illustration.

Expansion

In the previous examples we saw how Teacher B used the pupils' experiences, thoughts and feelings to make links to the text. She also used these to expand beyond the text. In the following interaction she encourages the pupils to speculate on how Veeb's father might have reacted to finding out that the dog came on the trip to Earth.

Teacher:	What do you think dad would say to Veeb?
Pupil 1:	He would say 'Veeb I told you not to bring him here!'
Teacher:	And he would be angry?
Pupil 4:	I think he would.
Pupil 3:	And he will go like this [*stands hands on hips and looks stern*].
Pupil 2:	I think he will go like this: [*develops Pupil 3's action*] 'Why did you bring the dog?'
Pupil 5:	And then he might, and then he might get him back in the sack and keep him in the spaceship in the sack.
Teacher:	So have you ever done anything like that before? Where you've done something secretly and you haven't told anyone that you've done it? And then somebody's found out in the end?
Pupil 2:	Well I brang a toy to school when my, when my mum said 'no' but I secretly put it in my coat pocket and brang it to school.
Teacher:	<u>Brought</u> it to school.
Pupil 2:	Yeah, and mummy didn't know and then – she figured out – at the end because she checked in my pockets.
Pupil 3:	Do you know what? When I went to Asda I brung Rabbit with me and I put him under my jumper.
Teacher:	<u>Brought.</u>
Pupil 3:	Brought him and I put him under my jumper, and then I took him out in the shop and mummy was very angry because the last time I lose one teddy.
Teacher:	You lost a teddy.

In this instance, the teacher encourages speculation on a character's feelings by making links to previous knowledge and experiences. By doing this Teacher B gives the pupils the framework to justify why their speculation might be logically plausible.

At a later point in the story, Veeb finds Speezy playing with an Earth boy. He becomes worried that the boy might try to keep Speezy. Teacher B uses this scenario as an opportunity to expand the discussion to encompass questions of moral choice.

Teacher:	'L' [Pupil 4] said that Veeb might be worried that that little boy might take Speezy home with him. Would that be the right thing for that little boy to do?
Pupil 5:	No.
Pupil 1:	No.

Teacher: Why not?

Pupil 1: Because, if you like, if somebody actually gave you a toy to play with, and you are at somebody else's house and they said can I have it back now and you said 'no', you might've taken it home when it was their toy. And the person didn't notice.

Teacher: What could that be called if you took something from somebody?

Pupil 3: Stealing.

Pupil 5: Yeah, stealing

Teacher: It could be called stealing, couldn't it?

Pupil 2: Only if it was on purpose.

Teacher: Well yes, sometimes you can take something by mistake.

Pupil 2's response in this interaction is an interesting one. The first point to note is that he is listening very carefully to the comments of the other group members. His comment also paves the way for a discussion as to what is – or isn't – stealing. This once again emphasises the point that texts we present children with exist within a wider social context.

TEACHER C: YEAR 5

Teachers I have worked with on numerous reading comprehension projects have found that pupils in years 5 and 6 (9–11 year olds) engage well with the Australian writer Paul Jennings, regardless of their perceived reading ability. One reason for this is that many of Jennings' texts present little difficulty in terms of readability – or so it appears. In actual fact many of Jennings' texts deal with some quite complex issues, such as death, bullying and love. One example is the short story, 'The Copy' (1997).

In this story, Dr Woolley, an eccentric inventor, creates a cloning machine. Anything that is placed in the machine can be copied simply by flicking the switch to the label 'Copy'. The object is replicated exactly – the only difference is that it comes out as a mirror-image. For example, at one point in the story, a frog with a spot on the right-hand side of its body is placed in the machine. When it is copied another frog appears exactly the same as the first one, but with the spot on the left-hand side of its body. This switch can also be flicked to the label 'reverse' which means that the copied object can be destroyed when placed back in the machine. Dr Woolley strikes up a friendship with a curious young boy called Tim. Tim has a girlfriend but is being bullied at school. One day when Tim visits Dr Woolley's inventing shed he finds it empty. Mysteriously, Dr Woolley has disappeared, leaving only a note telling Tim to destroy the cloning machine.

Teacher C used this text with a group of Year 5 children. The group was selected by ability and consisted of two girls and two boys. All the children were from minority ethnic backgrounds, reflecting the catchment area of the school. None of the children was considered to have second language issues.

The text was divided into four sections with one section covered each week, so the story was covered in four sessions over a period of four weeks. The following analysis relates to the second session. Teacher C used an adapted form of reciprocal teaching whereby the children had read the section of text to themselves the previous day and located words they didn't know. The teacher described this as a 'pre-read'. The teacher's rationale for this 'pre-read' is that he wanted to create more time for discussion and dialogue in the actual teacher and learner interaction. As part of the 'pre-read' he also gave them three questions to consider. As with Teacher B, these related to specific question types: a 'looking question' that aimed to expose the text; a 'clue question' that sought to 'explore' the text; and a 'thinking question' that required the children to expand upon the text by bringing ideas from outside of it. During the session, the teacher gave the group time to read over the text again to refresh their memory. Unknown or interesting words were clarified and the three questions were each used as a launching point for discussion and dialogue.

Exposition

To begin with, Teacher C clarified a number of words. One of these words was 'fink', which is what Matt Hodson, the bully in the story, called Tim. The children couldn't find this in the dictionary in the 'pre-read' session. In this instance the following interaction took place:

> *Teacher:* What do think it might mean? Do you want to read the context and let's see if we can make a good guess? Where did you see it?
>
> *Pupil 2:* When Matt Hodson said it, [*reads from the text*] 'I've been waiting for you, you little fink'.

The group then looked back in the text but could not come up with an exact definition. They did decide, however, that Matt Hodson was being nasty. The interaction closed with the teacher stating the following:

> *Teacher:* It's a slang word and these stories are from Australia, aren't they? I think what you did is that you kind of worked out what 'fink' means by looking at the context – by reading the bit before.

In this interaction Teacher C emphasises the strategy of using the context to work out the meaning of words, which takes us back to the cueing strategies that early readers are encouraged to develop. This example shows that these strategies are just as relevant for older developing readers. We cannot assume that they have become embedded skills, particularly as they are now likely to be dealing with more extended written texts. Here, Teacher C is supporting the group's metacognition by getting them to reflect on how they tried to work out the word, thus encouraging comprehension monitoring. Teacher C also touches upon wider language issues. By reminding the children it is a slang word that seems to have a clear meaning in Australia, the group are reminded that language exists in a social and cultural context.

The term 'cameo brooch' also needed clarification. In the story, Tim placed one of these in the cloner. The dictionary definition (of the words separately) did not help the group in the 'pre-read' session. Teacher C then produced a photograph of a cameo brooch and explained how they were commonly worn in Victorian times; he pointed out the fact that they featured the silhouetted profile of a face. In this instance Teacher C has anticipated a possible vocabulary-related difficulty that might hinder the literal comprehension of the text and tailored his teaching to address it. He didn't spend time discussing the meaning of the word as he was sure they wouldn't know what a 'cameo brooch' was. He just explained it to them, and in doing so his teacher talk became instructive, or expository. This example also shows that it is important to be familiar with texts before we use them with learners.

Having addressed vocabulary-related issues, Teacher C then went on to expose the learners' understanding of the events that took place in this section. As a way into this he introduced a 'looking question', which aimed to tap literal comprehension: 'What did Tim notice about the copies he had made?'

This question led to the following interaction:

Pupil 1:   When he copied the frog one of them had – on the right – he had a spot. And when he copied the other one it was like an exact mirror, only it was on the other side. The one on the left. So everything, was the same except that little dot.

Pupil 2:   So it's like a mirror image. It was like – you know – like [K] said. [*Pupil 2 points to the cameo brooch picture*] It was looking to the left and when he copied it, it was looking to the right. The face is the opposite way.

Teacher: Do you want to show us with the mirror? [*Gives Pupil 2 a small mirror*]

Pupil 2:   Can you see that here? When you put it in the middle one face is looking to the left and one is looking to the right.

The question that instigated this dialogue is an interesting one because if the learners had missed the answer they might have misunderstood events that took place later in the story. (I'm not going to tell you how. Read it for yourself – it's brilliant!). So Teacher C prepared this question with care. This emphasis on careful preparation was also evident when he invited Pupil 2 to demonstrate a mirror image by using an actual mirror. The mirror wasn't there by good fortune. What is interesting here is the way Pupil 2 shows her understanding of how the cameo brooch is significant. When it is copied in the story, the silhouetted face is looking in the opposite direction, reinforcing the idea of the cloned articles in the story appearing as a mirror image. Pupil 2 has exposed the text further for her peers by making the link with the cameo brooch, but this was instigated by Teacher C's initial clarification of what a cameo brooch is. A final point to make is the manner in which Pupil 2's first statement follows directly from Pupil 1's. Pupil 2 doesn't wait to be invited to talk but waits her turn. Of greater importance is the point that Pupil 2 was clearly listening to Pupil 1 because her ideas build on Pupil 1's statement. This would indicate a dialogue is being encouraged.

The dialogue then develops, with the teacher turning to Pupil 3.

Teacher: What do you think, 'U'? Did you notice that?

Pupil 3:   Yeah because the frog had the black spot on his left and when he made the copy he had it on the right.

The teacher has drawn Pupil 3 into the discussion, and Pupil 3 offers a response that indicates he has understood the difference between the cloned images and the real ones. If Pupil 3 had not offered this response, presumably the teacher would have probed his understanding through further questioning. The response given, however, makes it clear that Pupil 3 has understood the point about the mirror-imaged clones, and interestingly this may have been supported by Pupil 1's initial exposition.

As the interaction develops, the teacher reiterates what Tim noticed about the cloned copies but then moves the interaction forward with another question that further develops the text exposition.

Teacher: So it's like a mirror – copy – image. So, we're clear on that? So we looked at the text to find that one. Umm ... Did he copy lots of things or just one thing?

Pupil 4:   He copied everything in the workshop.

Teacher: Did he?

Pupil 4:   Yeah, it said in the text.

Teacher: Do you want to find it then? [*Children look for it.*] Just to check we know exactly what's happening.

In this interaction we see Teacher C using his opening question of 'What did Tim notice about the copies he had made?' not as an end in itself, but as a way to further investigate the group's literal comprehension. The question acts as a 'jumping-off point' for further exposition.

Exploration

Teacher C then moved on to explore the text to deepen understanding. The discussion focused initially on the following 'clue question' (because the clues are in the text): 'Why did Tim and his clone both say, "Hello there, welcome to earth?"'

This relates to the action in the story where the main character, Tim, gets into the cloning machine and makes a clone of himself. Paul Jennings does not explicitly say why the clone stated the same thing as Tim when they met. The group explore this:

Pupil 2: Maybe like because it's a mirror image so whatever the real Tim says the copy will say it. And because Tim said 'Hello, and welcome to earth?' maybe the copy said it too. Because it's like a mirror.

Pupil 1: He said what it ... [*inaudible*]

Pupil 2: Like, if you go to a mirror and start talking to it you will see yourself talking.

Teacher: It's like that is it ... So if Tim says welcome to earth and there's his clone, is he thinking – is <u>Tim</u> thinking – that the clone is new?

Pupil 1: Yeah, that it hasn't been here, or something.

Pupil 2: Yeah, but the other one has the same mind and he thinks the same thing.

Teacher: What do you mean by that?

Pupil 2: Because then the copy does exactly the same it's just like a mirror image. So then they both have the same thoughts and everything else. They have the same – what they can – same talents and stuff.

Pupil 1: Tim thought he would only have the same actions as him.

Pupil 2: Yeah, Tim thought it would just look the same and do the same.

Through this interaction led initially by Pupil 1 and Pupil 2, the group begin to explore Tim's clone further and find out something that might not have been obvious initially – that Tim's clone is not some sort of cardboard cut-out that looks the same; it also has a character and personality that resemble Tim's.

If we note the teacher talk, we notice that Teacher C is listening carefully to what the pupils are saying and encouraging them to outline their thinking with greater clarity. Later in the interaction this line of enquiry is developed further.

Pupil 4: If I said hello to 'U' [Pupil 3] he wouldn't say the same thing as me – everything.

Teacher: What, so you think Tim is surprised that he says the same thing?

Pupil 4: Yeah because he thought he would reply.

Pupil 2: Yeah but not just exactly the same and just be a copy. And that he would have his own mind and – personality and stuff.

Pupil 4: Yeah.

Teacher: OK, if Tim thinks the clone is new, what do you think the clone thinks?

Pupil 1: He thinks he's new too. Because that's what he's thinking.

Teacher: This is really hurting my brain now. [*Laughter from the group.*] You're saying there are two Tims and both think they are new.

Pupil 1: Yeah.

Pupil 2: The other one is new.

Pupil 1: Yeah.

Teacher: Right. That takes us back to Dr Woolley. What do you think might have happened with Dr Woolley? There were signs of a fight in the workshop.

This segment of the interaction opens with Pupil 4 making links to real-life greetings – people do not copy each other exactly when they meet. Here again, we can see how Pupil 2 builds on Pupil 4's point and provides greater clarity. The important point to pick out here is that it is the teacher's talk which instigates it. The emphasis in each question asked by the teacher aims to explore the *pupil's* thinking, not his. And once again, as with the exposition section, the opening question acts as a jumping-off point for further questions, this time with the aim of exploration. The group then starts to make links between what happened to Tim and what happened to Dr Woolley, thus making links across different parts of the story. The line of questioning has allowed the group to analyse the text closely.

Expansion

Teacher C then asked a 'thinking' question. This question sought to expand upon the events and actions in the text by making links to the pupils' wider knowledge, understanding and values. The question that opened this section was as follows: 'What do you think Tim could have done instead of copying himself?' As you will notice in the following section of dialogue, it encouraged some interesting speculation.

Pupil 1: I never knew he was going to copy himself. I thought he was going to copy some gold. That would be fine but he copied himself that's what made it worse.

Teacher: You think that's where he went wrong?

Pupil 1: Yeah, he could have just copied some gold and some money and that's it.

Teacher: So how would that solve the Matt Hodson situation?

Pupil 1: Buy him some guards?

Teacher: Buy him<u>self</u> some guards with his new gold.

What is also interesting in this dialogue is the way the teacher stays with Pupil 1 and undertakes a series of questions that aim to make Pupil 1 think about the justification for his point of view. Following this, another interesting exchange takes place whereby the teacher is completely absent from the interaction. It begins with Pupil 3 addressing the teacher, but it is Pupil 3's peers who respond:

Pupil 3: He could make a deal with Matt Hodson and like give him something and in return for not bullying him and not punching him and stuff. 'Leave me alone. I'll give you something.' But then he gets whatever his deal was and keeps copying it. He could keep on copy it.

Pupil 2: What if Matt Hodson lies and says I'll take it and carries on.

Pupil 1: Mmm. He <u>is</u> a bully.

Pupil 2: He <u>is</u> a bully.

Pupil 1: He hasn't got Matt Hodson's control [meaning power, presumably].

Pupil 2: That's a good idea, 'U', but it might not work.

Pupil 3 begins this interaction with a speculation as to what Tim could have done instead of cloning himself. This idea comes from his wider knowledge of the world as there is no sense of deals being made in the text. However, Pupil 1 links this idea from the wider world with the perception he has developed from the text of Matt Hodson's character. Pupil 2 joins in and makes a further link that equates lying with bullying. At this point we are beginning to see elements of argumentation.

School-based activity

Shaping the dialogue

In the previous chapter the school-based activity involved recording a guided group interaction and analysing the type of talk that was taking place.

This time, record a guided group interaction but consciously attempt to shape the dialogue so that it encompasses the following:

- Exposition
- Exploration
- Expansion

Analyse your talk and notice how your talk, and the talk of the learners, was different for each of these.

Share your findings with colleagues.

CONCLUSION

In this chapter we have investigated how comprehension can be promoted across the primary years. The first example used paintings in the nursery; the second used a reading scheme book that incorporated pictures and a limited amount of written text; and finally we looked at an extended piece of text in the form of a short story used in the upper primary years. At the centre of this was the type of talk that teachers use, and the type of talk that has been elicited from the learners. By shaping the dialogue carefully, teachers can help learners to expose the text, to explore the text and to expand upon the text. To re-iterate a point made in the previous chapter, a three-part lesson that moves from exposition, exploration and expansion is not being suggested; in the cut and thrust of an actual lesson teachers are likely to move between these depending upon the direction the dialogue is taking. However, the teaching of comprehension should aim to incorporate these consciously.

Central to all these examples is the fact that the teachers listened carefully to what the learners were saying and responded carefully by considering the learners' comments. Thus these teachers promoted talk with a clear purpose.

CONCLUSION

TEXT COMPREHENSION IS IMPORTANT, BUT IT'S WHERE IT TAKES YOU THAT COUNTS

Journey to Jo'burg by Beverly Naidoo, originally published in 1985, is set in South Africa during the apartheid years. The story focuses on two children, Naledi and her younger brother, Tiro, who travel to Johannesburg to find their mother. Their mother is working in Johannesburg as a maid and returns to the village only occasionally. Johannesburg is over 300 kilometres from their village but the children choose to undertake this journey because their baby sister, Dineo, is seriously ill. They do not have enough money to pay for a doctor.

> 'If only Mma was here,' Naledi wished as she and Tiro walked down to the village tap with their empty buckets. She clutched tightly at the coins in her hand.
>
> Each morning the children had to pass the place of the graves on their way to buy the day's water and only last week another baby in the village had died.

Slipping away from their grandmother, they embark on the long, difficult and dangerous journey with no money and very little to eat.

To comprehend the story to this point, the reader will have accessed all three of the broad domain areas outlined in Chapter 2 and explored further in the Processes section of this book. They will have applied linguistic processes relating to vocabulary and syntax. The section of text from the story gives a flavour of the demands the text makes in these areas. It is not particularly demanding in terms of vocabulary beyond the word 'Mma' – the Tswana word for mother – and the fact that the children's names are (likely to be) uncommon for most readers.

The syntax uses common structures. Cognitive processes are also applied; for example, the reader might make the inference that Naledi is carrying the coin so she can pay for the water. Knowledge factors are also relevant here. While the reader may not be familiar with the impact of apartheid, they are likely to have a prior knowledge relating to childhood and sickness, amongst other things. They may also apply story knowledge, as the children seem to be on a quest.

The application of these three domain areas and their associated components are applied by all readers (as much as is possible) whenever text – written or otherwise – is encountered. In each chapter of this book we have seen this to be the case across a wide variety of texts, from a picture book for young children, Sendak's *Where the Wild Things Are*, to a complex novel, Faulkner's *The Sound and the Fury*. We used them to comprehend non-fiction texts such as the newspaper article on the 'literate' baboons, and Applegate et al.'s (2009) academic study in Chapter 2; as well as the poetry of Lewis Carroll in Chapter 3, a Colin Thompson picture book in Chapter 8, and various fictional texts. This reinforces the point that these components of comprehension are applied by readers of all ages, across a range of texts.

For readers in the primary years, however, the ability to use these component skills needs to be developed; and this is where teaching comes in. In Chapter 10 it was noted that we need to address the teaching of comprehension from a pedagogically informed position; and it was suggested that the best way to achieve this was through scaffolded learning, which emphasises a dialogic teaching approach. The importance of dialogue to comprehension teaching cannot be understated. We saw in Chapter 8 that in all likelihood children will comprehend text in different and unique ways, because readers do not apply the components of comprehension, such as inference making, in the same way. No two readers do. If we want to discover how children have comprehended text, the best way is to ask them. One approach to structuring the dialogic interactions when teaching comprehension was also suggested in Chapter 10. This encompassed the three ways to focus our questions in these interactions. Our questions should aim to expose literal understanding; explore this literal understanding through evidence in the text; and expand upon it by making links to the knowledge the reader brings to the text. Examples of how this might look in practice were presented in Chapter 11. The process of deepening understanding allows children to make evaluations, offer opinions and justify their thinking.

In the Practices section some time was spent thinking about the texts we present young readers with. One of the important parts of this analysis related specifically to written texts and considered the issue of readability. If texts are too complex it might be difficult for young readers to comprehend them – and it was noted that this complexity is not simply related to issues of decoding.

At this point there is something else to consider in relation to this. Most chapters in this book begin with reference to a piece of fictional literature. This has been done for a reason. We were able to see the challenges they presented to text comprehension, and how we apply the components of comprehension to overcome these. As a result we are able to read literature like *Journey to Jo'burg* and develop an understanding of it, as shown in the short summary of the events that take place at the beginning of the story, and which is outlined at the start of this concluding chapter. This summary is likely to be different from one you might make; but they would probably be similar. The point to make here is that by applying the components we have been able to comprehend the text. All well and good.

Well, actually no. It is not all well and good. If our engagement with *Journey to Jo'burg* ends at this point – at the point we can say 'I understand what's happened' – then we miss much of what the text can offer. The text deals with apartheid South Africa with all its inequalities and injustices. Children are sensitive to this. They want to know why the children are paying for water; they want to know why the children's mother lives and works 300 kilometres away; they want to know why Naledi and Tiro can't just take their sister, Dineo, to the hospital. Indeed, what is particularly interesting about using *Journey to Jo'burg* in the classroom is watching children try to make sense of adult stupidity.

As Janet Maybin (2013: 65) states,

> Comprehension techniques are not an end in themselves, as they sometimes appear to be in official activities, but are used by children in the context of an intense emotional, moral and humorous engagement with texts.

It is important for us as teachers to ensure that children develop the skills to comprehend text. However, this is not an end in itself. The key point is what we ask – or allow – them to do with this understanding.

REFERENCES

Aaron, P.G., Joshi, R.M. and Williams, K. (1999) Not all reading disabilities are alike. *Journal of Learning Disabilities*, 32: 120–37.

Abadzis, N. (2002) *The Dog from Outer Space*. London: Heinemann/Rigby.

Afflerbach, P., Pearson, P.D. and Paris, S.G. (2008) Clarifying differences between reading skills and strategies. *The Reading Teacher*, 61: 364–73.

Aitchison, J. (2003) *Words in the Mind: An Introduction to Mental Lexicon*, 3rd edn. Oxford: Blackwell.

Alborough, J. (1992) *Where's My Teddy?* London: Walker Books.

Alexander, R. (2001) *Culture and Pedagogy: International Comparisons in Primary Education*. Oxford: Blackwell.

Alexander, R.J. (2008a) *Towards Dialogic Teaching: Rethinking Classroom Talk*, 4th edn. York: Dialogus.

Alexander, R. (2008b) Principle, pragmatism and compliance. In *Essays on Pedagogy*. Abingdon: Routledge. pp. 43–71.

Alexander, R. (2012) Improving oracy and classroom talk in English schools: achievements and challenges. Available at: www.primaryreview.org.uk/downloads_/news/2012/02/2012_02_20 DfE_oracy_Alexander.pdf [accessed 16 March 2014].

Alfassi, M. (1998) Reading for meaning: the efficacy of reciprocal teaching in fostering reading comprehension in high school students in remedial reading classes. *American Educational Research Journal*, 35 (2): 309–32.

Anderson, R. and Nagy, W. (1992) The vocabulary conundrum. *American Psychologist*, 30: 821–8.

Anglin, J. (1993) Vocabulary development: a morphological analysis. *Monographs of the Society for Research in Child Development*, 58 (10, Serial No. 238).

Applegate, M., Applegate, A.J. and Modla, V.B. (2009) 'She's my best reader; she just can't comprehend': studying the relationship between fluency and comprehension. *The Reading Teacher*, 62 (6): 512–21.

Au, K. (2004) An expanded definition of literacy. In D. Wray (ed.), *Literacy: Major Themes in Education*, volume 1. London: RoutledgeFalmer.

Australian Curriculum, Assessment and Reporting Authority (ACARA) (2011) *Australian Curriculum*. Available online at: www.australiancurriculum.edu.au/Home [accessed 16 March 2014].

Baddeley, A.D. (2000) The episodic buffer: a new component of working memory? *Trends in Cognitive Sciences*, 4 (11): 417–23.

Baddeley, A.D. (2004) *Your Memory: A User's Guide*. London: Carlton.

Baddeley, A. and Hitch, G. (1974) Working memory. In G. Bower (ed.), *The Psychology of Learning and Motivation*. New York: Academic Press. pp. 47–89.

Baker, L. (1984) Spontaneous versus instructed use of multiple standards for evaluating comprehension: effects of age, reading proficiency, and type of standard. *Journal of Experimental Child Psychology*, 38: 289–311.

Baker, L. and Brown, A.L. (1984) Metacognitive skills and reading. In P.D. Pearson, R. Barr, M.L. Kamil and P. Mosenthal (eds), *Handbook of Reading Research*. White Plains, NY: Longman. pp. 353–94.

Barnes, M.A., Dennis, M. and Haefele-Kalvaitis, J. (1996) The effects of knowledge availability and knowledge accessibility on coherence and elaborative inferencing in children from six to fifteen years of age. *Journal of Experimental Child Psychology*, 61: 216–41.

Bartlett, F.C. (1932) *Remembering: A Study in Experimental and Social Psychology*. New York: Cambridge University Press.

Barton, D. (2007) *Literacy: An Introduction to the Ecology of Written Language*. Oxford: Blackwell.

Baumann, J., Kame'enui, E. and Ash, G. (2003) Research on vocabulary instruction: Voltaire redux. In J. Flood, D. Lapp, J. Squire and J. Jensen (eds), *Handbook of Research on Teaching the English Language Arts*. Mahwah, NJ: Erlbaum. pp. 752–85.

Beare, H. (2000) *Creating the Future School*. London: RoutledgeFalmer.

Bentley, D. (1985) *The How and Why of Readability*. Reading: Centre for the Teaching of Reading, University of Reading School of Education.

Biemiller, A. (2005) Size and sequence in vocabulary development: implications for choosing words for primary grade vocabulary instruction. In A. Hiebert and M. Kamil (eds), *Teaching and Learning Vocabulary: Bringing Research to Practice*. Mahwah, NJ: Erlbaum. pp. 223–42.

Biemiller, A. and Boote, C. (2006) An effective method for building meaning vocabulary in primary grades. *Journal of Educational Psychology*, 98 (1): 44–62.

Black, J.B. (1985) An exposition on understanding expository text. In B.K. Britton and J.B. Black (eds), *Understanding Expository Text: A Theoretical and Practical Handbook for Analyzing Explanatory Text*. Hillsdale, NJ: Lawrence Erlbaum Associates.

Blaiklock, K. and Haddow, S. (2007) Incorporating phonics within a New Zealand whole language programme. *New Zealand Journal of Educational Studies*, 42: 143–59.

Bloom, C.P., Fletcher, C.R., Van den Broek, P., Reitz, L. and Shapiro, B.P. (1990) An on-line assessment of causal reasoning during comprehension. *Memory and Cognition*, 18: 65–71.

Blundell, T. (1993) *Beware of Boys*. Harmondsworth: Puffin Books.

Braine, M.D.S. (1990) The 'natural logic' approach to reasoning. In W.F. Overton (ed.), *Reasoning, Necessity and Logic: Developmental Perspectives*. Hillsdale, NJ: Lawrence Erlbaum Associates.

Bransford, J.D. and Franks, J.J. (1971) The abstraction of linguistic ideas. *Cognitive Psychology*, 2: 331–50.

Bransford, J.D., Barclay, J.R. and Franks, J.J. (1972) Sentence memory: a constructive vs. interpretive approach. *Cognitive Psychology*, 3: 193–209.

Britton, B.K., Van Dusen, L., Glynn, S.M. and Hemphill, D. (1990) The impact of inferences on instructional text. In A.C. Graesser and G.H. Bower (eds), *The Psychology of Learning and Motivation: Inferences and Text Comprehension*, volume 25. New York: Academic Press. pp. 53–70.

Bromley, K. (2007) Nine things every teacher should know about words and vocabulary instruction. *Journal of Adolescent and Adult Literacy*, 50 (7): 528–37.

Brown, A. and Palincsar, A. (1989) Guided, cooperative learning and individual knowledge acquisition. In L.B. Resnick (ed.), *Knowing, Learning and Instruction: Essays in Honor of Robert Glaser*. Hillsdale, NJ: Lawrence Erlbaum Associates. pp. 393–451.

Brown, A.L., Palinscar, A. and Armbruster, B. (1984) Instructing comprehension-fostering activities in interactive learning situations. In H. Mandl, N.L. Stein and T. Trabasso (eds), *Learning and Comprehension of Text*. Hillsdale, NJ: Lawrence Erlbaum Associates. pp. 225–81.

Bruner, J.S. (1974) *Beyond the Information Given: Studies in the Psychology of Knowing*. London: George Allen and Unwin.

Bruner, J.S. (1986) *Actual Minds, Possible Worlds*. Cambridge, MA: Harvard University Press.

Bruner, J.S. (2002) *Making Stories: Law, Literature and Life*. Cambridge, MA and London: Harvard University Press.

Cain, K. (2007) Syntactic awareness and reading ability: is there any evidence for a special relationship? *Applied Psycholinguistics*, 28: 679–94.

Cain, K. (2010). *Reading Development and Difficulties: An Introduction* (BPS Textbooks in Psychology). Oxford: Wiley–Blackwell.

Cain, K. and Oakhill, J.V. (1999) Inference making and its relation to comprehension failure. *Reading and Writing*, 11: 489–503.

Cain, K. and Oakhill, J.V. (2004) Reading comprehension difficulties. In T. Nunes and P.E. Bryant (eds), *Handbook of Children's Literacy*. Dordrecht: Kluwer. pp. 313–38.

Cain, K. and Oakhill, J. (2006) Assessment matters: issues in the measurement of reading comprehension. *British Journal of Educational Psychology*, 76: 697–708.

Cain, K. and Oakhill, J. (eds) (2007) *Children's Comprehension Problems in Oral and Written Language: A Cognitive Perspective*. New York: Guilford Press.

Cain, K., Oakhill, J. and Bryant, P.E. (2004) Children's reading comprehension ability: concurrent prediction by working memory, verbal ability and component skills. *Journal of Educational Psychology*, 96: 31–42.

Cain, K., Oakhill, J.V. and Elbro, C. (2003) The ability to learn new word meanings from context by school-age children with and without language comprehension difficulties. *Journal of Child Language*, 30: 681–94.

Cairney, T.H. (1990) *Teaching Reading Comprehension: Meaning Makers at Work*. Milton Keynes: Open University Press.

Carlisle, J.F. and Fleming, J. (2003) Lexical processing of morphologically complex words in the elementary years. *Scientific Studies of Reading*, 7: 239–53.

Carroll, L. (2003) *Jabberwocky*. London: Walker Books Ltd. (Originally published in 1871 in *Through the Looking-Glass, and What Alice Found There*.)

Casteel, M.A. and Simpson, G.B. (1991) Textual coherence and the development of inferential generation skills. *Journal of Research in Reading*, 14: 116–30.

Catts, H.W., Hogan, T.P. and Adlof, S.M. (2005) Developing changes in reading and reading disabilities. In H.W. Catts and A.G. Kahmi (eds), *The Connections between Language and Reading Disabilities*. Mahwah, NJ: Erlbaum. pp. 50–71.

Chall, J., Jacobs, V. and Baldwin, L. (1990) *The Reading Crisis: Why Poor Children Fall Behind*. Cambridge, MA: Harvard University Press.

Clark, H.H. (1977) Bridging. In P.N. Johnson-Laird and P.C. Wason (eds), *Thinking: Readings in Cognitive Science*. Cambridge: Cambridge University Press. pp. 243–63.

Clay, M. (1993) *Becoming Literate*. New Zealand: Heinemann Education.

Clymer, T. (1968) What is 'reading'? Some current concepts. In H. Richie and H. Robinson (eds), *Innovation and Change in Reading Instruction*. Chicago: National Society for the Study of Education. pp. 7–29.

Concannon-Gibney, T. and Murphy, B. (2010) Reading practice in Irish primary classrooms: too simple a view of reading? *Literacy*, 44 (3): 122–30.

Conway, M.A. (1990) *Autobiographical Memory: An Introduction*. Milton Keynes: Open University Press.

Cook, A.E., Limber, J.E. and O'Brien, E.J. (2001) Situation-based context and the availability of predictive inferences. *Journal of Memory and Language*, 44: 220–34.

Cross, G. (1995) *Posh Watson*. London: Walker Books.

Cunningham, A.E. (2005) Vocabulary growth through independent reading and reading aloud to children. In E.H. Hiebert and M.L. Kamil (eds), *Teaching and Learning Vocabulary: Bringing Research to Practice*. Mahwah, NJ: Erlbaum. pp. 45–68.

Cunningham, A.E. and Stanovich, K.E. (1997) Early reading acquisition and its relation to reading experience and ability 10 years later. *Developmental Psychology*, 33: 934–45.

Davis, M. (2006) *Reading Instruction: The Two Keys*. Charlottesville, VA: Core Knowledge Foundation.

Deacon, S.H. and Kirby, J. (2004) Morphological awareness: just 'more phonological'? The roles of morphological and phonological awareness in reading development. *Applied Psycholinguistics*, 25: 223–38.

Demont, E. and Gombert, J.E. (1996) Phonological awareness as a predictor of decoding skills and syntactic awareness as a predictor of comprehension skills. *British Journal of Educational Psychology*, 66 (3): 315–32.

Department for Education (DfE) (2014) National Curriculum in England: Framework for Key Stages 1 to 4. Available at: www.gov.uk/government/publications/national-curriculum-in-england-framework-for-key-stages-1-to-4 [accessed 16 March 2014].

Department for Education and Employment (DfEE) (1998) *The National Literacy Strategy*. London: DfEE.

Department of Education, Science and Training (2005) *National Inquiry into the Teaching of Literacy: Teaching Reading*. Commonwealth of Australia.

Duke, N.K. (2005) Comprehension of what for what: comprehension as a non-unitary construct. In S. Paris and S. Stahl (eds), *Current Issues in Reading Comprehension and Assessment*. Mahwah, NJ: Erlbaum. pp. 93–104.

Durkin, D. (1993) *Teaching Them to Read*, 6th edn. Boston, MA: Allyn and Bacon.

Ehrlich, M.-F., Remond, M. and Tardieu, H. (1999) Processing of anaphoric devices in young skilled and less skilled comprehenders: differences in metacognitive monitoring. *Reading and Writing: An Interdisciplinary Journal*, 11: 29–63.

Fincher-Kiefer, R. and D'Agostino, P.R. (2004) The role of visuospatial resources in generating predictive and bridging inferences. *Discourse Processes*, 37: 205–24.

Fountas, I.C. and Pinnell, G.S. (1996) *Guided Reading: Good First Teaching for All Children*. Portsmouth, NH: Heinemann.

Fountas, I.C. and Pinnell, G.S. (2010) Research Base for Guided Reading as an Instructional Approach. Available online at: http://teacher.scholastic.com/products/guidedreading/pdfs/GR_Research_Paper_2010.pdf [accessed 16 March 2014].

Franks, B. (1998) Logical inference skills in adult reading comprehension: effects of age and formal education. *Educational Gerontology*, 24 (1): 47–68.

Freire, P. (1973) *Pedagogy of the Oppressed*. New York: Seabury Press.

Frith, U. (1985) Beneath the surface of developmental dyslexia. In K. Patterson, J. Marshall and M. Coltheart (eds), *Surface Dyslexia: Neuropsychological and Cognitive Studies of Phonological Reading*. London: Lawrence Erlbaum Associates. pp. 301–30.

Fung, I., Wilkinson, I.A.G. and Moore, D.W. (2003) L1-assisted reciprocal teaching to improve ESL students' comprehension of English expository text. *Learning and Instruction*, 13: 1–31.

Garnham, A. (2001) *Mental Models and the Interpretation of Anaphora* (Essays In Cognitive Psychology). Phildelphia: Psychology Press.

Garnham, A. and Oakhill, J.V. (1992) Discourse representation and text processing from a 'mental models' perspective. *Language and Cognitive Processes*, 7: 193–204.

Garnham, A. and Oakhill, J.V. (1996) The mental models theory of language comprehension. In B.K. Britton and A.C. Graesser (eds), *Models of Understanding Text*. Hillsdale, NJ: Lawrence Erlbaum Associates. pp. 313–39.

Garrod, S. and Sanford, A. (1990) Referential processing in reading: focusing on roles and individuals. In D.A. Balota, G.B. Flores-Arcais and K. Rayner (eds), *Comprehension Processing in Reading*. Hillsdale, NJ: Lawrence Erlbaum Associates. pp. 465–84.

Garrod, S. and Sanford, A.J. (1994) Resolving sentences in a discourse context: how discourse representation affects language understanding. In M. Gernsbacher (ed.), *Handbook of Psycholinguistics*. New York: Academic Press. pp. 675–98.

Garton, A. and Pratt, C. (1989) *Learning to Be Literate: The Development of Spoken and Written Language*. New York: Basil Blackwell.

Gathercole, S.E. (1998) The development of memory. *Journal of Child Psychology and Psychiatry and Allied Disciplines*, 39: 3–27.

Gee, J.P. (1999) Reading and the new literacy studies: framing the National Academy of Sciences report on reading. *Journal of Literacy Research*, 31 (3): 355–74.

Gernsbacher, M.A. (1990) *Language Comprehension as Structure Building*. Hillsdale NJ: Lawrence Erlbaum Associates.

Gernsbacher, M.A. and Robertson, R.R.W. (1992) Knowledge activation versus sentence mapping when representing fictional characters' emotional states. *Language and Cognitive Processes*, 7: 353–71.

Goff, D., Pratt, C. and Ong, B (2005) The relations between children's reading comprehension, working memory, language skills and components of reading decoding in a normal sample. *Reading and Writing*, 18: 583–616.

Goldman, S.R., Lawless, K and Manning, F. (2013) Research and development of multiple source comprehension assessment. In M.A. Britt, S.R. Goldman and J-F. Rouet (eds), *Reading – from Words to Multiple Texts*. Abingdon: Routledge.

Gough, P.B. and Tunmer, W.E. (1986) Decoding, reading and reading ability. *Remedial and Special Education*, 7: 6–10.

Gough, P.B., Hoover, W.A. and Peterson, C.L. (1996) Some observations on a simple view of reading. In C. Cornoldi and J. Oakhill (eds), *Reading Comprehension Difficulties*. Mahwah, NJ: Lawrence Erlbaum Associates. pp. 1–13.

Graesser, A.C. (1981) *Prose Comprehension Beyond the Word*. New York: Springer-Verlag.

Graesser, A.C., Singer, M. and Trabasso, T. (1994) Constructing inferences during narrative text comprehension. *Psychological Review*, 101: 371–95.

Graesser, A.C., Swamer, S.S., Baggett, W.B. and Sell, M.A. (1996) New models of deep comprehension. In A.C. Graesser and B.K. Britton (eds), *Models of Understanding Text*. Mahwah, NJ: Lawrence Erlbaum Associates.

Greenway, C. (2002) The process, pitfalls and benefits of implementing a reciprocal teaching intervention to improve the reading comprehension of a group of Year 6 pupils. *Educational Psychology in Practice*, 18 (2): 113–37.

Guardian, The (2007) To cut a long story short. *The Guardian*, Saturday 24 March. Available at: www.theguardian.com/books/2007/mar/24/fiction.originalwriting [accessed 16 March 2014].

Guardian, The (2011) Philip Pullman: a life in writing. *The Guardian*, Thursday 3 March. Available at: www.theguardian.com/culture/2011/mar/03/philip-pullman-life-in-writing [accessed 16 March 2014].

Hacker, D.J. (1997) Comprehension monitoring of written discourse across early-to-middle adolescence. *Reading and Writing: An Interdisciplinary Journal*, 9 (3): 207–40.

Hacker, D. and Tenent, A. (2002) Implementing reciprocal teaching in the classroom: overcoming obstacles and making modifications. *Journal of Educational Psychology*, 94 (4): 699–718.

Hall, K. (2003) *Listening to Stephen Read*. Buckingham: Open University Press.

Harris, T.L. and Hodges, R.E. (1995) *The Literacy Dictionary: The Vocabulary of Reading and Writing*. Newark, DE: International Reading Association.

Harrison, C. (1980) *Readability in the Classroom*. Cambridge: Cambridge University Press.

Haynes, J. and Murris, K. (2012) *Picturebooks, Pedagogy and Philosophy*. Abingdon: Routledge.

Hildyard, A. (1979) Children's production of inferences from oral texts. *Discourse Processes*, 2: 33–56.

Holdaway, D. (1979) *The Foundations of Literacy*. Portsmouth, NH: Heinemann.

Horowitz, A. (2007) The eye of the cyclops. In *Myths and Legends*. London: Kingfisher.

Houck, B. and Ross, K. (2012) Dismantling the myth of learning to read and reading to learn. ASCD Express. 7, 11. Alexandria, VA: ASCD. Available at: www.ascd.org/ascd-express/vol7/711-houck.aspx [accessed 16 March 2014].

Irwin, J.W. (1991) *Teaching Reading Comprehension Processes*, 2nd edn. Boston, MA: Allyn and Bacon.

James, M. (2004) Assessment, teaching and theories of learning. In J. Gardner (ed.), *Assessment and Learning*. London: SAGE.

Jennings, P. (1997) The copy. In *Thirteen Unpredictable Tales*. London: Puffin Books.

Johnson-Laird, P.N. (1983) *Mental Models: Towards a Cognitive Science of Language, Inference and Consciousness*. Cambridge: Cambridge University Press.

Johnston, R. and Watson J. (2005) The effects of synthetic phonics teaching on reading and spelling attainment: a seven-year longitudinal study. Available at: www.scotland.gov.uk/ [accessed 16 March 2014].

Just, M.A. and Carpenter, P.A. (1980) A theory of reading: from eye fixations to comprehension. *Psychological Review*, 87 (4): 329–35.

Kamil, M.L. and Hiebert, E.H. (2005) Teaching and learning vocabulary: perspectives and persistent issues. In E.H. Hiebert and M.L. Kamil (eds), *Teaching and Learning Vocabulary: Bringing Research to Practice*. Mahwah, NJ: Erlbaum. pp. 1–23.

Kamil, M.L., Borman, G.D., Dole, J., Kral, C.C., Salinger, T. and Torgesen, J. (2008) *Improving Adolescent Literacy: Effective Classroom and Intervention Practices. A Practice Guide* (NCEE 2008–4027). Washington, DC: National Center for Education Evaluation and Regional Assistance, Institute of Education Sciences, US Department of Education. Available online at: http://ies.ed.gov/ncee/wwc/pdf/practiceguides/adlit_pg_082608.pdf [accessed 16 March 2014].

Kelly, M., Moore, D.W. and Tuck, B.F. (1994) Reciprocal teaching in a regular primary school classroom. *Journal of Educational Research*, 88 (1): 53–61.

Kieffer, M.J. and Lesaux, N.K. (2007) Breaking words down to build meaning: vocabulary, morphology and reading comprehension in the urban classroom. *The Reading Teacher*, 61: 134–44.

Kim, Y-S., Petscher, Y., Schatschneider, C. and Foorman, B. (2010) Does growth rate in oral reading fluency matter for reading comprehension? *Journal of Educational Psychology*, 102: 652–67.

King, C. and Johnson, L. (1999) Constructing meaning via reciprocal teaching. *Reading Research and Instruction*, 38 (3): 169–86.

Kintsch, W. (1998) *Comprehension: A Paradigm for Cognition*. New York: Cambridge University Press.

Kintsch, W. and Kintsch, E. (2005) Comprehension. In S.G. Paris and S.A. Stahl (eds), *Current Issues in Reading Comprehension and Assessment*. Mahwah, NJ: Lawrence Erlbaum Associates. pp. 71–92.

Kintsch, W. and Rawson, K.A. (2005) Comprehension. In M.J. Snowling and C. Hulme (eds), *The Science of Reading: A Handbook*. Malden, MA: Blackwell. pp. 209–26.

Kintsch, W. and Van Dijk, T.A. (1978) Toward a model of text comprehension and production. *Psychological Review*, 85 (5): 363–94.

Kolić-Vehovec, S. and Bajšanski, I. (2007) Comprehension monitoring and reading comprehension in bilingual students. *Journal of Research in Reading*, 30 (2): 198–211.

Kress, G. and Knapp, P. (1992) Genre in a social theory of language. *English in Education*, 26 (2): 92–8.

Lanes, S. (1980) *The Art of Maurice Sendak*. New York: Harry N. Abrams.

Leadholm, B. and Miller, J. (1992) *Language Sample Analysis: The Wisconsin Guide*. Madison, WI: Wisconsin Department of Public Instruction.

Levinson, S. (1983) *Pragmatics*. Cambridge: Cambridge University Press.

Levy, R. (2011) *Young Children Reading at Home and at School*. London: SAGE.

Linderholm, T., Virtue, S., Tzeng, Y. and van den Broek, P. (2004) Fluctuations in the availability of information during reading: capturing cognitive processes using the Landscape Model. *Discourse Processes*, 37: 165–86.

Long, D.L., Golding, J.M., Graesser, A.C. and Clark, L.F. (1990) Goal, event and state inferences: an investigation of inference generation during story comprehension. In A.C. Graesser and G.H. Bower (eds), *The Psychology of Learning and Motivation: Inferences and Text Comprehension*, volume 25. New York: Academic Press. pp. 89–102.

Lumbelli, L. (1996) Focusing on text comprehension as a problem solving task: a fostering project for culturally deprived children. In C. Cornoldi and J. Oakhill (eds), *Reading Comprehension Difficulties: Processes and Intervention*. Mahwah, NJ: Erlbaum. pp. 301–30.

Maybin, J. (2103) What counts as reading? PIRLS, EastEnders and The Man on the Flying Trapeze. *Literacy*, 47 (2): 59–66.

McCutchen, D. and Logan, B. (2011) Inside incidental word learning: children's strategic use of morphological information to infer word meanings. *Reading Research Quarterly*, 46 (4): 334–49.

McKoon, G. and Ratcliff, R. (1992) Inference during reading. *Psychological Review*, 99: 440–66.

McTear, M. and Conti-Ramsden, G. (1992) *Pragmatic Disability in Children*. London: Whurr.

Mercer, N. (1995) *The Guided Construction of Knowledge: Talk amongst Teachers and Learners*. Clevedon: Multilingual Matters.

Mercer, N. (2000) *Words and Minds: How We Use Language to Think Together*. London: Routledge.

Mercer, N. and Littleton, K. (2007) *Dialogue and the Development of Children's Thinking: A Sociocultural Approach*. Abingdon: Routledge.

Miller, J. and Schwanenflugel, P.J. (2008) A longitudinal study of the development of reading prosody as a dimension of oral reading fluency in early elementary school children. *Reading Research Quarterly*, 43: 336–54.

Millis, K.K., Morgan, D. and Graesser, A.C. (1990) The influence of knowledge-based inferences on the reading time of expository texts. In A.C. Graesser and G.H. Bower (eds), *The Psychology of Learning and Motivation: Inferences and Text Comprehension*, volume 25. New York: Academic Press. pp. 197–212.

Moravcsik, J.E. and Kintsch, W. (1993) Writing quality, reading skills and domain knowledge as factors in text comprehension. *Canadian Journal of Experimental Psychology*, 47 (2): 360–74.

Moshman, D. (1990) The development of metalogical understanding. In W.F. Overton (ed.), *Reasoning, Necessity and Logic: Developmental Perspectives*. Hillsdale, NJ: Lawrence Erlbaum Associates.

Moyle, D. (1972) *The Teaching of Reading*, 3rd edn, London: Ward Lock Educational.

Muter, V., Hulme, C., Snowling, M.J. and Stevenson, J. (2004) Phonemes, rimes and language skills as foundations of early reading development: evidence from a longitudinal study. *Developmental Psychology*, 40: 665–81.

Myers, M. and Paris, S.G. (1978) Children's metacognitive knowledge about reading. *Journal of Educational Psychology*, 70: 680–90.

Nagy, W.E., Anderson, R.C. and Herman, P.A. (1987) Learning word meanings from context during normal reading. *American Educational Research Journal*, 24: 237–70.

Naidoo, B. (1996) *Journey to Jo'burg*. London: HarperCollins. (Originally published in 1985.)

Nation, K. (2005) Children's reading comprehension difficulties. In M.J. Snowling and C. Hulme (eds), *The Science of Reading: A Handbook*. Oxford: Blackwell. pp. 248–65.

Nation, K. and Snowling, M.J. (1997) Assessing reading difficulties: the validity and utility of current measures of reading skill. *British Journal of Educational Psychology*, 67: 359–70.

Nation, K. and Snowling, M.J. (2000) Factors influencing syntactic awareness skills in normal readers and poor comprehenders. *Applied Psycholinguistics*, 21: 229–41.

Nation, K., Adams, J.W., Bowyer-Crane, C.A. and Snowling, M.J. (1999) Working memory deficits in poor comprehenders reflect underlying language impairments. *Journal of Experimental Child Psychology*, 73: 139–58.

National Reading Panel (2000) *Teaching Children to Read: An Evidence Based Assessment of the Scientific Research Literature on Reading and Its Implications for Reading Instruction.* Washington, DC: National Institute of Child Health and Human Development.

Nicholas, D.W. and Trabasso, T. (1981) Toward a taxonomy of inferences. In F. Wilkening and J. Becker (eds), *Information Integration by Children*. Hillsdale, NJ: Lawrence Erlbaum Associates.

Nippold, M. (1998) *Later Language Development: The School-age and Adolescent Years*. Austin, TX: PRO-ED.

Nye, R. (1997) *Lord Fox and Other Spine-Chilling Tales*. London: Orion.

Nystrand, M., Gamoran, A., Kachur, R. and Prendergast, C. (1997) *Opening Dialogue: Understanding the Dynamics of Language and Learning in the English Classroom*. New York: Teachers College.

Oakhill, J. (1982) Constructive processes in skilled and less-skilled comprehenders' memory for sentences. *British Journal of Psychology*, 73: 13–20.

Oakhill, J. (1984) Inferential and memory skills in children's comprehension of stories. *British Journal of Educational Psychology*, 54: 31–9.

Oakhill, J. and Cain, K. (2007) Issues of causality in children's reading comprehension. In D. McNamara (ed.), *Reading Comprehension Strategies: Theories, Interventions and Technologies*. New York: Lawrence Erlbaum Associates. pp. 47–72.

Oakhill, J.V., Cain, K. and Bryant, P.E. (2003) The dissociation of word reading and text comprehension: evidence from component skills. *Language and Cognitive Processes*, 18: 443–68.

Oakhill, J.V., Hartt, J. and Samols, D. (2005) Levels of comprehension monitoring and working memory in good and poor comprehenders. *Reading and Writing*, 18: 657–86.

O'Brien, E.J., Plewes, P.S. and Albrecht, J.E. (1990) Antecedent retrieval processes. *Journal of Experimental Psychology: Learning, Memory and Cognition*, 14: 410–20.

Omanson, R.C., Warren, W.H. and Trabasso, T. (1978) Goals, inferential comprehension and recall of stories by children. *Discourse Processes*, 1: 355–72.

Oullette, G.P. (2006) What's meaning got to do with it? The role of vocabulary in word reading and reading comprehension. *Journal of Educational Psychology*, 98: 554–66.

Pahl, K. and Rowsell, J. (2011) *Literacy and Education: Understanding New Literacy Studies in the Classroom*, 2nd edn. London: SAGE.

Palincsar, A.S. and Brown, A.L. (1984) Reciprocal teaching of comprehension-fostering and comprehension-monitoring activities. *Cognition and Instruction*, 1: 117–75.

Pardo, L. (2004) What every teacher needs to know about comprehension. *The Reading Teacher*, 58 (3): 272–80.

Paribakht, T.S. and Wesche, M. (1997) Vocabulary enhancement activities and reading for meaning in second language vocabulary. In J. Coady and T. Huckin (eds), *Second Language Vocabulary Acquisition*. New York: Cambridge University Press. pp. 174–200.

Paris, S.G. and Upton, L.R. (1976) Children's memory for inferential relations in prose. *Child Development*, 47: 660–8.

Patel, S. (2010) Reading at risk: why effective literacy practice is not effective. *Waikato Journal of Education*, 15 (3): 51–68.

Pearson, P.D. and Johnson, D.D. (1978) *Teaching Reading Comprehension*. London: Holt, Rinehart and Winston.

Perfetti, C.A., Landi, N. and Oakhill, J. (2005) The acquisition of reading comprehension skill. In M.J. Snowling and C. Hulme (eds), *The Science of Reading: A Handbook*. Oxford: Blackwell. pp. 227–47.

Perfetti, C.A., Marron, M.A. and Foltz, P.W. (1996) Sources of comprehension failure: theoretical perspectives and case studies. In C. Cornoldi and J. Oakhill (eds), *Reading Comprehension Difficulties: Processes and Intervention*. Mahwah, NJ: Lawrence Erlbaum Associates. pp. 137–65.

Perkins, M. (2012) *Observing Primary Literacy*. London: SAGE.

Pickering, S.J. (2006) *Working Memory and Education*. London: Elsevier Academic Press.

Pressley, M. and Wharton-McDonald, R. (1997) Skilled comprehension and its development through instruction. *School Psychology Review*, 26 (3): 448–66.

Primary National Strategy (2006) *Literacy Framework*. London: Department for Education and Skills.

Pritchard, A. (2009) *Ways of Learning: Learning Theories and Learning Styles in the Classroom*. London: Routledge.

Pullman, P. (1985) *The Ruby in the Smoke*. Oxford: Oxford University Press.

RAND Reading Study Group (2002) *Reading for Understanding: Toward a Research and Development Program in Reading Comprehension*. Santa Monica, CA: Office of Education Research and Improvement.

Rasinski, T.V. and Padak, N.D. (2008) *Evidence-based Instruction in Reading: A Professional Development Guide to Comprehension*. London: Pearson/Allyn and Bacon.

Rose, J. (2006) *Independent Review of the Teaching of Early Reading: Final Report*. London: Department for Education and Skills.

Ruffman, T. (1996) Do children understand the mind by means of simulation or a theory? Evidence from their understanding of inference. *Mind and Language*, 11: 388–414.

Scarborough, H.S. (2001) Connecting early language and literacy to later reading (dis)abilities: evidence, theory and practice. In S.B. Neuman and D. Dickinson (eds), *Handbook of Early Literacy Research*. New York: Guilford Press. pp. 97–110.

Schank, R.C. (1976) The role of memory in language processing. In C. Cofer (ed.), *The Nature of Human Memory*. San Francisco: Freeman. pp. 162–89.

Schmalhofer, F., McDaniel, M.A. and Keefe, D. (2002) A unified model for predictive and bridging inferences. *Discourse Processes*, 33: 105–32.

Seifert, C. (1990) Content-based inferences in text. In A.C. Graesser and G.H. Bower (eds), *The Psychology of Learning and Motivation: Inferences and Text Comprehension*, volume 25. New York: Academic Press. pp. 103–22.

Sendak, M. (1963) *Where the Wild Things Are*. London: Bodley Head.

Shears, C. and Chiarello, C. (2004) Knowledge-based inferences are NOT general. *Discourse Processes*, 38: 31–55.

Simpson, M. (1966) *Suggestions for Teaching Reading in Infant Classes*. London: Methuen Educational.

Sinatra, R. and Dowd, C.A. (1991) Using syntactic and semantic clues to learn vocabulary. *Journal of Reading* 35 (3): 224–9.

Singer, M. (1994) Discourse inference processes. In M.A. Gernsbacher (ed.), *Handbook of Psycholinguistics*. San Diego, CA: Academic Press.

Singer, M. and Ferreira, F. (1983) Inferring consequences in story comprehension. *Journal of Verbal Learning and Verbal Behaviour*, 22: 437–48.

Singer, M., Halldorson, M., Lear, J.C. and Andrusiak, P. (1992) Validation of causal bridging inferences. *Journal of Memory and Language*, 31: 507–24.

Smith, F. (1985) *Reading*, 2nd edn. Cambridge: Cambridge University Press.

Snow, C.E., Burns, M.S. and Griffin, P. (1998) *Preventing Reading Difficulties in Young Children*. Washington, DC: National Academy Press.

Snowling, M.J. and Hulme, C. (2005) Learning to read with a language impairment. In M.J. Snowling and C. Hulme (eds), *The Science of Reading: A Handbook*. Oxford: Blackwell. pp. 397–412.

Soler, J. and Openshaw, R. (2007) 'To be or not to be?': the politics of teaching phonics in England and New Zealand. *Journal of Early Childhood Literacy*, 7: 333–53.

Spache, G.D. (1974) *Good Reading for Poor Readers*. Champaign, IL: Garrard.

Stahl, S.A. (1999) *Vocabulary Development*. Cambridge, MA: Brookline Books.

Stahl, S.A. and Murray, B. (1994) Defining phonological awareness and its relationship to early reading. *Journal of Educational Psychology*, 86: 221–34.

Stanovich, K.E. and Stanovich, P.J. (1999) How research might inform the debate about early reading acquisition. In J. Oakhill and R. Beard (eds), *Reading Development and the Teaching of Reading*. Oxford: Blackwell. pp. 12–41.

Strauss, S.L. and Altwerger, B. (2007) The logographic nature of English alphabetics and the fallacy of direct intensive phonics instruction. *Journal of Early Childhood Literacy*, 7 (3): 299–319.

Swinney, D. A. and Osterhout, L. (1990) Inference generation during auditory language comprehension. In A.C. Graesser and G.H. Bower (eds), *The Psychology of Learning and Motivation: Inferences and Text Comprehension*, volume 25. New York: Academic Press. pp. 17–34.

Tannenbaum, K.R., Orgesen, J.K. and Wagner, R.K. (2006) Relationships between word knowledge and reading comprehension in third-grade children. *Scientific Studies of Reading*, 10: 381–98.

Templeton, S. (2012) Teaching and learning morphology: a reflection on generative vocabulary instruction. *Journal of Education*, 192 (2/3): 101–7.

Tennent, W., Stainthorp, R. and Stuart, M. (2008) Assessing reading at Key Stage 2: SATs as measures of children's inferential abilities. *British Educational Research Journal*, 34 (4): 431–46.

Tharp, R.G. and Gallimore, R. (1988) *Rousing Minds to Life: Teaching, Learning and Schooling in Social Context*. Cambridge: Cambridge University Press.

Thompson, C. (1995) *How to Live Forever*. London: Julia MacRae.

Tomlinson, J. (1988) *The Owl Who Was Afraid of the Dark*. Basingstoke: Macmillan Education. (Originally published in 1968.)

Torgerson, C., Brooks, G. and Hall, J. (2006) A systematic review of the research literature on the use of phonics in reading and spelling. Research Report, 711. London: Department for Education and Skills. Available at www.education.gov.uk/publications/eOrderingDownload/RB711.pdf [accessed 16 March 2014].

Torgesen, J.K. (1999) Phonologically based reading disabilities: toward a coherent theory of one kind of learning disability. In R.J. Sternberg and L. Spear-Swerling (eds), *Perspectives on Learning Disabilities*. New Haven, CT: Westview Press. pp. 231–62.

Tulving, E. (1983) *Elements of Episodic Memory*. New York: Oxford University Press.

van den Broek, P. (1994) Comprehension and memory of narrative texts: inferences and coherence. In M.A. Gernsbacher (ed.), *Handbook of Psycholinguistics*. San Diego, CA: Academic Press. pp. 539–88.

van den Broek, P., Kendeou, P., Kremer, K., Lynch, J.S., Butler, J., White, M.J. and Lorch, E.P. (2005) Assessment of comprehension abilities in young children. In S. Stahl and S. Paris (eds), *Children's Reading Comprehension and Assessment*. Mahwah, NJ: Lawrence Erlbaum Associates. pp. 107–30.

van den Broek, P., Risden, K., Fletcher, R.C. and Thurlow, R. (1996) A 'landscape' view of reading: patterns of activation and the construction of a stable memory representation. In A.C. Graesser and B.K. Britton (eds), *Models of Understanding Text*. Mahwah, NJ: Lawrence Erlbaum Associates. pp. 165–88.

van der Schoot, M., Vasbinder, A.L., Horsley, T.M., Reijntjes, A. and van Lieshout, E.D.C.M. (2009) Lexical ambiguity resolution in good and poor comprehenders: an eye fixation and self-paced reading study in primary school children. *Journal of Educational Psychology*, 101 (1): 21–36.

van Dijk, T.A. and Kintsch, W. (1983) *Strategies of Discourse Comprehension*. New York: Academic Press.

Von Radowitz, J. (2012) 'Literate' baboons can tell genuine words from nonsense. *The Independent*, Friday 13 April. Available at: www.independent.co.uk/news/science/literate-baboons-can-tell-genuine-words-from-nonsense-7640679.html [accessed 16 March 2014].

Vorstius, C., Radach, R., Mayer, M.B. and Lonigan, C.J. (2013) Monitoring local comprehension monitoring in sentence reading. *School Psychology Review*, 42 (2): 191–206.

Vygotsky, L.S. (1978) *Mind in Society: The Development of Higher Psychological Processes.* Cambridge, MA: Harvard University Press.

Wagener-Wender, M. and Wender, K.F. (1990) Expectations, mental representations and spatial inferences. In A.C. Graesser and G.H. Bower (eds), *The Psychology of Learning and Motivation: Inferences and Text Comprehension*, volume 25. New York: Academic Press. pp. 137–58.

Wilkinson, I.A.G., Freebody, P. and Elkins, J. (2000) Reading research in Australia and Aotearoa/New Zealand. In M.L. Kamil, P.B. Mosenthal, P.D. Pearson and R. Barr (eds), *Handbook of Reading Research*, volume 3. Mahwah, NJ: Lawrence Erlbaum Associates. pp. 3–16.

Winograd, P. and Johnston, P. (1987) Some considerations for advancing the teaching of reading comprehension. *Educational Psychologist*, 22 (3/4): 213–30.

Wolf, M. (2008) *Proust and the Squid: The Story and Science of the Reading Brain.* Cambridge: Iconbooks.

Wood, D., Bruner, J.S. and Ross, G. (1976) The role of tutoring in problem solving. *Journal of Child Psychology and Psychiatry*, 17: 89–100.

Woolley, G.E. (2007) A comprehension intervention for children with reading comprehension difficulties. *Australian Journal of Learning Difficulties*, 12(1): 43–50.

Wyse, D. and Styles, M. (2007) Synthetic phonics and the teaching of reading: the debate surrounding England's Rose report. *Literacy*, 41: 35–42.

Wyse, D., Jones, R., Bradford, H. and Wolpert, M.A. (2013) *Teaching English, Language and Literacy*, 3rd edn. Abingdon: Routledge.

Yekovich, F.R., Walker, C.H., Ogle, L.T. and Thompson M.A. (1990) In A.C. Graesser and G.H. Bower (eds), *The Psychology of Learning and Motivation: Inferences and Text Comprehension*, volume 25. New York: Academic Press. pp. 259–78.

Yuill, N. and Oakhill, J. (1988) Effects of inference awareness training on poor reading comprehension. *Applied Cognitive Psychology*, 2 (1): 33–45.

Yuill, N. and Oakhill, J. (1991) *Children's Problems in Text Comprehension: An Experimental Investigation.* Cambridge: Cambridge University Press.

Yuill, N.M., Oakhill, J.V. and Parkin, A.J. (1989) Working memory, comprehension skill and the resolution of text anomaly. *British Journal of Psychology*, 80: 351–61.

Zwaan, R.A. (1996) Toward a model of literary comprehension. In B. Britton and A.C. Graesser (eds), *Models of Understanding Text*. Mahwah, NJ: Erlbaum. pp. 241–56.

INDEX